POETRY:

A Modern Guide to Its Understanding and Enjoyment

POETRY:

A Modern Guide to Its Understanding and Enjoyment

BY ELIZABETH DREW

W · W · NORTON & COMPANY · INC ·
NEW YORK

Published by arrangement with Dell Publishing Co., Inc.

Library of Congress Catalog Card No. 59-10937

PRINTED IN THE UNITED STATES OF AMERICA

7 8 9 0

ACKNOWLEDGMENTS:

The following poems or portions of poems are reproduced by permission of the poets, their publishers or their agents:

James Agee, "Sunday: Outskirts of Knoxville, Tennessee," by permission of the James Agee Trust.

W. H. Auden, "Now the leaves are falling fast," from THE COLLECTED POETRY OF W. H. AUDEN. Copyright 1940 by W. H. Auden. From "In Memory of W. B. Yeats," in THE COLLECTED POETRY OF W. H. AUDEN. Copyright 1940 by W. H. Auden. "The Shield of Achilles" from the W. H. Auden collection, THE SHIELD OF ACHILLES. Copyright 1952 by W. H. Auden. Reprinted by permission of Random House, Inc., and of Faber and Faber.

John Betjeman, "In Westminster Abbey," from SLICK BUT NOT STREAMLINED by John Betjeman, published by Doubleday and Co., 1947. Reprinted by permission of the poet. In British Commonwealth and Empire, "In Westminster Abbey" from COLLECTED POEMS, by permission of the poet and John Murray Ltd.

Robert Bridges, "On a Dead Child," from THE SHORTER POEMS OF ROBERT BRIDGES by permission of The Clarendon Press, Oxford.

Emily Dickinson, "After great pain. . . ," from THE POEMS OF EMILY DICKINSON, Little, Brown & Company, 1937. Copyright 1929 by Martha Dickinson Bianchi. Reprinted by permission of Little, Brown & Company.

Contents

APPENDIX

Foreword

Any book about poetry must be written in the hope that it will win new hearts and minds to both the pleasures and the profits in the reading of poems. Poetry can be enjoyed without reading books about it; the taste for it is often innate, like the impulse to write it. But as Bacon said: "Natural abilities are like natural plants, they need pruning by study." Such fostering of natural abilities is the task of criticism. It is not to lay down laws for what is good or bad in poetry, nor to be like a college professor described in one of the novels of H. G. Wells: "He was one of those who teach us how to appreciate poetry and prose, and when to say Oh! and Ah! and when to shake one's head about it discouragingly, like a bus conductor who is proffered a doubtful coin." The aim of any critic who is a lover of poetry must be to make the reading of it an exploration, which constantly reveals new insights to the reader about himself as well as about the writers and writing of poems. It must be an invitation to look, to listen, to linger in the presence of poetry and to feel its spell.

And because the only purpose of talking about poetry is to say "Come hither" and read it, this book is full of poems; poems by many writers, old and new, familiar and unfamiliar. As with other tastes, both temperament and fashion play parts in any appreciation. Response must always be a personal thing. We have the same sympathies and antipathies toward writers that we have toward other human beings. These may be mitigated by critical detachment, but personal tastes must always differ according to our individual needs and moods. As Oscar Wilde said, only an auctioneer can be equally enthusiastic about all forms of art. In the same way we can't escape the outlook we inherit by belonging to our own times. What we vaguely call "the spirit of the age" unconsciously affects us, however independent we may think we are or try to be. Our own climate of culture and consciousness tends to make us cherish certain artistic conventions and to put others in mothballs. Each age, like each person, has its own likes and dislikes, and the idols of one generation often turn into the skittles of the next. No choice of poems can please everyone, and like the Irishman's evidence, this book is "chock full of omissions."

Yet obviously the more widely we can extend our interests, the more enjoyment we can get from reading. The only real need is to come to poetry with an open mind and a willing ear, and to be prepared to use sympathetically all the faculties we possess. For as Wordsworth says, genius represents an advance or a conquest made by the poet in the sphere of human sensibility and it is not to be supposed that the reader can share in that conquest by following "like an Indian prince or general—stretched on his palanquin and borne by his slaves. No, he is invigorated and inspirited by his leader in order that he may exert himself; for he cannot proceed in quiescence, he cannot be carried like a dead weight." And he adds: "To create taste is to call forth and bestow power."

Since poetry is an art, with language as its medium, and art and craft are indivisible, some of the early chapters in the book deal in detail with the basic verbal techniques practiced by all poets—sound patterns, imagery, word-texture, structure and design. These are the poet's means to his ends, his workmanship, and it is part of the critic's job to do his best to reveal such artistic skills and cunning. We need not be afraid that "we murder to dissect." Good poetry never loses anything by analysis and discussion, and it may make a fuller experience of it possible by discovering some of the sources of its power. But the general reader may prefer to skip this introductory material and to dip at once into any of the later chapters where the emphasis is on the subject matter. For a training in poetic means is of value only that we may respond more fully to the ends of poetry, which must always be its communication of human experience. So the larger part of the book is a collection and discussion of poems creating the human themes that recur over and over in the poetry of every age; the common themes of all living, that are given their most intense and memorable expression by the poets. We come back always to Dr. Johnson's simple and bedrock wisdom: "The only end of writing is to enable the reader better to enjoy life, or better to endure it."

PART I

The Poetic Process

1. Poetry and the Poet

"A man speaking to men."
William Wordsworth

Very old are the woods;
    And the buds that break
Out of the briar's boughs,
    When March winds wake,
So old with their beauty are
    Oh, no man knows
Through what wild centuries
    Roves back the rose.

Very old too is the art in which Walter de la Mare sings of the ever-self-renewing life on our planet. For though the sociologists tell us that man's basic needs are food, sleep, shelter and sexual fulfillment, it seems that he has always had another need—something that on the face of it seems quite superfluous and useless—the urge to self-creation in art. Life under natural conditions may be, as Hobbes described it, "nasty, brutish and short," but one of the things that has always distinguished man from his brothers the brutes, is his compulsion to make things of beauty out of his own experience, which embody his consciousness in some more enduring form. Even in his most primitive stage he adorned his cave walls with drawings. As he developed his civilizations, he fashioned jewelry and metal work and decorated his dishes and pots and funeral urns. He danced and chanted rhythmical incantations, and for the last two to three thousand years we have records of how he used his speech, not only for the utilitarian purpose of communicating directly with his fellows, but to create in musical patterns the stories of his people and the records of his thoughts, his feelings and his sensations.

The psychologist Jung bases a great deal of his observation of psychological phenomena on the existence of what he calls the Collective Unconscious. He sees this as an inherited storehouse of related images and of large symbolic patterns which he thinks exists unconsciously within every human being. He believes this inheritance accounts for the appearance of these same patterns again and again in dream, in myth, and in imaginative art. Whether the presence of a collective unconscious can be proved is very uncertain, but it is quite certain that literature can well be called the written record of the collective *consciousness* of man. "Man is the great venture in consciousness" said D. H. Lawrence, and we have an inheritance of thousands of years of this growing consciousness recorded in script on papyrus and vellum and parchment, and for the last five hundred years in the printed word.

Man's consciousness develops new insights and complexities; it holds different standards at different periods, but basically it does not change. No one indeed would bother to read the literature of the past if it didn't continue to illumine life in the present. All down the ages man has had the same experiences—emotional, moral and physical; the same ecstasies and agonies, triumphs and frustrations, glories and shames. He has faced the same human problems and asked the same human questions. He has found himself entangled in the same emotional and moral conflicts in his relations with others and with himself. But we know this only because a certain few among the millions of men in every age have always felt the compulsion to communicate in the form of speech what they have observed and felt; to make their experience *fully conscious* by selecting, combining, shaping and lighting its outlines in different ways, and so isolating its special, intrinsic qualities by giving it *form,* through the medium of language.

Poetry is the earliest and remains the most concentrated and intense form of communication among the arts of language. Its uses of words are finer, richer and more powerful than those of prose, and it has played a larger part in the whole literary tradition. Today the pessimists are very gloomy about the state of poetry. They point out that, like the behavior of the younger generation and of the weather, it isn't what it used to be. They complain that poetry is written only for a small and specialized audience; that it has become a private cult; that it is unintelligible to the ordinary reader; and that as a result, the appreciation of poetry by the public has dwindled to a shadow of what it once was.

No one could argue that poetry has the importance it once had in the life of the whole community. The classical epics and dramas appealed to all classes among their peoples. The same is true of the medieval romances and the Elizabethan plays. Yes, poetry has lost its public entertainment value and its mass appeal, though this is largely because all its old narrative territory has been taken over by prose. As far as lyric poetry is concerned the public for it has never been large, and the pessimists forget or ignore how much of the now familiar and admired poetry of the past was private when it was first written. Literary history is strewn with examples of poetry written in new forms that has had to establish itself slowly, and which proves the truth of Wordsworth's remark that the revolutionary poet must himself create the taste by which he is judged. He will be recognized by the public only when the public has recognized itself in the work of the poet.

The only cause for pessimism would be if men and women ceased to write poetry, and they don't. In spite of all we hear of the sterilizing effects on the arts of our mass civilization and materialistic standards, there is no slackening of artistic output. Poets write, just as painters paint and musicians compose, because they possess the creative urge within them. What this strange impulse *is* may remain mysterious, but it is clearly an instinct common to certain individuals in all ages, which will always

[*Poetry and the Poet*] 15

find its own outlet. All the talk of the incapacity of the artist to flourish in this, that or the other social and economic environment can be disproved by any study of the past. It is indeed impossible to say what social soil is the richest for the production of literary masterpieces; they have been produced in all conditions. Poetry has been written under monarchies, democracies and dictatorships, in times of religious and political persecution, in war and in peace. It has been written by princes and by peasants, by scholars and scamps, by hermits and cosmopolitans, by revolutionists and by quietists, by priests, by rationalists and by madmen.

What then is peculiar to these individuals in all ages who have felt compelled to use patterned language to embody their experiences of living? What is a poet?

This is how Thomas Gray describes "The Bard" in the late eighteenth century.

> On a rock, whose haughty brow
> Frowns o'er old Conway's foaming flood,
> Robed in the sable garb of woe,
> With haggard eyes the Poet stood;
> (Loose, his beard and hoary hair
> Streamed, like a meteor, to the troubled air)
> And with a Master's hand, and Prophet's fire,
> Struck the deep sorrows of his lyre.

We get a different picture from A. W. E. O'Shaughnessy in the late nineteenth century.

> We are the music-makers,
>   And we are the dreamers of dreams,
> Wandering by lone sea-breakers,
>   And sitting by desolate streams;
> World-losers and world-forsakers,
>   On whom the pale moon gleams:
> Yet we are the movers and shakers
>   Of the world for ever, it seems.

Here are two romantic pictures and poses, in which it would be difficult to imagine Mr. T. S. Eliot or Mr. Archibald MacLeish. Perhaps Yeats was the last poet who looked and dressed the part, and consciously thought of himself as a man called to be the mouthpiece of his own country and mankind. But poets see themselves and their art in many different ways. To Wordsworth the poet is "a man speaking to men . . . who rejoices more than other men in the spirit of life that is in him." This is not very specific, and in spite of its moderation, in a sense it claims too much. A great many people besides poets have exceptional vitality and exceptional sensitivity and impart direct stimulus to their fellows by speaking to them. It suggests too an outstanding "personality," while the poet seems often to feel that what we usually think of as "personality" is unimportant to him, or at least of secondary importance. The "personality" lives in the daylight world of earning a living, and direct relation with others and domesticity and sociabilities, but when he is possessed by creation, the poet is a stranger in the daylight world. Beneath it is the poet's real world, where his experiences of actual and factual living, freed from the control of time and place, combine and transform themselves into new kinships and patterns. In this world the poet is alone, and in a way, anonymous. Keats declared the essence of the poetical character to be that it had no identity, because it was always filling some other body. Yeats too has the same thought when he says: "My *character* is so little my *self* that all my life it has thwarted me. It has affected my poems, my true self, no more than the character of a dancer affects the movements of the dance." The most extreme statement is that of Eliot: "Poetry is not the expression of personality, but an escape from personality. . . . The poet has not a 'personality' to express, but a particular medium, which is only a medium and not a personality, in which impressions and experiences combine in peculiar and unexpected ways."

Yet however matter-of-fact the poet may be about his make-up, from earliest times he has felt himself subject to a power beyond his workaday self. The classical writers of the ancient world embodied it in Apollo or the Muses. The

Romantics set this power in the Imagination, regarded as something magical, apart from man's normal faculties. To Wordsworth it was

> The Power so called
> Through sad incompetence of human speech,

that "rose from the mind's abyss" and took possession of him; while Shelley saw it as "that imperial faculty whose throne is curtained within the invisible nature of man." A modern poet, Randall Jarrell, speaks of the same thing in more colloquial terms: "A good poet is someone who manages, in a lifetime of standing out in thunderstorms, to be struck by lightning five or six times; a dozen or two dozen times and he is great."

But other poets suggest much quieter processes. The poet in Shakespeare's *Timon of Athens* says:

> Our poesy is as a gum which oozes
> From whence 'tis nourished: the fire i' the flint
> Shows not till it be struck; our gentle flame
> Provokes itself, and like the current flies
> Each bound it chafes.

Shakespeare suggests no transcendental quality of inspiration. He feels his art as coming from a creative inner source which is self-nourished. It needs no flint or lightning to kindle its flame. But it's a compulsive, though quiet energy, and holds its own steady flow in the face of any outer checks. A. E. Housman, without the suggestion of the fire and the current, which expand Shakespeare's oozing gum from a passive to an active movement, has something of the same idea:

> If I were obliged not to define poetry, but to name the class of things to which it belongs, I should call it a secretion; whether a natural secretion, like turpentine in the fir, or a morbid secretion, like the pearl in the oyster.

The poets do seem to agree, in spite of their very different terminology, that the origin of their art lies outside

[The Poetic Process] 18

their purely conscious faculties. It is an energy that cannot be commanded. It comes and goes. All artists are familiar with the capriciousness of its visitations, and with the frustrations that attend its withdrawal, leaving only the impotent will.

> O! 'tis an easy thing
>   To write and sing;
> But to write true, unfeignèd verse
> Is very hard! O God, disperse
> These weights, and give my spirit leave
> To act as well as to conceive!
>
> (Henry Vaughan)

But what of the product itself? Has any poet or critic successfully defined poetry? They talk about it in such very different terms that it is difficult to believe that they are describing the same activity. "Poetry is the breath and finer spirit of all knowledge." (Wordsworth) "Poetry is that which comprehends all science, and that to which all science must be referred." (Shelley) "Poetry is properly speaking a transcendental quality . . . and we can no more define this quality than we can define a state of grace." (Herbert Read) "The poet, described in ideal perfection, brings the whole soul of man into activity." (Coleridge) And in opposition to all this romantic exuberance, Coleridge's other terse statement that poetry is "the best words in their best order"; Frost's simple description of it as "a performance in words"; Eliot's almost contemptuous dismissal of it as "a superior amusement"; or a textbook definition which declares, in a somewhat chilling abstraction: "a poem is a form of expression in which an unusual number of the resources of language are concentrated into a patterned organic unit of significant experience."

Yet in a way these last quotations, bringing us down to earth after the flights of the romantics, insist on the basic fact about the art, that it is something *made* with words. Auden once wrote that if a young man with ambitions to write came to him and said, "I have important things to say," he was not a poet; but that if he confessed,

"I like hanging around words, listening to what they say," then maybe he would become a poet. The personality of the poet may play a greater part in poetry than some poets suggest, but unless he is master of his medium, his personality remains unrevealed in his work and cannot communicate itself to others. As Hart Crane wrote: "Oh, it is hard! One must be drenched in words, literally soaked in them, to have the right ones form themselves into the proper patterns at the right moment." Eliot says the *first* duty of the poet is toward the language he inherits from the past, toward its preservation and growth. The "familiar compound ghost" who appears to him in the last of the *Four Quartets,* and who is the spirit of poetry itself, says:

> Our concern was speech, and speech impelled us
> To purify the dialect of the tribe
> And urge the mind to aftersight and foresight. . . .

To urge the mind to human insight is the final aim of the poet, but it is his "speech" which produces that result. And since "to purify the dialect of the tribe" is the translation of a line of Mallarmé, Eliot has smuggled in the suggestion that the poetic heritage from the past is one of the poet's great possessions, which he must preserve, and from which he draws part of his own being. But the poet also extends what he has inherited by his creation of his own unique idiom, the product of being both servant to and master of his medium. No facile fluency will write "true, unfeignèd verse." Whether it appear simple or complex, the poet has struggled to make it as exact and as rich and as buoyant as he knows how.

Hence the impatience of poets with the popular view that to write poetry is only a matter of waiting on the Muse to supply a magic carpet to Parnassus, or of going into a trance in which the unconscious produces a finished work of art. Coleridge himself said of "Kubla Khan," the visionary fragment he wrote under the influence of opium, that he published it at the request of Byron, and "as far as the Author's own opinions are concerned, rather as a psychological curiosity, than on the grounds of any supposed poetic merits." Baudelaire acidly defined "inspiration" as "working every day"; William Morris declared that to talk of it was sheer nonsense: "there is no such thing, it is a mere matter of craftsmanship." Gerard Manley Hopkins said flatly: "Nothing but fine execution survives long." And Dylan Thomas, with all his apparent profuse excess, described the writing of a poem as "the physical and mental task of constructing a formally watertight compartment of words . . . to hold a little of the real causes and forces of the creative brain and body. To me the poetical impulse and inspiration is only the sudden, generally physical coming of energy to the constructional, craftsman ability."

It is clear from all these contradictory statements by the poets that an essential *doubleness* exists at the heart of poetic creation itself and of any analysis of it. The poet has a twofold nature, as man and as artist; poetry comes from a twofold source—a mysterious inner compulsion and a fully conscious technical discipline; it is a process in which both living and language mingle, in which both meaning and method marry, and in which both visions and revisions play their parts.

Jung holds that we can never isolate for examination the inner core of any of the fine arts. "Any reaction to stimulus may be causally explained; but the creative act, which is the absolute antithesis of mere reaction, will for ever elude the human understanding." This may be largely true. Certainly no amount of examination of poets' worksheets and drafts does more than scratch the surface of the subject. Alterations and emendations at that stage can always be "causally explained," and though interesting in proving the sharpening of perceptions and subtleties of craft, give us no light on the mysteries of artistic conception. We can say perhaps that all conception is the result of a union and fusion that brings forth new life. Some poets use the physical analogy. Auden says: "The poet is the father who begets the poem which the language bears." Hopkins, lamenting that his own fire has left him, speaks of the union of "rapture" and mind by which poetry is conceived:

> The fine delight that fathers thought; the strong
> Spur, live and lancing like the blowpipe flame,
> Breathes once and, quenched faster than it came,
> Leaves yet the mind a mother of immortal song.

Or again Coleridge, in the most famous statement on the quality of the poetic imagination, sees in every detail of the creative process this union and reconciliation of opposites: "of sameness with difference; of the general with the concrete; the idea with the image; the individual with the representative; the sense of novelty and freshness with old and familiar objects; a more than usual state of emotion with more than usual order."

"A more than usual state of emotion with more than usual order." When we move from the conception of the poem to its making, this statement seems central. The emotion must be there, whatever the kind of poetry. "Poetry lives in *gusto*," says the "romantic" Keats; its distinctive quality is "that *energy*, which collects, combines, amplifies and animates" says the "classical" Dr. Johnson. Wordsworth called it "emotion recollected in tranquillity," but as he points out in pursuing the point further, this does not mean that poetic composition itself is a tranquil and serene occupation. What Eliot calls "the pains of turning blood into ink," cannot be escaped. "Recollected" is Wordsworth's key word. Art is not life as it is lived and acted, it is life seen in the mode of contemplation, re-created into a new kind of life under the power of a new kind of drive, the activity of re-collecting, combining, amplifying and animating it by getting it into an organic *order*.

"Organization" is a somewhat forbidding word, suggesting big business or bureaucracy rather than artistic creative process; yet it is really very rich in its suggestion of both life and order. Vitality and pattern are never absent from fine poetry, or indeed from any successful creation. Organic design is the synthesizing of perceptions, the final subduing of multiplicity into unity, the emergence of cosmos from chaos.

The work of art is not conceived and then followed to its final birth by any natural process of gestation. Alfred North Whitehead speaks of "the state of imaginative muddled suspense which precedes any successful inductive generalization." I suspect this is true of the creative process in any field. Certainly the poet's final clarification seems to emerge from a similar condition. It is true that Shelley argues on the other side that the mind in creation is a fading coal, that when composition begins inspiration is already on the wane, and that even the finest poetry is a feeble shadow of the original conception of the poet. But Shelley was more interested in feeling than in form, and most poets seem to find composition is discovery rather than loss; not the production of a phantom in place of the imagined substance, but the creation of new life where it did not before exist.

For whatever embryo the poem starts from—an event, an emotion, a character, a scene, an insight, an idea—its theme never exists in isolation. It spreads and proliferates. The poet becomes in that state of "imaginative muddled suspense." There may be dead-ends and discards, periods of blind searching, even total recastings. But his complete being is involved. It is not only his "whole soul," as Coleridge says, that is brought into activity, for poetry is as much sensuous as of the spirit. His consciousness is stored with swarms of physical and emotional impressions and associations, which jostle and fertilize one another in the creative process. Words and memories are inextricably intertwined. "How can I know what I think till I see what I say" might be the poet's motto. The interplay and transmutation which goes on perpetually in him between life and language makes the poem as much a discovery of himself as a communication of his theme to his readers. We shall see much more of the workings of this process in later chapters. Yeats knew the truth of

[*Poetry and the Poet*]   23

it very well. When he was criticized for revising some of his early poems his answer proved it.

> Those friends that have it I do wrong
> Whenever I remake a song
> Should know what issue is at stake
> It is myself that I remake.

2. Poetry and the Reader

"Blood, imagination and intellect
running together."

W. B. Yeats

"Art is a human activity consisting in this, that one man
consciously, by means of certain external signs, hands
on to others feelings he has lived through, and that others
are infected by those feelings and also experience them."
Tolstoy's definition is simple, but comprehensive. The cre-
ative act may be mysterious and complex in origin, but
its aim is communication. The poet is a man speaking to
men; a man striving passionately to find "the best words
in their best order" to make his own experience live again
for others. Here again it is a "double" activity. When the
poet is at work, says Eliot, "he is no more concerned with
the social consequences than the scientist in his laboratory
—though without the context of use to society, neither
the poet nor the scientist could have the conviction which
sustains him."

Poetry has been put to some strange uses. I have heard
of a teacher whose class was reading *The Ancient Mar-
iner,* who sent the children to the Museum of Natural His-
tory to learn the wing-span of an albatross; and of an
instructor of Greek who smacked his lips over the treat
in store for his students of Sophocles's *Oedipus at Colonus,*
telling them that they could look forward to "a veritable
treasure-trove of grammatical peculiarities." But what are
its real uses to society, or to the individuals who make up
society? Are they important or superfluous? central or
peripheral?

It has always been something of a puzzle why Plato excluded poets from his ideal Republic, especially since he himself had the imagination of a poet, and saw so much of his thinking through the vision of a myth-maker. But Plato lived in a society very different from our own, a society so sensitive to art and so steeped in its magic, that he felt that youth might easily become corrupted by its sorcery and seduced from using the practical energies of life for the moral welfare of the state. In fact he was afraid that the very gifts which had made Athens the cultural center of the ancient world might cause its political disintegration.

No danger of that sort exists today. Our academies have their visiting and resident poets, to give the right cultural tone. But any idea that the poets might lead those training for politics, finance, industry or technology into choosing instead the worlds of artistic fulfillments, would be laughable. The poets count themselves lucky if they can communicate a glimmering of those worlds to small groups whose minds are flexible enough to include both practical and contemplative interests.

Yet the presence of the resident artists and poets proves that society does still value their calling, and any teacher practicing the applied art of introducing young minds to works of literature, is aware that the response to it is easy to arouse. But what is the "use" of this "infection"? Since we have said that in writing the poet discovers himself and the world, the communication of this to readers must be of the same order. The range of feelings handed on from poet to reader is as wide as human experience itself, all the way from a kind of superficial hypnosis to the deepest and truest stimulus of the whole being. Poetry probably started as magical chanting to accompany the dance, producing either a lulling of the senses and emotions or a whip to them, and it will always exist as the music and the dance of words. Its pleasures can be purely those of sensation. Take the soothing melody of the opening verses of Shelley's "Night."

[*The Poetic Process*]   26

Swiftly walk over the western wave,
    Spirit of Night!
Out of the misty eastern cave,—
Where, all the long and lone daylight,
Thou wovest dreams of joy and fear
Which make thee terrible and dear,—
    Swift be thy flight!

Wrap thy form in a mantle grey,
    Star-inwrought!
Blind with thine hair the eyes of Day;
Kiss her until she be wearied out.
Then wander o'er city and sea and land,
Touching all with thine opiate wand—
    Come, long-sought!

Or the awakening of all the senses in the last verse of Ben Jonson's "The Triumph of Love."

Have you seen but a bright lily grow
    Before rude hands have touch'd it?
Have you mark'd but the fall of the snow
    Before the soil hath smutch'd it?
Have you felt the wool of the beaver,
    Or swan's down ever?
Or have smelt o' the bud o' the brier,
    Or the nard in the fire?
Or have tasted the bag of the bee?
O so white, O so soft, O so sweet is she!

Or the sense of exultation in the climactic verse of Spenser's "Epithalamion."

Open the temple gates unto my love,
Open them wide that she may enter in,
And all the posts adorn as doth behove,
And all the pillars deck with garlands trim . . .
And let the roaring organs loudly play
The praises of the Lord in lively notes;
The whiles, with hollow throats,
The choristers the joyous anthem sing,
That all the woods may answer, and their echo ring.

Some readers take little from poetry except its simple music and movement. Pope was bitter about such frivolous readers:

> In the bright Muse, though thousand charms con-
>   spire,
> Her voice is all these tuneful fools admire,
> Who haunt Parnassus but to please their ear,
> Not mend their minds; as some to Church repair,
> Not for the doctrine, but the music there.

From earliest times critics have claimed another "doubleness" for poetry, that it must both delight and instruct. It is a deep human instinct to seek moral stimulus in poetry, and just as some readers isolate sensuous pleasure as their response, so others go to it mainly for its "message." Even Matthew Arnold (who really knew much better) insisted that the touchstone was "high seriousness," and excluded Chaucer from the great names because of his lack of it. The extremists here filter out anything except the useful maxims for living:

> O, but a man's reach should exceed his grasp
> Or what's a heaven for.   (Browning)

> I am the master of my fate,
> I am the captain of my soul.   (Henley)

> O, yet we trust that somehow good
>   Will be the final goal of ill.   (Tennyson)

There's no need to be superior about the value of such mottoes on the wall: they have helped most of us in times of need. But we don't want poetry to be all moral propaganda. As Keats said, we hate poetry that has a palpable design upon us, feeling instinctively that it is not its true function to preach. It is too much like Alice in Wonderland trying to use a flamingo as a croquet mallet.

Shelley declared that poets are the unacknowledged legislators of the world, which, unfortunately, is not true. Yet in any imaginary court for the arraignment of mankind, they might be called as some of the chief witnesses for the defense. Yeats believed them to be "the chief voice of the conscience," and that which the great poets have affirmed in their finest moments is the nearest we can come to an authoritative religion. The humanist, who requires nothing authoritarian or dogmatic in his creed, would subscribe to this, but poetry is not a religion, and we mustn't hope to get more from it than it can give. It can salve but not solve the conflicts of the human condition. The author of the Book of Job, or Milton in *Paradise Lost,* set out "to justify the ways of God to men," but neither poem ever made a convert of an unbeliever, and no one has to share the theological beliefs in order to enjoy the poems. The best religious poetry never preaches; it communicates what it *feels* like to have the poet's faith. Poetry's mountain top is Parnassus, not Olympus or Sinai. Yet this is certainly not to exclude ethical significance from poetry, and what true lover of it could ever agree with Oscar Wilde that "all art is quite useless" and that "they are the elect to whom beautiful things mean only Beauty"?

Nowadays we don't bandy about the word Beauty, with a capital B, as vaguely and glibly as they did in the 1890s. A school of critics, stemming from Wilde, did for a time promote what they called "pure poetry," poetry with all the "ideas" bleached out of it. This was no doubt largely a rebellion against the Victorian obsession with direct moral preachments. It was possible to make an anthology of good poems appealing purely to the senses and the emotions. But why limit poetry to such responses? From the time that Homer built his great epic out of the tragic consequences of the jealous wrath of Achilles, the presentation of human moral and emotional choices, and their effects, have been great poetic themes; naturally so, since they are rooted so deeply in the stuff of human experience, and in the fatally "double" nature of man:

> Created half to rise, and half to fall;
> Great Lord of all things, yet a prey to all;
> Sole judge of truth, in endless error hurled;
> The glory, jest and riddle of the world!

> (Pope)

[*Poetry and the Reader*]   29

It is the province of poetry to *show* rather than to teach.
It isn't the ethical content we rebel at in didactic poetry;
it is the way it reaches us. When Wordsworth writes:

> One impulse from a vernal wood
> May teach you more of man,
> Of moral evil and of good,
> Than all the sages can.

he's a bore, and we don't want to listen to his prosy ser-
mon, but when he creates the full emotional truth of an
impulse from a vernal wood into "Daffodils" it becomes
alive in a new way. In its most romantic and transcen-
dental form, Wordsworth himself tells us of the alchemy
that turns life into language.

> Visionary Power
> Attends upon the motion of the winds
> Embodied in the mystery of words.
> There darkness makes abode, and all the host
> Of shadowy things do work their changes there
> As in a mansion like their proper home.

The poet hardly knows what goes on in the process where-
by his experience is stirred by a new force, "the motion
of the winds," to take shape in words. It isn't a direct
process, but works in the inner world of creative darkness
to make *changes* until a form is found which is "their
proper home."

These changes are the secret of the power. Two of the
"opposites" which Coleridge says are harmonized in the
poetic process are "the sense of novelty and freshness with
old and familiar objects." Whitehead feels that "the soul
cries aloud for release into change" and that this release
is the heart of artistic fulfillment.

> It is something which adds to the permanent rich-
> ness of the soul's self-attainment. It justifies itself
> both by its immediate enjoyment, and also by its dis-
> cipline of the inmost being. Its discipline is not dis-
> tinct from enjoyment, but by reason of it. . . . The
> fertilization of the soul is the reason for the necessity
> of art.

[*The Poetic Process*]   30

The "change" may simply be the expression in a simple and memorable form of one of the great commonplaces of the human lot:

> They also serve who only stand and wait.
>
> (Milton)

or:

> 'Tis better to have loved and lost
> Than never to have loved at all.   (Tennyson)

or it may be some intricate fashioning of a complex situation. In fact perhaps we can distinguish two differing responses in reading poetry: those of *recognition* and of *revelation*. Keats said that poetry "should strike a reader as a wording of his own highest thoughts, and appear almost a remembrance." Pound exclaims: "No one can read Hardy's poems but that his own life, and forgotten moments of it, will come back to him, a flash here and an hour there. Have you a better test of true poetry?" It is a good test, but only a partial one. For one thing the memories are changed through the poet's vision, we are made more *conscious* of our own feelings by his words. And then poetry does more than remind us of "what oft was thought, but ne'er so well expressed." As Whitehead suggests, it fertilizes the soul by creating entirely new insights. Browning, in the person of Fra Lippo Lippi, speaks of painting, but what he says is equally true of poetry:

> We're made so that we love
> First when we see them painted, things we have
>   passed
> Perhaps a hundred times nor cared to see . . .

And Frost is noting the same sense of sudden discovery when he says that success in "taking" figures of speech is as intoxicating as success in making them; which certainly applies to whole poems as well as to the details of imagery.

Poetry indeed is not "like life," but awakens and quickens new life. The poets find the right words in the

[Poetry and the Reader]   31

right order for what we already dimly and dumbly feel, and they also fertilize in our consciousness responses which were lying inert and cloddish. The poet "remakes himself" in his poems, finding, sorting, selecting, rejecting, shaping among the "host of shadowy things" jostling one another to become words and sounds; and the reader in turn finds not only the poet, another more gifted human being, but discovers "new thresholds, new anatomies" unsuspected in himself. It is as Tanner says in Shaw's *Man and Superman:*

> The artist's work is to show us ourselves as we really are. Our minds are nothing but this knowledge of ourselves; and he who adds a jot to such knowledge creates new mind as surely as any woman creates new men.

But the poet doesn't accomplish this by the direct means of logical analysis. A prose "meaning" can be detached from most poems, but good poems are never just ornamental versions of a prose content, and I doubt if poetry ever has any "message" that could not be said equally forcibly in prose. We don't judge it by the excellence of its principles, by what it says *about* life, but by the intensity and illumination of its perceptions.

For poetry vitalizes the whole man. As Yeats says: "It is blood, imagination, intellect running together," and again, "It bids us touch and taste and hear and see the world, and shrink from all that is of the brain only, from all that is not a fountain jetting from the entire hopes, memories and sensations of the body." The very verbs he uses, *running, jetting,* suggest the zest and vigor in the process.

The fountain jets from the body, and whatever magical, mystical qualities inhere in poetry, they can never be separated from the senses. Language is itself a sense medium and it creates a new physical body for the poet's own consciousness; but in addition to that, the sense world and the inner world of thought and emotion are inseparable to the poet. Each melts into the other in his words. Two more of Coleridge's "opposites" which the imagination

[*The Poetic Process*]   32

combines, are the general and the concrete, the idea and the image, and these reconciliations are everywhere in poetry. Indeed the "idea" is often completely absorbed into the physical and the concrete and communicated to us purely by that impact. An editorial, pleading the cause of civil rights, might say: *"We may unhesitatingly assert that we shall not lessen our efforts nor cease to struggle in this great conflict for human happiness and moral welfare, until our objectives have been clearly obtained."* But this is what Blake writes:

Bring me my Bow of burning gold!
Bring me my Arrows of desire!
Bring me my Spear! O clouds, unfold!
Bring me my Chariot of fire!

I will not cease from Mental Fight,
Nor shall my Sword sleep in my hand,
Till we have built Jerusalem
In England's green and pleasant land.

How has Blake transformed and enriched the effect of the prose statement? The horror of social injustice is the theme of the verses, and he has referred in a previous verse to "the dark Satanic Mills" which blacken the English countryside, and the industrial slavery which blackens the Christian message. It is a deeply moral poem, but it has no overt moral ideas in it. It is all created in images of concrete, physical action. The poet is a fighter; his weapons are a bow and arrow, a spear, a chariot, a sword. But these physical objects become charged with emotional significance by the other words that surround them. His fight is a spiritual one and for the spirits of men. His bow is of burning gold, created from the fire and light and glory of his dedication. His arrows are his piercing aspirations; his chariot glows like that of Phoebus, the sun-god, driving in the heavens. And these are not only weapons of destruction against the darkness of evil, they are instruments of creation. They will build Jerusalem, and all that that name implies, and the placid English countryside can become charged with that burning vision of hope and joy. Finally the whole feeling of the verses is embodied in the active, triumphant sound pattern and rhythm.

Here is "blood, imagination and intellect running together." It awakens life in the physical senses, the emotions, the mind, and gives us that shock of change and intensity that fertilizes the soul. The poet is not a man of action in the usual sense of that term; his form of action is the writing of poetry, of turning the material of living into a verbal design, into "words that have become deeds," as Frost says. His poem doesn't only transfer experience, it *is* an experience in itself. Matthew Arnold proved that he felt poetry much more truly than we would guess from his touchstone of "high seriousness," or his definition of it as "criticism of life," when he wrote:

> The grand power of poetry is its interpretive power, by which I mean, not the power of drawing out in black and white an explanation of the mystery of the universe, but the power of so dealing with things as to awaken in us a wonderfully full, new and intimate sense of them.

3. Sound Patterns

"The sound must seem an echo to the sense."

Alexander Pope

The Blake stanzas quoted in the preceding chapter are different in three ways from the prose statement of their theme: they have a rhythmical pattern, the language is metaphorical, and the words, though perfectly simple and familiar, seem to carry more significance than we give them in ordinary use. Since a poem is a unity, this trinity of effects is in fact indivisible, but for the purposes of analysis we can speak of each in turn.

When we open a book of verse and see short lines of print on the page, unconsciously we prepare ourselves immediately for an experience different from that of reading a page of solid print. The response is an instinctive mental adjustment, like the mobilization of the necessary muscles to perform any simple physical action, and in the same way it is in fact a multiple movement. At once we prepare to meet a use of language which cuts off the words on the page from their practical, simple uses in our daily lives. Then, since we expect the language to be more concentrated, we also expect an intensification of our faculties of feeling; but the one thing we *know* will differentiate verse from prose is an experience in the ear: poetry is rhythmically patterned language.

Rhythmical patterns are widely varied, however, and lead at once into the question of how "free" verse can be. In the first quarter of this century it was the fashion to hold that poetry could dispense with any regular metrical pattern, either of rhyme or beat. Edith Sitwell declared poetry to be a sister of horticulture, "each poem growing according to the laws of its own nature." Laura Riding and Robert Graves, in their *Survey of Modernist Poetry* (1927) insist on the same irregularity. To them poetry is "a very sensitive substance which succeeds better when allowed to crystallize by itself than when put into prepared molds." D. H. Lawrence went so far as to say that the pattern "doesn't depend on ear, particularly, but on the sensitive soul." Pound's cult of "Imagism" demanded no rhythmical stress at all, only a clear visual image in lines alleged to be in the pattern of the musical phrase. When read aloud, these patterns couldn't possibly be distinguished from prose. The result was a flood of poems such as William Carlos Williams's "Red Wheelbarrow," which proves perhaps only that words can't take the place of paint.

> So much depends
> upon
> a red wheel
> barrow
> glazed with rain
> water
> beside the white
> chickens.

Whether this kind of thing pleases must be a matter of personal taste, but it should not be called "verse," since that word means that the rhythm "turns" and repeats itself; just as "prose" means that it runs straight on. Eliot made a good point when he called the term "free verse" a misnomer in another sense: "no verse is free for the man who wants to do a good job." He declared that there is never any escape from meter in poetry, but only mastery of it, and gave as his own formulation: "The ghost of some simple meter should lurk behind the arras in even the 'freest' verse; to advance menacingly as we doze, and withdraw as we rouse. Or, freedom is only true freedom when it appears against the background of an artificial limitation." Frost expressed the same idea more simply: "Freedom is feeling easy in your harness," and he declared roundly: "I'd as soon write free verse as play tennis with no net."

Besides the question of the liberty to abolish regular rhythmical pattern altogether, the subject of *rhyme* has also been hotly debated. Classical poetry was unrhymed, and rhyme wasn't introduced into English poetry until the Middle Ages, when it came into fashion from France and Italy. The Elizabethans all used blank verse as their dramatic medium, but they carried on a keen controversy on the merits and demerits of rhyme for lyrical writing. Samuel Daniel declared, in a prose pamphlet:

> For be the verse never so good, never so full, it seems not to satisfy nor breed that delight as when it is met and combined with a like sounding accent: which seems as the jointure without which it hangs loose, and cannot subsist, but runs wildly on, like a tedious fancy without a close.

Ben Jonson argued the other side—in rhyming verse!

> Rhyme, the rack of finest wits,
> That expresseth but by fits,
>   True conceit,
> Spoiling senses of their treasure,
> Cozening judgment with a measure,
>   But false weight;
> Wresting words, from their true calling;
> Propping verse, for fear of falling
>   To the ground;
> Jointing syllables, drowning letters,
> Fastening vowels, as with fetters
>   They were bound!
> Soon as lazy thou wert known,
> All good poetry hence was flown—

Thomas Campion, most delicate and musicianly of poets, chose to argue too against the "altogether intolerable" faults of rhyme—though in practice he generally used it. He could, however, write in an unrhymed syllabic pattern which has a magic of graceful movement.

Rose-cheeked Laura, come;
Sing thou smoothly with thy beauty's
Silent music, either other
Sweetly gracing.

Lovely forms do flow
from concent[1] divinely framèd;   [1] *concord*
Heaven is music, and thy beauty's
Birth is heavenly.

These dull notes we sing
Discords need for helps to grace them;
Only beauty purely loving
Knows no discord;

But still moves delight,
Like clear springs renewed by flowing,
Ever perfect, ever in them-
Selves eternal.

No poets have used unrhymed sound patterns as often as have those of our own day. They rebelled against the very conventional and lax rhyming of the late nineteenth century. Swinburne, in a stanza which is, unfortunately, a just comment on a great deal of his own poetry, summed up both the sentimentality of content and the feeble technical achievement of his contemporaries.

A month or twain to live on honeycomb
Is pleasant; but one tires of scented thyme,
Cold sweet recurrence of accepted rhyme,
And that strong purple under juice and foam
When the wine's heart has burst;
Nor feel the latter kisses like the first.

It's a far cry from that kind of thing to Pound's "The Bath Tub":

As a bath tub lined with white porcelain,
   When the hot water gives out or goes tepid,
    So is the slow cooling of our chivalrous passion,
  O my much praised but-not-altogether-satisfactory
    lady.

But apart from this rather crude kind of rebellion, the break in the tradition of rhymed verse produced many most successful experiments. In his introduction to Pound's *Selected Poems*, Eliot makes a distinction between verse as *speech* and verse as *song*. It was the first that the twentieth-century revolution in poetry emphasized. At its best it illustrated that the lyric could be founded as well on the rhymeless speech rhythm as on the traditional song. The first verse of a love song by Auden is a good example:

> Lay your sleeping head, my love,
> Human on my faithless arm;
> Time and fevers burn away
> Individual beauty from
> Thoughtful children, and the grave
> Proves the child ephemeral:
> But in my arms till break of day
> Let the living creature lie,
> Mortal, guilty, but to me
> The entirely beautiful.

Only one true rhyme appears here, but the lines have a beautiful pattern of echoing consonant and vowel similarities and a rhythmical melody which is very satisfying.

Nowadays rhyme is back in fashion, much freshened by its combination with easy speech rhythms, and subtle-ized by the use of half-rhyme, internal rhyme, the rhyming of unstressed syllables, and any other variety our versatile poetic craftsmen care to develop. Here are the first three verses from Richard Wilbur's "Statues."

> These children playing at statues fill
> The garden with their shrillness; in a planned
> And planted grove they fling from the swinger's hand
> Across the giddy grass and then hold still
>
> In gargoyle attitudes,—as if
> All definition were outrageous. Then
> They melt in giggles and begin again.
> Above their heads the maples with a stiff

Compliance entertain the air
In abrupt gusts, losing the look of trees
In rushed and cloudy metamorphoses,
Their shadows all a brilliant disrepair. . . .

Each age develops or invents new sound effects from words, and in the course of its history poetry has named an enormous variety of its rhythmical patterns. With the exception of free verse, these all differ from prose by their root in *meter*. Meter means "measure." Verse is written in lines, which are measured according to the number and arrangement of accented and unaccented syllables in them, the unit of measurement being the "foot." The average reader of poetry, however, doesn't spend much time on noting these things, and one suspects that many poets have the same feelings about them as T. S. Eliot in his essay "The Music of Poetry:"

> I have never been able to retain the names of feet and meters, or to pay the proper respect to the accepted rules of scansion. . . . This is not to say that I consider the analytical study of metric, of the abstract forms which sound so extraordinarily different when handled by different poets, to be utter waste of time. It is only that a study of anatomy will not teach you how to make a hen lay eggs. . . .

Since, however, it is part of the study of poetry to have a knowledge of metrical facts, and rhyme schemes, the practical information about these will be found in an appendix at the end of this book.

The common application of the term "musical" to verse means nothing more than "pleasant sounding"; it does not mean that the sound of poetry carries any analogy to the organization of sounds in music. Interesting studies have been made of poetry where the verbal arrangements do parallel musical notation. The Elizabethans, particularly Ben Jonson and Campion, often consciously practiced this, as did later poet-musicians such as Milton and Hopkins. Yet to speak of one art in the terms of another is never a very fruitful criticism, since their differences must always be so very much greater than their resemblances. Any comparison between music and poetry founders very early on the fact that in poetry *sounds suggest nothing apart from meaning.* Pope demanded that "the sound must seem an *echo* to the sense," and that is all it does do in even the most deliberate imitative effects. When Coleridge writes of the ice:

It cracked and growled, and roared and howled,
Like noises in a swound.

Or Tennyson describes

The moan of doves in immemorial elms,
And murmuring of innumerable bees.

the sounds *support* the meaning, they have no independent esthetic value of their own.

This is the basis of sound pattern, large or small. Nor is the meter more than one component in the sound. A metrical scheme in itself is simply a mechanical framework, a convention, within which, and against which, the poet orders his individual poetic movement. The convention sets up a pattern of recurrent sound effects which is pleasant to the ear. But if the poem does nothing but repeat these with absolute monotony, the result is sheer boredom. To the skilled poet, the regular metrical beat is a foundation, a norm from which to depart and return. It is an element in a larger movement, his rhythm. Rhythm mean "flow," and flow is determined by meaning more than meter, by feeling more than feet. It represents the freedom the poet can use within his own self-imposed necessity. It is the personal voice speaking through the formal convention.

Hence it is never the regular number and kind of "feet" which control the sound pattern of a poem, but the placing of the particular and varied accents or stresses or beats (these three words are interchangeable). No precise rules of rhythm can ever be evolved, so there can never be any absolute laws of scansion (the placing of the stresses in reading). The human ear is variable in its responses and different readers hear the poet's voice differently. But whatever the changes in detail in the reading of a poem, the entirely regular metrical scheme will always be subordinate to the sense of what is being said, and to the varieties in the pattern required by the thought and feeling. The poet will use reversals of the expected beat, omissions or additions of syllables, surprises, postponements and even shocks. These are all deliberate and calculated: "It is not inspiration that exhausts one," said Yeats, "it is art." And he confesses that he often spent a whole day working on a single stanza.

The differences can be heard very clearly if we listen to several "voices" using the same verse forms, and note the various rhythmical possibilities that emerge. Take blank verse. This is what it sounded like in *Gorboduc* (1561), the earliest play written in that meter:

> The royal king and eke his sons are slain;
> No ruler rests within the regal seat;
> The heir, to whom the scepter 'longs, unknown; . . .
> Lo, Britain's realm is left an open prey,
> A present spoil for conquest to ensue.

It is clumsily regular. Its five iambs (two syllable feet, with the accent on the second syllable) all end-stopped, plod along in regimented uniformity, and the result is a lifeless monotony.

Christopher Marlowe changed all that, and brought a new ease and flexibility to blank verse by varying the accents, by breaking the line in the middle, by indicating dramatic pauses, and by allowing the sense to flow into a freer sentence structure.

> Was thís the fáce that láunched a thóusand shíps,
> And búrnt the tópless tówers of Ílium?—
> Swéet Hélen, máke me immórtal with a kíss,—
> Her líps suck fórth my sóul; sée, where it flíes!
> Cóme, Helen, cóme, gíve me my sóul agáin.
> Hére will I dwéll, for heáven is in these líps,
> And áll is dróss that is not Hélena.

Shakespeare's intonations are still nearer the speaking voice.

> That it should cóme to thís!
> But twó mónths déad! Náy, not so múch, nót twó.
> So éxcellent a Kíng, that wás, to thís,
> Hypérion to a sátyr. So lóving to my móther
> That he might not beteém the wínds of heáven
> Vísit her fáce too roúghly. Héaven and eárth!
> Múst I remémber? Whý, she would háng on him
> As if increase of áppetite had grówn
> By what it féd on. And yét withín a mónth—
> Let me not thínk on 't—

This is truly dramatic blank verse: no single line is entirely regular, and the almost strangling fury and disgust come out in the broken, uneven rhythms and gasps of angry pain and nausea.

Milton's blank verse is not dramatic, but epic. It depends for its magnificence on sustained rhythmic nobility and sonorous sweep. But again, his finest effects are gained by playing the thought and feeling structure of his larger rhythms against the expected regular beat. Take his description of the fall of Satan:

> Hím the Almíghty Pówer
> Húrled héadlong fláming from the ethéreal sky
> With hídeous rúin and combústion dówn
> To bóttomless perdítion, thére to dwéll
> In ádamántine cháins and pénal fíre,
> Who dúrst defý the Omnípotent to árms.

Here one line only, the fifth, keeps the regular metrical pattern. It supplies the conventional order against which the freedom and irregularity of the other lines are counterpointed. Their magnificent energy, indeed, is not only in the splendor of their diction, but in the movement which, in the sweep of a single sentence, creates the sense of Lucifer falling through space. The rush of the opening with its powerful beats carries through without pause to "perdition," and after this toppling descent, "there to dwell / In adamantine chains and penal fire," checks the rush into the feeling of the permanence of Satan's doom.

In "Samson Agonistes" Milton allows himself not only variations within the pentameter line, but variations of line length itself to give specific effects.

> O dárk, dárk, dárk, amíd the bláze of noón,
> Irrecóverably dárk, tótal eclípse
> Withóut all hópe of dáy!

Although the first line has ten syllables, it has six stresses; the second has eleven syllables, but only four beats; and the third, with only three beats, stands as a complete line. The sound goes underground, as it were, and the pause which completes the line is filled with the echo of "dark" and Samson's silent hopelessness.

If we turn to Browning from Milton, it is difficult to realize that they are both using the same meter:

> I am poor brother Lippo, by your leave!
> You need not clap your torches in my face.
> Zooks, what's to blame? you think you see a monk!
> What, 'tis past midnight, and you go the rounds,
> And here you catch me at an alley's end
> Where sportive ladies leave their doors ajar?
> The Carmine's my cloister; hunt it up,
> Do—

Again we hear speech rhythms in individual tones. The parentheses, the quick shifts and breaks in thought, the questions, the ejaculations, carry all the immediacy and spontaneity of the natural voice. But the rhythms are facile rather than subtle.

An equal variety of rhythmic flow and tone can be heard in the heroic couplet. Marlowe in "Hero and Leander" loads it with descriptive richness, but the end-stopped lines tend toward monotony.

> Upon her head she wore a myrtle wreath,
> From whence her veil reached to the ground beneath.
> Her veil was artificial flowers and leaves
> Whose workmanship both man and beast deceives.
> Many would praise the sweet smell as she passed,

When 'twas the odor which her breath forth cast;
And there for honey bees have sought in vain,
And, beat from thence, have lighted there again.

Donne was only nine years younger than Marlowe, but his
heroic couplets certainly sound very different.

> On a húge híll
Crágged, and stéep, Trúth stánds, and hé that will
Réach her, abóut múst, and abóut múst gó;
And whát the híll's súddenness resísts, wín só;
Yet stríve so, that befóre áge, déath's twílight,
Thy sóul rést, for nóne can wórk in thát níght.

Though this is in rhymed couplets, it has more of the
quality of Elizabethan blank verse than of the nondra-
matic poetry of the period. The pressure of the thinking
mind bends the rhyme out of regularity. In some lines it
is emphasized with heavy stress; in others ignored. The
reader must slow up to get the force of the ideas, must
identify himself, in an almost physical way, with the
breath pauses, with the image of reaching and striving
and resisting "the hill's suddenness" by patient struggle.
In the third and fourth lines the slow, plodding effort
lengthens the lines by stresses on the last two single
words, and in the last line the Biblical echo, "for the night
cometh when no man can work," brings home the delib-
erate *laboriousness* which Donne is creating in the place
of that easy musical rhythm.

The rhythm of Donne's couplets moves slowly with its
burden of personal emotional meaning, while that of
Pope's has the brisk tone of the man of the world con-
versing with his friends. Instead of speaking in a sus-
tained sentence of several lines, he makes each couplet a
unit in itself, with its rhythm based on the symmetry and
neat opposition of its two halves. The closed couplet is an
artificial convention, but within its framework of formal
decorum Pope packs pithy terseness, and the effect is very
different from the same thing in Marlowe.

> First slave to words, then vassal to a name,
Then dupe to party; child and man the same;

> Bounded by Nature, narrowed still by art,
> A trifling head, and a contracted heart.

Browning used the couplet, as he used blank verse, to carry the tones of the ordinary speaking voice. The sense is never enclosed within the two lines; the rhymes are unemphatic, and the meaning flows across them and ignores them.

> Who'd stoop to blame
> This sort of trifling? Even had you skill
> In speech—(which I have not)—to make your will
> Quite clear to such an one, and say, "Just this
> Or that in you disgusts me; here you miss,
> Or there exceed the mark"—

Just as the feeling and thought in poetry can be created or enhanced by the flow of the verse form, so it can be ruined by it too. William Cowper, for instance, doomed his "Verses Supposed to Be Written by Alexander Selkirk" (the original of Robinson Crusoe) by choosing to write them in the tripping anapest (a foot of two unaccented syllables followed by an accented one).

> I am monarch of all I survey,
> My right there is none to dispute;
> From the center all round to the sea,
> I am lord of the fowl and the brute.
> Oh, Solitude! where are thy charms
> That sages have seen in thy face?
> Better dwell in the midst of alarms,
> Then reign in this horrible place.

No amount of variation could change the rhythm from being more suited to comic opera than to expressing the horrors of shipwrecked isolation.

Or again a poem may become monotonous, even if the monotony is one of the pleasant sounds. The opening of George Meredith's "Love in the Valley" is delightful:

> Under yonder beech-tree single on the green-sward,
> Couched with her arms behind her golden head,

Knees and tresses folded to slip and ripple idly,
Lies my young love sleeping in the shade.
Had I the heart to slide an arm beneath her,
Press her parting lips as her waist I gather slow,
Waking in amazement she could not but embrace me:
Then would she hold me and never let me go?

But when this is followed by twenty-five stanzas of the same rippling melody, the ear cloys and the senses become comatose; the sound pattern is *too* fluid, *too* flexible. To hear triumphant love created in rhythm, take the first stanza of Donne's "The Anniversary," where the mind works to keep a complex stanza pattern and to fill the lines with intellectual as well as with emotional intensity.

Aĺl kíngs, and áll their fávorites,
Aĺl glóry of hónors, beáuties, wíts,
The sún itsélf, which mákes tímes, as they páss,
Is élder by a yeár, nów, than it wás
When thóu and I fírst one anóther sáw:
All óther thíngs to théir destrúction dráw,
    Ónly óur lóve hath nó decáy;
Thís no tomórrow háth, nor yésterday,
Rúnning it néver rúns from ús awáy,
But trúly kéeps his fírst, lást, éverlásting dáy.

The sixth line is a regular iambic, but until that is reached, the accents are wrenched to enforce a slowing up in the reading, so that all the weight of the temporal, and the passing, and the material, shall contrast with the light, sweeping movement of the triumph over time in the last half of the verse. After the summing up of the theme of mortality, "All other things to their destruction draw," the firm beats of "Only our love hath no decay," announce that triumph, and then the syllables move easily, with their four chiming rhymes, to end in that long, lingering, seven-beat exultation of eternal constancy.

Rhythmic creation of a totally opposing mood—empty despair—is well illustrated in the opening lines of Eliot's "The Hollow Men."

> We are the hollow men
> We are the stuffed men
> Leaning together
> Headpiece filled with straw. Alas!
> Our dried voices, when
> We whisper together
> Are quiet and meaningless
> As wind in dry grass
> Or rats' feet over broken glass
> In our dry cellar
>
> Shape without form, shade without colour,
> Paralysed force, gesture without motion; . . .

The theme of the paragraph is the sense of banishment from human vitality, vitality either for good or for evil. That condition of meaningless neutrality is evoked in the unrhymed couplet at the end. It has no directed movement toward anything else, its language is as static and negative as its feeling, and the lifelessness of the hollow men is expressed in the very faint heartbeat of the rhythm in the introductory lines, with their halting uneven stresses. The "dried voices" are entirely without resonance or vigor; the words they whisper "lean together" with no interlocking harmony; and they are likened to the meaningless inhuman sounds of the wind in dry grass or "rats' feet over broken glass." The halting, harsh cacophony of vowels and consonants in that image carries something of the shattered fragments which is all "our dry cellar" contains.

Yet of course there's no need for poetic rhythm to be dramatic and complicated in order to delight us. It spans the whole gamut from sonorous rhetoric to simple colloquialism. The modern taste among poets themselves is for the most skillful ingenuities of craft. The lyric has to be condensed and intense and its technical achievement must be sophisticated and impeccable. As a result the level of workmanship is very high. This is a fine ideal, yet the final test of lyric poetry is that it should get off the ground, and should not be so cumbered with craft that it can't use its wings. We miss the rhythms of pure song in most contemporary verse. Yeats and Walter de la Mare were perhaps the last in that tradition, and James Joyce in his "Chamber Music," which is full of flowing and limpid sound effects.

All day I hear the noise of waters
        Making moan,
Sad as the sea-bird is, when going
        Forth alone,
He hears the winds cry to the waters'
        Monotone.

The grey winds, the cold winds are blowing
        Where I go.
I hear the noise of many waters
        Far below.
All day, all night, I hear them flowing
        To and fro.

This has all the simple melody we seldom hear nowadays, and though the tone and movement is not Elizabethan, its sensuous satisfaction and easy resolutions of words and sounds remind us of the sixteenth-century song writers.

Weep you no more, sad fountains;
        What need you flow so fast?
Look how the snowy mountains
        Heaven's sun doth gently waste!
But my Sun's heavenly eyes
        View not your weeping,
        That now lies sleeping
Softly, now softly lies
        Sleeping.

Sleep is a reconciling,
        A rest that peace begets;
Doth not the sun rise smiling
        When fair at even he sets?

Rest you then, rest, sad eyes!
　　Melt not in weeping,
　　While she lies sleeping
Softly, now softly lies
　　　Sleeping.

4. Imagery

"Saying one thing and meaning another."
Robert Frost

"I hope Philosophy and Poetry will not neutralize each other, and leave me an inert mass," said Coleridge; and again: "A whole essay might be written on the danger of *thinking* without images." Indeed poetry without images would be an inert mass, for figurative language is an essential part of its energy. "There are many other things I have found myself saying about poetry," writes Robert Frost, "but the chiefest of these is that it is metaphor, saying one thing and meaning another, saying one thing in terms of another."

It is perhaps questionable whether this is precisely true. The "chiefest thing" about poetry would seem to be that it has a rhythmical pattern, and it is equally true of prose that its liveliness depends largely on its success in reinforcing "thought" by concrete figures of speech. Moreover a poetry which ignores plain logical statement altogether (which Frost never does) is a specialized taste, and the modern vogue for it has provoked Ogden Nash to the sardonic comment:

> One thing that literature would be greatly the better
> for
> Would be a more restricted employment by authors
> of simile and metaphor.

Yet rhythm and imagery run together in poetic harness, and Sir Philip Sidney links them as indivisible: "that exquisite observing of number and measure in words, and that high-flying liberty of conceit proper to the poet."

The very nature of language itself is metaphorical, and our common speech is strewn with metaphors which have become so worn with use that we no longer notice them. We boil with anger or an idea dawns on us; the years roll by or the votes cast become a landslide. We can't respond freshly to such comparisons; they are too familiar. But the poet has always expanded and intensified his ideas or his descriptions by likening one thing to another in new ways: by simile, an explicit comparison; or by metaphor, an implicit one. The poet's mind is stored with memories, alliances, affiliations. What Coleridge calls "the streamy nature of association" blends these together in infinite variety. This image-making faculty has always been the mark of the poet. Homer is full of similes, and it was Aristotle who first said that metaphor was essential to poetry and was the one thing that the poet could not be taught. It's an *intuitive* perception of similarities between dissimilars, resulting in fresh vision or insight.

At their simplest both simile and metaphor are visual. When Shakespeare describes bees as "the singing masons building roofs of gold," or Browning writes:

> The wild tulip, at the end of its tube, blows out its
> great red bell
> Like a thin clear bubble of blood,

we *see* more intensely. Or again D. H. Lawrence evokes a bat in a series of vivid comparisons:

> A twitch, a twitter, an elastic shudder in flight
> And serrated wings against the sky,
> Like a glove, a black glove, thrown up at the light
> And falling back.

These are what we might call "picture images." They reveal external similarities which stimulate our senses freshly and pleasurably. They don't get beyond the senses, however, and metaphor works more deeply in poetry if mind or emotion, or both, are fused with the sensuous image. Indeed it isn't really necessary to have any precise sensuous image at all. If Shakespeare writes:

> When to the sessions of sweet silent thought
> I summon up remembrance of things past,

we don't visualize a troop of memories appearing before a court of law; or when Keats addresses the Grecian urn as "Thou still unravished bride of quietness" it doesn't call up an image of the marriage bed. In these examples the abstract emotional content is made stronger than the concrete association. But the two may be equally balanced. When Macbeth says of Duncan, "After life's fitful fever he sleeps well," we get not only the conventional picture of death as sleep, but the emotional addition of life as a fitful fever to which the deep sleep of death comes as a release. When Hart Crane describes the sea as "this great wink of eternity," he condenses into one image a suggestion of the momentary and the timeless, as well as the actual gleam of the sea's wide surface and the good humor of its mood.

This concentration is a very common quality in poetic metaphor. When Mr. Prufrock says, "I have measured out my life with coffee spoons," he telescopes two suggestions into one: that of partaking of life in tiny sips, instead of savoring it fully and freely; and that of spacing it out in conventional parties which never go beyond the surface of social exchanges. Or when Dylan Thomas opens a poem with the line "The force that through the green fuse drives the flower," the natural energy that generates the stem and the blossom of the plant is blended in our minds with the mechanical explosive "fuse" that is destructive, not creative. At once he has created the eternal presence of life and death together as one process, which is the theme of the poem.

A metaphor may give a vivid climactic sense of revelation to the plain statements that lead up to it. Emily Dickinson's "A Light Exists in Spring" is a good example. The first four verses describe the strange quality of this impalpable light. It communicates a particular emotion to the poet, it almost has a voice. Then as the months move, it passes, "without the formula of sound," leaving

> A quality of loss
> > Affecting our content,
> As trade had suddenly encroached
> > Upon a sacrament.

The final image suddenly tightens the meaning of everything that has gone before and gives it fresh emotional intensity.

Or at the opposite extreme from this, an entire poem may be a sustained image. Indeed I think it is this sort of poem that Frost had in mind when he said that poetry is "saying one thing in terms of another." A perfect example is his own "A Silken Tent."

> She is as in a field a silken tent
> At midday when a sunny summer breeze
> Has dried the dew and all its ropes relent,
> So that in guys it gently sways at ease,
> And its supporting central cedar pole,
> That is its pinnacle to heavenward
> And signifies the sureness of the soul,
> Seems to owe naught to any single cord,
> But strictly held by none, is loosely bound
> By countless silken ties of love and thought
> To everything on earth the compass round,
> And only by one's going slightly taut
> In the capriciousness of summer air
> Is of the slightest bondage made aware.

Chekov said: "When a man spends the least possible movements on some definite action: that is grace." It is a definition that fits this poem well. Within a single sentence, Frost has fashioned a flowing, supple sonnet, and within the single simile of the silken tent he has made us feel the woman's unobtrusive strength and "sureness"; her radiation of love and thoughtfulness for others; and at the same time her human dependence on others for her own happiness. It's a beautiful fusion of idea and image, of form and content.

The test of the success of metaphor is never its mere profusion. "All thought is sorting," says I. A. Richards, and the poet's achievement is the result of this process. It might be possible indeed to transpose Coleridge's remark and say that a whole essay might be written on the danger of image-making without thinking, or the danger of relying solely on the wealth of response to experience which an acute sensibility intuitively makes. As Eliot says, a reading of Spinoza and the noise of the typewriter and the smell of dinner cooking may be all together in a moment's experience; and the truthful poet, he reminds us, must look into more than the heart: the cerebral cortex, the nervous system and the digestive tract are equally important. But the fine poet doesn't take everything he finds as of equal value. He "sorts" it. It is quite as easy to have too many images as too few. Unlike a logical argument, a poem is not the sum of its individual parts; it's a pattern of living relationship among statements and images, the way they kindle or support or modify one another by the poet's arrangement. Sometimes, though the individual metaphors are all vivid, the whole effect is blurred. In this passage from Tennyson's "In Memoriam," for instance, if we stop to think of each image it becomes a struggle to keep up with the number of pictures and sensations that are called up, and which don't seem to lead from one to another with any associative sequence, or to fuse into any powerful whole.

> Be near me when my light is low,
>   When the blood creeps, and the nerves prick
>   And tingle; and the heart is sick,
> And all the wheels of being slow.
>
> Be near me when the sensuous frame
>   Is racked with pangs that conquer trust;
>   And Time, a maniac scattering dust,
> And Life, a Fury slinging flame.
>
> Be near me when my faith is dry,
>   And men the flies of latter spring,
>   That lay their eggs, and sting and sing
> And weave their petty cells and die.

[*Imagery*] 55

Be near me when I fade away,
    To point the term of human strife,
    And on the low dark verge of life
The twilight of eternal day.

Compare this with another passage where the emptiness
and senselessness of life and time are also presented to
us in a rush of imagery.

Tomorrow, and tomorrow, and tomorrow
Creeps in this petty pace from day to day
To the last syllable of recorded time;
And all our yesterdays have lighted fools
The way to dusty death. Out, out, brief candle!
Life's but a walking shadow, a poor player,
That struts and frets his hour upon the stage
And then is heard no more. It is a tale
Told by an idiot, full of sound and fury,
Signifying nothing.

Here everything holds together; every image reinforces
and is absorbed into Macbeth's mood of total despair and
disgust. First all the suggestions of time; the slow mo-
notony of tomorrows and yesterdays, the creeping petty
pace toward the final doom. Then those of the impotence
and insignificance of life blending with them; the brief
candle, the walking shadow, the ham actor, the empty
wild gibbering. Each image is itself striking, but the ef-
fect of the whole is far greater than the mere enumeration
of its parts.

Donne was a contemporary of Shakespeare, and the
kind of poetry he and his disciples wrote gains its effects
too from close-packed imagery. But in general its mate-
rials are different. It was Dr. Johnson who first called
these poets "metaphysical," and the name has stuck to
them, though it has nothing to do with the philosophy
that Coleridge feared. Johnson meant only that they were
learnèd or ingenious in their use of metaphor. In their
poetry, as he says, "the most heterogeneous ideas are
yoked by violence together; nature and art are ransacked

for illustrations, comparisons and allusions." Johnson
didn't much approve the fashion, though he does admit
that "if their conceits were far-fetched, they were often
worth the carriage." The game of finding and working out
queer analogies, and the judging of the success and "wit"
of a comparison by the width of the leap between the
things compared, produced some strange results. This,
for example from Francis Quarles's *Divine Fancies* (1632).

> My sins are like the hairs upon my head,
> And raise their audit to as high a score;
> In this they differ: these do daily shed,
> But, ah, my sins grow daily more and more:
> If by my hairs thou number out my sins,
> Heaven make me bald before that day begins.

And indeed is Donne's famous metaphor of the com-
passes really the success it is claimed to be? It concludes
"A Valediction: Forbidding Mourning," written on the
occasion of one of his absences abroad.

> Our two souls therefore, which are one,
>   Though I must go, endure not yet
> A breach, but an expansion,
>   Like gold to airy thinness beat.
>
> If they be two, they are two so
>   As stiff twin compasses are two,
> Thy soul the fixed foot, makes no show
>   To move, but doth, if th' other do.
>
> And though it in the center sit,
>   Yet when the other far doth roam,
> It leans, and hearkens after it,
>   And grows erect, as that comes home.
>
> Such wilt thou be to me, who must
>   Like th' other foot, obliquely run;
> Thy firmness makes my circle just,
>   And makes me end, where I begun.

This is very different in intensity and rhythmical satisfac-
tion from the Quarles, but what about its emotional con-

tent? It may be said that we cannot visualize it too carefully, that it's the feel of a pair of compasses we must get, the sense of leaning and firmness, the pull between the two feet. But doesn't Donne *force* the visual on us with his "stiff, twin compasses" and his detailed concrete exactness? And is the emotional comparison between the compasses and the lovers a just one? The compass feet don't come together again at the end of the circle: the one remains in the center, the other on the periphery. There is no sense of happy reunion. If, as it is thought, the poem was addressed to his wife, I can't believe that poor Anne Donne, left alone in poverty and expecting a tenth child, could find much comfort in it: or that other lovers turn to it for help in easing the pains of separation.

To feel Donne's extraordinarily agile and forceful mind and emotions at work controlling and unifying what would seem a swarm of incongruous metaphors, look at one of his famous religious sonnets.

> Batter my heart, three personed God; for you
> As yet but knock, breathe, shine, and seek to mend;
> That I may rise and stand, o'erthrow me and bend
> Your force to break, blow, burn and make me new.
> I, like an usurped town, to another due,
> Labour to admit you, but Oh, to no end;
> Reason, your viceroy in me, me should defend,
> But is captived and proves weak or untrue.
> Yet dearly I love you and would be lovèd fain,
> But am betrothed unto your enemy:
> Divorce me, untie or break that knot again,
> Take me to you, imprison me, for I
> Except you enthrall me, never shall be free,
> Nor ever chaste, except you ravish me.

When Henry James discussed the fiction of George Eliot he said that in spite of her depth and power in presenting the human condition, her conception of the novelist's task was never in the least as the *game* of art. No one could bring such a criticism against Donne. At the same time no one could feel here that he isn't profoundly moved by his subject, or that the fun he must have had working out his analogies in any way falsifies his faith and fervor. The complexity of the verbal pattern communicates the conflict in his own being: his burning emotional need for religious fulfillment on the one hand, and on the other, his unsuccessful efforts to achieve it by any rational or impersonal approach.

Violent emotion indeed is at the center of the whole poem. The paradoxical theme is the achievement of final peace only through the violent conflicts and ultimate surrenders of war and of love. "Batter my heart," he starts, combining at once the two metaphorical strands. The address, though, is to "three personed God," and he is going to weave "trinities" into the formal elements of his design. Though the final unity is that of the sonnet, the structure is divided into three clusters of metaphors, two in the octet and one in the sestet. Beyond that, the first metaphor, the direct prayer to the three-in-one God not to use gentle ways, but to re-create after destruction, presents the argument in two groups of three words each, then summed up in a phrase unifying them. God must not "knock, breathe, shine, and seek to mend," but "break, blow, burn and make me new." In the thematic scheme, each of the words in the first line suggests a quiet action, while each of the second group intensifies it into a vehement one.

Various words in the first quatrain, *batter, o'erthrow, burn,* make links to the next cluster of metaphors, dominated by that of the captive town. The poet's heart, though true to its rightful owner, has been overpowered and is helpless. Reason, reigning in the place of God, should be an aid, but has no power. It again is not active enough. This quatrain is also colored by the love imagery, which develops as the main strand in the last six lines. The "usurped town, to another due" has a suggestion of a betrayed maiden, and the "weak or untrue" reason implies a faithless friend. In the same way when the sexual imagery comes to the fore, suggestions of capture and imprisonment keep the war theme alive. Again the pattern of the need for the violent to invade what is too gentle is played out in the language. The betrothal to another sounds like an inert drifting, and the language is inert too. It comes to life again in the violent, crowded, rushing images of the last four lines and the startling paradox of the consummation.

The metaphors of Donne and his disciples often make a first reading of their poems difficult, partly because they use images based on seventeenth-century ideas now outdated, and partly, as in the preceding sonnet, because of the density and concentration of the material. But they are always *logical* beneath their quick shifts and queer analogies; a backbone of rational argument always links their farfetched metaphors together. The use of symbols is more elusive, for interpretation often depends on a purely emotional association which has no basis in any logical comparison. In a religious or national context, for instance, a cross or a crescent or a hammer and sickle may be loaded with symbolic significance and associations which it doesn't have at all by itself. In the same way in poetry, some physical thing—a human figure, a broken statue, a worm-eaten rose—may symbolize to the poet a whole cluster of thoughts and emotions which surround it in his own mind, and which it is his purpose to evoke from it for the reader in the pattern of his poem. Or alternatively certain deep emotions may become, for him, inextricably associated with certain physical scenes. Thomas Hardy describes such an association in "Neutral Tones."

We stood by a pond that winter day,
And the sun was white, as though chidden of God,
And a few leaves lay on the starving sod;
    —They had fallen from an ash, and were gray.

Your eyes on me were as eyes that rove
Over tedious riddles of years ago;
And some words played between us to and fro
    On which lost the more by our love.

The smile on your mouth was the deadest thing
Alive enough to have strength to die;

> And a grin of bitterness swept thereby
> Like an ominous bird a-wing . . .
>
> Since then, keen lessons that love deceives,
> And wrings with wrong, have shaped to me
> Your face, and the God-curst sun, and a tree,
> And a pond edged with grayish leaves.

Hardy presents us plainly with both the emotional content of the scene and the group of physical details which ever after became to him the symbol of his feelings. Wordsworth does the same thing in "Resolution and Independence." The poet goes out on a lovely spring morning, rejoicing in the life and growth around him and in his own well-being and good fortune. Then he is assailed by memories of other young poets, Chatterton and Burns, who started out with equal hope, and perished in unhappiness. But in this mood there's "a something given" to his spirit. He sees the old leech-gatherer, solitary on the moor, who still has "a fire about his eyes," in spite of his age and poverty and the uncertainty of his occupation. The old man melts into a symbolic figure for the poet.

> The Old Man still stood talking by my side;
> But now his voice to me was like a stream
> Scarce heard; nor word from word could I divide;
> And the whole body of the man did seem
> Like one whom I had met with in a dream;
> Or like a man from some far region sent;
> To give me human strength, and strong admonish-
>   ment.
>
> My former thoughts return'd; the fear that kills;
> The hope that is unwilling to be fed;
> Cold, pain, and labour, and all fleshly ills;
> And mighty poets in their misery dead . . .

But in the face of this, the poet now has his symbol of the toughness of the human spirit.

This is symbolism at its simplest. A step further in its use is for the poet to create the scene and to build up the emotional suggestions from its details, without actually naming the theme which emerges from them. A straightforward example is Shelley's "Ozymandias."

> I met a traveller from an antique land
> Who said: Two vast and trunkless legs of stone
> Stand in the desert . . . Near them, on the sand,
> Half sunk, a shattered visage lies, whose frown,
> And wrinkled lip, and sneer of cold command,
> Tell that its sculptor well those passions read
> Which yet survive, stamped on these lifeless things,
> The hand that mocked them, and the heart that fed:
> And on the pedestal these words appear:
> "My name is Ozymandias, king of kings:
> Look on my works, ye Mighty, and despair!"
> Nothing beside remains. Round the decay
> Of that colossal wreck, boundless and bare
> The lone and level sands stretch far away.

We see the desert, the huge broken statue—first the enormous legs, supporting nothing, then the shattered face holding its "sneer of cold command"—and finally the inscription. The poet's comment isn't in moral or abstract terms; it's in further descriptive touches of the desolation of the "colossal wreck," and the sense of endless time created in the words "boundless and bare / The lone and level sands stretch far away." The reader interprets the symbols as a comment on the vanity of human wishes; on the irony of human pride and power; on the brevity of human life; and perhaps too on the immortality of the art which remains to carry these reminders to future generations of mortal men.

The little sketch Robert Frost gives us of his neighbor in "Mending Wall" has none of the *planned* symbolic significance of "Ozymandias," but a symbolic meaning grows naturally out of the picture. The poet develops his own tolerant, sensible view that no wall is needed between neighbors who have no cows to stray, and he waits for the other man to reply:

                                    I see him there
Bringing a stone grasped firmly by the top
In each hand, like an old-stone savage armed.
He moves in darkness as it seems to me,
Not of woods only and the shade of trees.
He will not go beyond his father's saying,
And he likes having thought of it so well
He says again, "Good fences make good neighbors".

Frost doesn't say what the figures symbolize to him, but
the association with the primitive, the reference to the
darkness and to the rigidity of mind that clings stubbornly
to dead tradition, all imply the forces of violence, igno-
rance and superstition which stand in the way of good
sense and good feeling between both neighbors and na-
tions.

These are simple but powerful examples of poetic sym-
bols, linking the sensuous with emotional and moral im-
plications, but visionary poets often use symbols in more
elusive ways, leaving with us as much a sense of mystery
as of clarity. Coleridge said that some of the best poetry
remained only "generally and not perfectly understood."
That is true of a poem like Blake's "The Sick Rose."

O Rose, thou art sick!
The invisible worm,
That flies in the night,
In the howling storm,

Has found out thy bed
Of crimson joy;
And his dark secret love
Does thy life destroy.

There's no simple equation here between a physical ob-
ject and an emotional and moral meaning. All three levels
are experienced simultaneously in a single sentence,
which creates a feeling of some sinister and violent pas-
sion behind the simple but ominous words. Ostensibly
the poem is about a flower and a garden pest—a rose and
a grub—but the language conveys at once that the real

intent is symbolic; the rose and the worm and the situation between them is an inner drama that has nothing to do with a flower garden.

The situation is not defined in logical terms at all: it comes to us through the interrelations suggested by the words—those quite simple words that have been charged with sensations and the possibility of extended significance. But it's impossible to be precise about this inner drama. The oppositions of rose and worm, of "joy" and "destroy," suggest the presence of corrupting evil in the moral and emotional order as in the natural order. This may be universal, but since the dark secret lover is "he," it carries the hint that it is womanhood, or a specific woman, who has been ruined in this calamity. Evil lives in every phrase except one. The rich, vital feel of *thy bed of crimson joy* is surrounded by the hostile forces hinted at in *sick, worm, night, howling storm, found out, dark secret love* and *destroy*.

What is this worm: lust, sin, death? We don't know. It is "invisible," which adds to the atmosphere of mystery. Its real nature is as dark as the night it flies in, and as deadly as the howling storm. Then again in contrast to its swift dark flight in the howling storm, there is something furtive and stealthy in "has found out thy bed" and "his dark secret love." This suggests some evil, devouring sexuality that destroys instead of creating, bringing mortal sickness to the crimson joy. The whole thing is extraordinarily alive, but probably no two people get quite the same "meaning" out of it.

The use of symbols by modern poets has been all in the direction of complexity such as Blake's. The two most distinguished poets of the age, Yeats and Eliot, are both visionaries to whom thought and idea embody themselves instinctively in symbolic shapes. As Yeats says: "Anyone who has any experience of any mystical state of the soul knows how there float up into the mind profound symbols whose meaning . . . one does not perhaps understand for years"; or again, completing that unconscious experience by the final revelation, he speaks of "a sudden sense of power and peace that comes when we have before our mind's eye a group of images, which obeys us . . . and which satisfies the needs of our soul." Moreover he believed that the memory of the individual at its deepest level became part of a "Great Memory" (which corresponds to Jung's Collective Unconscious) and thus unites the poet in the present with the myths of the past.

Out of such a belief comes his sonnet "Leda and the Swan," though the poem gives no answer to the final question the poet asks, and leaves its complex strangeness in its own symbolic outlines.

Yeats believed in a cyclical pattern of history, and in the notes to the volume in which the poem first appeared in 1923, he tells us that its origin was in thoughts of the exhausted political soil of Europe and of some new start. "Then I thought 'Nothing is now possible but some movement, or birth from above, preceded by some violent annunciation.' My fancy began to play with Leda and the Swan for metaphor, and I began this poem, but as I wrote, bird and lady took such possession of the scene that all politics went out of it . . ." All politics did go out of it, but the figures remain symbolic, though of universals instead of particulars.

A sudden blow: the great wings beating still
Above the staggering girl, her thighs caressed
By the dark webs, her nape caught in his bill,
He holds her helpless breast upon his breast.

How can those terrified vague fingers push
The feathered glory from her loosening thighs?
And how can body, laid in that white rush,
But feel the strange heart beating where it lies?

A shudder in the loins engenders there
The broken wall, the burning roof and tower
And Agamemnon dead.
                  Being so caught up,
So mastered by the brute blood of the air,
Did she put on his knowledge with his power
Before the indifferent beak could let her drop?

Yeats was remembering Michelangelo's painting of the same subject in Venice, and in the first eight lines we are certainly aware of nothing but "bird and lady," and the superb sensuous modeling of the strange, wild scene in its mingled terror and glory. Even when this is broken by the intrusion of *what* is "engendered there," and the abstract question of power and knowledge, the physical returns. From the first "sudden blow," to the slow, faint rhythm of the last line, we are in the presence of a momentous creative act. But what is Yeats implying by it all? What further inner vision is immanent in this physical union? What does the ancient myth of bird and lady signify to him?

The swan is Zeus, the eternal creative power and creative mind which descends, takes physical shape, becomes "the brute blood of the air" and mates with humanity. In another poem he says:

> The stallion Eternity
> Mounted the mare of Time
> 'Gat the foal of the world.

The union of Leda and the Swan contains the same idea. Spirit can fulfill itself only in body, and by so doing begets man, with his incurably dual nature, half creative, half destructive; half love, half war. This is what the symbolic union "engenders." From it came Helen, and thus the Trojan War and all the mythical history with its human implications stretching from it. Yeats centers the experience in Leda and her sense of being "mastered," and the unanswered question at the end takes us beyond the myth to the general mystery. Can any human creature understand the universal forces of which it seems to be the instrument? What is the secret of all the opposing passions inborn in every human creature, playing out their drama throughout the history of the human race?

Here again interpretation can vary with each reader, but the sense of the vitality and power of the symbol stays. The physical picture doesn't remain at the physical level, but engenders thoughts and feelings that go beyond it

[*The Poetic Process*]   66

and have no conclusion in the poem. It's interesting to compare this sonnet with Donne's. We might say of that that the poet starts with the silent prayer: "Make my faith active not passive," and then transforms that abstraction from the first word to the last into brilliantly graphic concrete and complex terms, drawn in metaphors of love and war. Yeats uses the same images, but gives us the whole symbolic picture first, alone in its sensuous impact, without interpretation. This is followed by further glimpses of mythic scenes, and then with the one abstract sentence, "Did she put on his knowledge with his power . . . ?" He too is contemplating the same "union of opposites" as Donne is: active-passive, body-mind, creation-destruction, conscious-unconscious, and their paradoxical mystery. Both poets are intense, dramatic and concentrated. But their effects are quite different. Donne strictly logical under all his strange interlocking analogies, leaving a completely worked out pattern; Yeats carrying us away on a great sweep of vision, creating a formal unity as complete as that of Donne, but leaving the "thought" all unresolved at the end, streaming off beyond the outline of the poem.

No one can say that one is "better" than the other. Both are beautiful works of poetic art. But for the focus of this chapter, the heart of one is in metaphor, and the heart of the other in symbol.

5. Words

"The best words in their best order."

S. T. Coleridge

The English language has had many harsh things said about it. To the Germans it is an impure product, without the dignity of an unbroken single tradition: the language of a mixed race, which lacks the quality of a speech that has formed native words from its own stock for every new need. To the French, it is a chaotic and illogical language unsuited to the expression of clear thinking, which has been allowed to run wild like an unschooled child, instead of being watched over carefully by a learnèd Academy. Both these criticisms are true, but there's much to be said on the other side. The English language is an unpredictable medley, but no other can communicate such subtle shades of thought and feeling, such fine discriminations of meaning. The riches of its mingled derivations supply a multitude of synonyms, each with its own distinction of implication, so that *fatherly* is not the same thing as *paternal,* nor *fortune* as *luck,* nor *boyish* as *puerile,* nor *pastor* as *shepherd.* There are the simple, almost prehistoric words for plain, primitive things, the common unchanging experience of life, the strongest human feelings: words like *sun* and *summer, heat* and *cold, sea* and *earth, hand* and *heart, father* and *mother, love* and *sin, blood* and *breath.* There are beautiful words of emotional significance from the French, *charity* and *grace* and *mercy* and *pity* and *comfort;* exotic words from the East, *azure* and *scarlet, damask* and *caravan;* and splendid classical words, trailing their ancestry from the ancient worlds of Greece and Rome: *apprehension* and

[The Poetic Process] 68

universal, magnanimity and *omnipotence, intelligence* and *ideal, tragedy* and *philosophy.*

This most vigorous and lively mongrel among languages is the medium of our poets. But the medium of poetry in any language differs from that of any of the other arts in that we use it all the time for another purpose. Language is our means of communication with our fellows. We carry on all our transactions of thought, feeling and the practical conduct of our lives in it. To a large degree, therefore, it is already alive in its own right. Words have an independent being; they come loaded with the values of their origin, with traditional usage, and personal emotional and sensuous associations. As a result of this common traffic, they differ also from other artistic media in that they wear out. As Eliot says, they

> Slip, slide, perish
> Decay with imprecision, will not stay in place,
> Will not stay still.

Language is like soil. However rich, it is subject to erosion, and its fertility is constantly threatened by uses that exhaust its vitality. It needs constant re-invigoration if it is not to become arid and sterile.

Poetry is one great source of the maintenance and renewal of language. The dead poets provide a heritage of tradition, of all the finest that still lives from the past; the living poets carry the language forward. For no generation feels in exactly the same way as its forerunners, and each must therefore inevitably use words differently. The history of poetry, in one way, is a history of the birth, maturing and decay of cycles of poetic diction. Each is born in revolution, runs its course of development and elaboration, and degenerates into formalism and mechanical imitation.

It is usual to give the name "poetic diction" to a peculiarly artificial use of words which became popular in the eighteenth century, when a breeze was always a zephyr; a girl a nymph; fishes, birds, and sheep, the finny prey, the feathered choir, and the fleecy care; and rats, the whiskered vermin race. We cannot by any stretch of imagination think of Donne calling a girl a nymph, or Wordsworth or Shelley calling birds the feathered choir, or of Eliot speaking of rats as the whiskered vermin race. But it was not only the eighteenth century which evolved a poetic diction; certain marked characteristics belong to each tradition. Before the enormous development of language which the Elizabethan and Jacobean dramatists illustrate, the early Elizabethan lyrists sang in a very simple vocabulary, using the surface of words only.

> Love in my bosom like a bee
>   Doth suck his sweet;
> Now with his wings he plays with me,
>   Now with his feet.
> Within mine eyes he makes his nest,
> His bed amidst my tender breast;
> And yet he robs me of my rest.
>   Ah, wanton, will ye?

But that convention was much too easy for the complexity of thought and dramatic intensity which Donne and his followers demanded that the lyric should carry, so that in their era words became close-packed and concentrated in their condensation of emotional and intellectual meaning. At the opposite extreme from Donne, Milton changed the Elizabethan vocabulary into the Latinized eloquence of formal grandeur. But to the poets of the eighteenth century the language of both Donne and Milton was equally unsuitable. They needed a social literary medium which would communicate to an audience which prided itself on standards of clarity, elegance and decorum in the use of a specified "poetic diction." This now seems forced and artificial to us. The biblical proverb: "Go to the ant, thou sluggard, consider her way and be wise . . . How long wilt thou sleep, O sluggard? When wilt thou arise out of thy sleep?" becomes in Dr. Johnson's version:

> Turn on the prudent ant thy heedless eyes,
> Observe her labours, sluggard, and be wise . . .
> How long shall sloth usurp thy useless hours,

Unnerve thy vigour, and enchain thy powers,
While artful shades thy downy couch enclose,
And soft solicitation courts repose?

Wordsworth rebelled violently from that convention and demanded a return to the language of ordinary men. The later Romantics, Keats, Shelley, and then Tennyson, Rossetti and Swinburne, developed more particularly the sensuous suggestions of words and loaded their poetry with them. That convention petered out in the nineties into the ultra-sensuous:

I have forgot much, Cynara, gone with the wind,
Flung roses, roses, riotously with the throng,
Dancing to put thy pale lost lilies out of mind . . .
(Ernest Dowson)

The twentieth century, among many changes in poetic language, has entirely discarded all such florid gestures, and demands again the language of speech. If a modern poet expresses something of the same situation as Dowson does, he uses a deliberately "unpoetic" vocabulary, and it comes out:

I have stuttered on my feet
Clinched to the streamlined and butter-smooth trulls
of the élite.
(Louis MacNeice)

Apart from a "poetic diction" belonging in a general way to the language of every age, diction in its simplest sense—words—is the foundation of every poem. And apart from a tendency of poets in every age to use certain conventions belonging to that age, each poet by taste and temperament may tend to an individual quality in his use of words. He may be thrifty like Housman or Hardy, spendthrift like Marlowe or Swinburne, calm like Herbert, boisterous like Browning, graceful like Herrick, or energetic like Hopkins or Yeats. In addition to his inherent bent, the whole conscious force of his artistry will be toward the most exact equivalence he can attain between the words he uses and the effects he wishes to communicate. The poet, in spite of Donne's declaration, can never be "a naked thinking heart that makes no show." He will use every resource of his language, from complete simplicity to complex eloquence, heightening his emotion now through compression, now through expansion; now through omission of detail, now through repetition.

Some of the most moving lines in poetry are bare of any ornament at all:

> O God! O God! That it were possible
> To undo things done, to call back yesterday.
>
> (Heywood)

or the final line of Milton's sonnet on his dead wife:

> I waked, she fled, and day brought back my night.

or Donne's impatient plea:

> For God's sake hold your tongue and let me love.

or Wordsworth's heartbreak:

> The memory of what has been
> And never more will be.

or Eliot's prayer:

> Teach us to care and not to care
> Teach us to sit still.

At the other extreme are magnificent pieces of rhetoric such as Macbeth's cry of horror:

> Will all great Neptune's ocean wash this blood
> Clean from my hand? No; this my hand will rather
> The multitudinous seas incarnadine,
> Making the green one red.

or Milton's description of Satan's embattled hosts, with its high-sounding, sonorous list of historic names. "Never, since created man" did such force assemble,

> though all the giant brood
> Of Phlegra with th' heroic race were join'd
> That fought at Thebes and Ilium, on each side

Mix'd with auxiliar Gods; and what resounds
In fable or romance of Uther's son,
Begirt with British and Armoric knights;
And all who since, baptized or infidel,
Jousted in Aspramont or Montalban,
Damasco, or Marocco, or Trebisond,
Or whom Biserta sent from Afric shore,
When Charlemain with all his peerage fell
By Fontarabia.

or Yeats's fury as he looks on the degradation of his country:

On this foul world in its decline and fall;
On gangling stocks grown great, great stocks run dry,
Ancestral pearls all pitched into a sty,
Heroic reverie mocked by clown and knave. . . .

Not the simple or majestic words themselves, but the energy or emotion or movement given them by the poet creates the value. Emily Dickinson's simplicity, often so heartfelt, can be embarrassing if it strains at originality, misses the mark, and falls flat:

I lost a world the other day
Has anybody found?
You'll know it by the row of stars
Around its forehead bound.

Rhetoric too can be out of place when James Thomson in *The Seasons* addresses the pineapple:

But O thou blest Anana, thou the pride
Of vegetable life . . .

or when Hart Crane addresses Brooklyn Bridge:

O Thou steeled Cognizance whose leap commits
The agile precints of the lark's return;
Within whose lariat sweep encinctured sing
In single chrysalis the many twain—

Browning can make a string of common little rhyming words very touching at the conclusion of "Confessions":

> We loved, sir—used to meet:
> How sad and bad and mad it was—
> But then, how it was sweet!

Whereas the same sequence is slightly ridiculous and very clumsy in Swinburne's refrain:

> Villon, our sad bad glad mad brother's name.

Yeats speaks of bringing expression "to that point of artifice where the true self can find its tongue." This seems a paradox. We think of artifice and truth as opposites. Actually it is not so. By grinding, a lens is brought to the point of artifice which brings true vision to the imperfect eye. A process similar to grinding, what Yeats calls "stitching and unstitching," brings its true tongue to imperfect human speech. The result may give an effect of pure spontaneity—must indeed, he says:

> A line will take us hours maybe;
> Yet if it does not seem a moment's thought,
> Our stitching and unstitching has been nought.

The poet's craft is to turn words into deeds, for the basic difference between words used in poetry and in prose is the amount of activity they transmit. A good prose writer doesn't waste words, and he uses them too with a keen ear to their balance, texture and sound; but the poet, especially the lyric poet, has to work in a narrow compass and must therefore use more precise qualities of compression and design. The greater the poet the more value he will wring from his medium: music, meaning, memory; simplicity and ornament; image and idea; dramatic force and lyrical intensity; direct statement and oblique suggestion; color, light, power—all are distilled from his words.

In a sense all poetry has a dramatic element. The poet, directly or indirectly, is addressing someone else. It may be a reader, or some figure in his own life, or different emotions playing out their parts in his consciousness. He is always in some role: prophet, lover, thinker, mourner, cynic, satirist; and within that role in some mood: joyous, defiant, despairing, embittered, questioning, assured. And it is to the degree that we feel an individual voice speaking the words, making language act out his "true self" of the moment, that we value the poem. Take the difference in expression between Cowper and Hopkins as they each lament the felling of a favorite row of poplars. Cowper writes:

> The poplars are fell'd, farewell to the shade
> And the whispering sound of the cool colonnade,
> The winds play no longer, and sing in the leaves,
> Nor Ouse on his bosom their image receives.
>
> Twelve years have elaps'd since I first took a view
> Of my favorite field and the bank where they grew,
> And now in the grass behold they are laid,
> And the tree is my seat that once lent me a shade.

The tripping rhythm at once destroys any sense of grief in the situation, and except for the neat antithesis in the last line, the language is banal in the extreme. So is the final sentiment.

> 'Tis a sight to engage me, if anything can,
> To muse on the perishing pleasures of man;
> Though his life be a dream, his enjoyments, I see,
> Have a being less durable even than he.

Hopkins also laments the loss of the shade, the shadow and the wind, but how differently!

> My aspens dear, whose airy cages quelled,
> Quelled or quenched in leaves the leaping sun,
> All felled, felled, are all felled;
>   Of a fresh and following folded rank
>   Not spared, not one
>   That dandled a sandalled
>   Shadow that swam or sank.
> On meadow and river and wind-wandering weed-
>   winding bank.

Here the life and light and movement of the poplars before they were cut down, and the poet's delight in their ever-changing beauty is created in every word of the description. First not only the beauty, but the power of the trees that could quell and quench even the leaping sun, then the springing curving line of them, and their loosely shifting slipper-like shadows on field and river and bank. And woven into the description, the poet's grief at man's outrage against this lovely scene. The heavy tolling doom of "all felled, felled, are all felled," and "not spared, not one" are the center of his emotion:

> Ten or twelve, only ten or twelve
> Strokes of havoc unselve
> The sweet especial scene.

That's the tragedy. This was something unique, with its own especial being. But Hopkins's "especial" voice remains; his extraordinary individual use of precise or invented words to create his unique vision and personal intensity of feeling.

Or take a famous, but surely rather commonplace, farewell of Burns and compare it with Shakespeare.

> Ae fond kiss, and then we sever;
> Ae farewell, alas, for ever!
> Deep in heartwrung tears I'll pledge thee,
> Warring sighs and groans I'll wage thee!
>
> Had we never loved sae kindly,
> Had we never loved sae blindly,
> Never met—or never parted,
> We had ne'er been broken-hearted.

This is an example perhaps where the reader puts more into the poem than he takes out, and in fact creates the emotion for himself. Since most people have suffered some similar feelings, they respond easily to the sentiment, and to the flat and insipid language. In contrast, this is Shakespeare's Troilus saying good-by to Cressida.

> We two, that with so many thousand sighs
> Did buy each other, must poorly sell ourselves
> With the rude brevity and discharge of one.
> Injurious time now with a robber's haste

Crams his rich thievery up, he knows not how.
As many farewells as be stars in heavens,
With distinct breath and consigned kisses to them,
He fumbles up into a loose adieu,
And scants us with a single famished kiss,
Distasted with the salt of broken tears.

This is truly tortured parting; rhetoric that gives full expression to the extravagant agony alive in the circumstance, and yet does not falsify it in the least. In spite of its extravagance, it is personal speech: the language isn't inflated into any general vague significance. It's that of a young lover frantic with grief, pouring out the essence of his passionate rebellion. He loads his speech with intricate metaphors of buying and selling, of robbery, of bitter tasting, but all enclosed in the single thought that what had seemed lavish, infinite and boundless, has shrunk to "a single famished kiss,/ Distasted with the salt of broken tears." And in spite of the magnificence of some of the vocabulary, Shakespeare uses too quite common words like *rude, crams, fumbled*. These bring it all within the human reality of the moment. Indeed it is much more "real" than the Burns verses.

In the last of the *Four Quartets,* Eliot describes the perfect sentence:

where every word is at home,
Taking its place to support the others,
The word neither diffident nor ostentatious,
An easy commerce of the old and the new,
The common word exact without vulgarity,
The formal word precise but not pedantic,
The complete consort dancing together.

He is emphasizing that it's the right *relationships* that make the harmony and activity of good writing. Mutual support among words has much to do with successful artistry. The use of familiar short words among "poetic" and unusual ones (as in the Troilus speech) is often very satisfying. The same "easy commerce" works in the Yeats lines:

Ancestral pearls all pitched into a sty
Heroic reverie mocked by clown and knave.

Or the mixture may be between abstract and concrete
words, as when Hamlet says to Horatio,

Absent thee from felicity awhile
And in this harsh world draw thy breath in pain,
To tell my story.

A further "commerce" is going on here between the short
Saxon words and the dignified Latinizations.

Or "the complete consort" may dance together because
a varied vocabulary has been woven into a single poetic
"tone." This verse of Housman is a simple illustration of
how the whole "feel" of a mood, here one of happy, active,
carefree youth, can come to life in a few lines:

Once in a wind of morning
    I ranged the thymy wold;
The world-wide air was azure
    And all the brooks ran gold.

But a much more complex skill in the same thing runs all
through Herrick's "Delight in Disorder."

A sweet disorder in the dress
Kindles in clothes a wantonness;
A lawn about the shoulders thrown
Into a fine distraction,
An erring lace, which here and there
Enthralls the crimson stomacher,
A cuff neglectful, and thereby
Ribands to flow confusedly,
A winning wave, deserving note,
In the tempestuous petticoat,
A careless shoe-string, in whose tie
I see a wild civility,
Do more bewitch me than when art
Is too precise in every part.

The poet creates his "delight in disorder" in an art that
is "precise in every part." The basis of the poem is in the

paired words which seem to deny each other. "Sweet disorder," "fine distraction," "wild civility" seem to be contradictions, but that is just what makes them delightful. He is implying, of course, that it is this quality of unselfconscious provocativeness that he enjoys in women, but he transposes it wittily to the clothes, so that they act out their "wantonness" in their own spontaneous fashion, and kindle excitement. The scarf is thrown into distraction, the lace is erring and enthralls the stomacher, ribands flow confusedly, the wave is winning, the petticoat tempestuous. The whole movement and meaning of the language adds up to the tone of playful amorous gaiety, and it is "deserving note" how deftly it is all conveyed in the character of the words. Moreover there's even a sweet disorder in the run of the verses. After the opening couplet announcing the theme, ten lines of variegated subjects tumble tempestuously into the verb "do more bewitch me," and then the poem subsides into the prim neatness of the final phrase.

Multitude is here subdued into unity of tone, but the poet may use the opposite way of creating harmony. He may make a single word the pivot of a poem, with everything else sustaining the suggestions that radiate from it. In the eleventh poem of "In Memoriam" Tennyson does this with the word *calm*.

> Calm is the morn without a sound,
>> Calm as to suit a calmer grief,
>> And only thro' the faded leaf
> The chestnut pattering to the ground:
>
> Calm and deep peace on this high wold,
>> And on these dews that drench the furze;
>> And all the silvery gossamers
> That twinkle into green and gold:
>
> Calm and still light on yon great plain
>> That sweeps with all its autumn bowers.
>> And crowded farms and lessening towers,
> To mingle with the bounding main:
>
> Calm and deep peace in this wide air,

These leaves that redden to the fall;
And in my heart, if calm at all,
If any calm, a calm despair:

Calm on the seas, and silver sleep,
And waves that sway themselves in rest,
And dead calm in that noble breast
Which heaves but with the heaving deep.

The beautiful calm and deep peace of the autumn land-
scape, spread out before us, and the quietly heaving sea at
rest, all speak of the lulling beauty of the natural sur-
roundings; first in the details immediately around, then
in those of the far distance. But the word takes on a com-
pletely different coloring and is in poignant contrast
when it becomes the "calm despair" and the "dead calm"
of the two human figures.

Or the coloring of the single word may be highly dra-
matic instead of quietly meditative. As Othello blows out
the candle at Desdemona's bedside, he says:

Put out the light, and then put out the light:
If I quench thee, thou flaming minister.
I can again thy former light restore,
Should I repent me: but once put out thy light,
Thou cunning'st pattern of excelling nature,
I know not where is that Promethean heat
That can thy light relume.

The word *light* is repeated five times in the seven lines,
shuttling between its meaning as a physical flame, and
as life itself. The simple opening of one-syllable words de-
velops into an intensity of magnificance at the end of the
sentence, yet the single word *light* holds its central power,
reminding us not only of Desdemona's warm, living body
and spirit, but of her innocence in the face of the dark
deed Othello is going to commit, and so soon to repent of.
Again the mixture of short and long words, abstract and
concrete, Saxon and Latin, ancient and modern, all sup-
port one another in consort.

A "commerce" between words much favored by Eliot
himself is to mingle with his own contemporary vocabu-

lary quotations or allusions from other writers, and thus to create a sense of irony in the implied contrast. The homecoming of the typist in Part III of *The Waste Land* is an example:

> At the violet hour, the evening hour that strives
> Homeward, and brings the sailor home from sea,
> The typist home at teatime, clears her breakfast, lights
> Her stove, and lays out food in tins.
> Out of the window perilously spread
> Her drying combinations touched by the sun's last rays. . . .

The central lines describe the sordid and unappetizing quality of the typist's "home" and her slovenly manner of living, in the most prosaic and direct words; but the picture they give is accentuated by framing it within other lines where allusive words recall memories of romantic scenes of evening, homecoming, and open windows. The "violet hour" suggests Sappho's lines to the evening star; "the sailor home from sea" echoes R. L. Stevenson's "Requiem"; while the conjunction of the window with the word "perilously" provokes a wry comparison with Keats's

> . . . magic casements, opening on the foam
> Of perilous seas, in faery lands forlorn.

The precise use of *epithets* by poets is in sharp contrast with our usual careless or conventional use of them in speech. Dorothy Wordsworth enters in her journal: "William tired himself seeking an epithet for the cuckoo," and Keats writes to Fanny Brawne, "I want a brighter word than bright, a fairer word than fair." The result may be a vivid concrete satisfaction like Milton's "meadows *trim* with daisies *pied*," or Rupert Brooke's "the *rough male* kiss of blankets," or Housman's "*twelve-winded* sky." Or the poet may achieve a concentration of sense-suggestion: Keats's *deep damasked* wings of the tiger moth contains the shimmer of silk, the sheen of damascened metal and the texture of a damask rose. The concentration may be both sensuous and emotional. Arnold's final line in "Isolation," (p. 146) "The *unplumbed, salt, estranging* sea," brings the sight and taste of the sea, along with the mystery of the bitterness and loneliness of the human condition in the flux of life and time. Another device is to blend an abstract and a concrete epithet, as Milton does in "the *lazy leaden-stepping* hours," or T. S. Eliot more startlingly in his description of

> the *damp* souls of housemaids
> *Sprouting despondently* at area gates.

Finally, from the rough drafts left by poets, or from revised editions of a published poem, we can often see them at work, rejecting, polishing and sharpening their language to the final "point of artifice where the true self can find its tongue." For instance, the first four lines of "Leda and the Swan" (p. 65) were originally:

> Now can the swooping godhead have his will
> Yet hovers, though her helpless thighs are pressed
> By the webbed toes; and that all-powerful bill
> Has suddenly bowed her face upon his breast.

It wasn't until five years later that the poem appeared in its final form, with the far more dramatic opening and the far more vivid physical outline.

Alterations are always directed toward making the language stronger, more precise or more full of rhythmic movement. This is how Meredith first published half of one stanza of "Love in the Valley," in 1851:

> Shy as a squirrel whose nest is in the pinetops;
>   Gentle—ah! that she were as jealous as the dove!
> Full of all the wildness of the woodland creatures,
>   Happy in herself is the maiden that I love!

In 1878 it had become:

> Shy as the squirrel that leaps among the pinetops,
>   Wayward as the swallow overhead at set of sun,
> She whom I love is hard to catch and conquer,
>   Hard, but O the glory of the winning were she won!

[*The Poetic Process*]   82

In the same way, the famous lines in Poe's "To Helen."

> the glory that was Greece
> And the grandeur that was Rome.

went through the feebler stage of

> the beauty of fair Greece
> And the grandeur of old Rome.

The exact truth of Keats's

> Not so much life as on a summer's day
> Robs not one light seed from the feathered grass.

might have remained

> Not so much life as on a summer's day
> Robs not at all the dandelion's fleece.

Of poetic speech we might use Donne's image of molding metal on a forge, and say that the poet takes words to batter them, to break, blow, burn and make them new; or that he has the power both to remint the old coinage of traditional use and to issue new currency. But the best metaphor is Eliot's organic one of growth. Poetry arises and takes its own specific form out of the formless flux of life.

> Out of the slimy mud of words, out of the sleet and
>   hail of verbal imprecisions,
> Approximate thoughts and feelings, words that have
>   taken the place of thoughts and feelings,
> There spring the perfect order of speech, and the
>   beauty of incantation.

6. The Design of Poems

"A performance in words."

Robert Frost

In his inaugural lecture as Professor of Poetry at Oxford in 1956, W. H. Auden said that the two questions which interest him most when reading a poem are: "1) Here is a verbal contraption, how does it work? and 2) What kind of a guy inhabits this poem?" As we have seen, these double interests, the technical and the psychological, run through any discussion of poetry. Perhaps we should add a third, the physiological. Housman said he recognized poetry by a shiver down the spine, a constriction of the throat, a precipitation of water to the eyes, and a sensation in the pit of the stomach. Emily Dickinson declared: "If I read . . . and feel physically as if the top of my head were taken off, I know that is poetry . . . is there any other way?" This is to consider poetry entirely in terms of the intuitive response, the "magic," which is certainly better than to limit it to the "message," for poetry is an art not a social service. But it can't really be separated from "meaning." It starts in something given from without and then transformed from within and re-created. Ultimately it is a verbal design, but it has designs upon us, in the sense that the poet is communicating not only a pattern of sounds but a theme, some personal response to life. These two are indivisible. The design is formed of words and sentences, just as prose is, though the arrangement is different. The final difference is in the sound pattern, and I doubt if the structural design of "meaning" in most long poems can be discussed any differently from that in a novel. In a short poem the theme can be presented in a variety of ways, according to the personality of the poet and the literary convention in which he is writing.

The impulse behind all art is to give a personal form to some part of the raw material presented by life. Living is both raw and confused, but in giving it a design the artist does not want to lose all its rawness, for that is the intensity with which it has been felt. Symmetry of outline is not enough. A dead body may be perfectly formed, but it is still dead. A poem may say true things and have a metrical scheme which is technically correct, and yet have no life in it. When Sir Ronald Ross had finally proved how the female anopheles mosquito transfers the infection of malaria, he wrote a poem about it, of which one stanza runs:

> I know this little thing
> A myriad men will save,
> O Death, where is Thy sting,
> Thy victory, O grave!

No one would question the sincerity of the feeling behind the words, and the meter is perfectly regular, but the reader is not "infected" by the feeling and does not share it. Emotion has not been converted into eloquence or warmth into fire. Unlike Shelley's skylark, the poet does not pour his full heart "in profuse strains of unpremeditated art": turning blood into ink is no mere chemical process.

In one of his notebooks Wordsworth describes, in very flat verse, how feeling in itself is valueless, how his passion for creation

> burst forth
> In verse which, with a strong and random light
> Touching an object in its prominent parts,
> Created a memorial which to me
> Was all sufficient, and to my own mind
> Recalling the whole picture, seemed to speak
> An universal language. Scattering thus
> In passion many a desultory sound,

[*The Design of Poems*] 85

I deemed that I had adequately clothed
Meanings at which I hardly hinted, thought
And forms of which I scarcely had produced
An arbitrary sign. . . .

He goes on to state that this is not the "poetic act," which

By slow creation doth impart to speech
Outline and substance even, till it has given
A function kindred to organic power,
The vital spirit of a perfect form.

To put it simply, poetry must *interest* us. It might be
true to say that there are no dull themes, only dull poems.
Donne can start with a flea, which seems as unpromising
material as a mosquito, but by the end the poem has be-
come an impassioned eulogy of sexual union; while
Wordsworth can often talk about the mystical union of
his own soul with that of Nature and make it nothing but
a prosy "sermon in stones." Or Blake (p. 33) can trans-
form a "social" theme into the exultation of the verses on
building Jerusalem, while Tennyson in "Locksley Hall
Sixty Years After" writes about the same thing like this:

Is it well that while we range with Science, glorying
in the Time,
City children soak and blacken soul and sense in
city slime?

There among the glooming alleys Progress halts on
palsied feet,
Crime and hunger cast our maidens by the thousand
on the street.

There the master scrimps his haggard sempstress of
her daily bread,
There a single sordid attic holds the living and the
the dead.

Poor old Tennyson is feeling with real intensity as he sees
"poor old Heraldry, poor old History, poor old Poetry pass-
ing hence" in the new age of Darwin and Huxley, and
compares the triumphs of contemporary scientific theories

with the actualities of social degradation. But while it isn't perhaps fair to dismiss the poem as what one critic calls "choicely cadenced hysteria," this passage is nothing better than a catalogue, though a vivid one.

The taste of the twentieth-century revolutionary poets for casting their "outline and substance" into image and symbol makes the reading of poetry more difficult than it has ever been before. Our contemporaries did not invent the most important change, which originated among the French symbolist poets of the late nineteenth century, but they introduced it to England and America, and it has been the dominating influence upon the poetry of our age. Pound announced its aim when he wrote: "General expressions in non-concrete terms are a laziness, they are talk, not art, not creation." General expressions in non-concrete terms meant all explanation, all commentary, all interpretive material. The "meaning" of a poem must not need any statement in abstract language; it must all be absorbed into and communicated through sensuous imagery. Moreover it isn't necessary that the images should be *logically* related. They must work intuitively on the emotions and sensations of the reader, and the associations and relationships they set up in the reader's mind must suggest all the ideas behind the words.

Of course the demand that poetry should be concrete was nothing new. The new thing in the theories of Pound and Eliot was that *no* abstract language must be used at all. We can see the change by comparing two poems, "Daffodils" by Wordsworth and "Now the leaves are falling fast" by Auden, each of which creates an emotional mood, though both the moods themselves and the methods by which they are created are completely different.

> I wandered lonely as a cloud
>   That floats on high o'er vales and hills,
> When all at once I saw a crowd,
>   A host of golden daffodils;
> Beside the lake, beneath the trees,
> Fluttering and dancing in the breeze.

Continuous as the stars that shine
  And twinkle in the Milky Way,
They stretched in never ending line
  Along the margin of the bay.
Ten thousand saw I at a glance,
Tossing their heads in sprightly dance.

The waves beside them danced, but they
  Outdid the sparkling waves in glee:
A poet could not but be gay
  In such a jocund company:
I gazed—and gazed—but little thought
What wealth the show to me had brought:

For oft, when on my couch I lie
  In vacant or in pensive mood,
They flash upon that inward eye
  Which is the bliss of solitude;
And then my heart with pleasure fills
And dances with the daffodils.

In this well-known poem, Wordsworth describes the profound experience which gave life its meaning to him. The poet, wandering "lonely as a cloud," floating, detached from earthly fellowship, suddenly sees the host of dancing flowers. They remind him of the stars at night in brightness and multitude; they match the waves in radiance and gaiety. In a flash, the poet's loneliness is transformed into fellowship: he becomes a part of all this "jocund company," this sense of joy and unity and continuity in the natural elements of air, water, earth. All this is now alive in his own being too. And this moment of vision and revelation, this "show," is a possession which enriches his life forever. Through that "inward eye" of memory, other moods of loneliness and listlessness can be animated with the sense of fulfillment which was captured on that first spring morning.

Now the leaves are falling fast,
Nurse's flowers will not last;
Nurses to the graves are gone,
And the prams go rolling on.

Whispering neighbours, left and right,
Pluck us from our real delight;
And the active hands must freeze
Lonely on the separate knees.

Dead in hundreds at the back
Follow wooden in our track,
Arms raised stiffly to reprove
In false attitudes of love.

Starving through the leafless wood
Trolls run scolding for their food;
And the nightingale is dumb,
And the angel will not come.

Cold, impossible, ahead
Lifts the mountain's lovely head
Whose white waterfall could bless
Travellers in their last distress.

This poem of Auden's too is a vision seen through the "inward eye," not in the bliss of solitude, but in the torture of isolation. Instead of the intuition of a vital union between himself and the forces around him, the poet is aware only of the sense of exclusion from any kind of fellowship.

It's a despairing glimpse of an individual in a fragmentary world, without a faith, without a center, without the safe dependence on a settled society and traditional ideals. We could say that it is a wonderful picture of a personal neurosis, but since it is only too true that this is an *age* of anxiety, anything personal in the picture extends itself easily into a general perspective.

But the first question is: What does it mean? For everything in it is communicated through a series of concrete impressionistic details, and the poet gives us no interpretation of them. They produce sensations and associations in our minds, but any precise exposition must be guess work in some lines, I think. One can say only: This is how I read it.

The whole scene is autumnal, the atmosphere that of a dying day. "Nurse's flowers will not last," that is, the safe dependence and the simple joys and innocence of child-hood are over. By extension of that into general terms, the sense of security is lost that comes from being born into a congenial, integrated society. The old safe bond between nannies and children is dead, and the tragedy is that no new independent maturity has taken its place. The nurses have gone, but the individual and the race remain in their baby-carriages, quite unequipped to control their own destiny.

The whispering neighbors may refer, at the public level, to rival totalitarian systems (the poem was written in 1936, in the days of Hitler and Stalin); or we can read it as meaning the personal distractions and conflicts we all know. But the vivid picture of the active hands freezing *lonely* on the *separate* knees is clearly the inca-pacity for any living union and warm fellowship of pur-pose, and that is what should be "our real delight."

Instead of any such close ties, we are shown these next puppet-like figures, dehumanized and regimented, which seem to represent rigid, hypocritical authority killing all spontaneity.

Perhaps the starving, scolding trolls symbolize instincts which should have been fed by natural free living, but have become suppressed and distorted into evil shapes with aggressive, compulsive demands. The nightingale must be the symbol for nature and romance and the voice of imagination; and the angel, the voice of spiritual com-fort.

The last verse suggests the absolute unattainability of peace and aspiration and healing, and their utter remote-ness from "the leafless wood." The will is paralyzed; any transcendence is "impossible"; frustration is complete.

The emotional moods of these two poems are obviously at extremes, but so are the methods of poetic design. For one thing the vocabularies belong to different periods. No contemporary poet could use the word "glee" and make it sound natural, or speak of being in a "pensive mood"; and I'm not sure that in this era of psychoanalysis he would risk lying on a couch! But beyond the use of words, the ways in which the moods reach us are quite unlike.

"Daffodils" is crystal clear and lucid. The poet recounts a little episode, gives a description of the scene and of the feelings that match it. Then he abstracts the total emotional value of the experience and concludes by summing that up. The whole thing is written out in a logical, linear, syntactical progression. But that's not all. If we look below the immediate surface, we find that all the realistic detail of the flowers, the trees, the waves, the wind, and all the accompanying sensations of active joy, are absorbed into an over-all concrete metaphor, the recurrent image of the *dance*, which appears in every verse. The flowers, the stars, the waves are units in this gay dancing pattern of order in diversity, of linked eternal harmony and vitality. Through the revelation and recognition of his kinship with nature, the poet himself becomes as it were a part of the whole cosmic dance.

Auden makes his whole poem out of this last element in Wordsworth's design. He tells no story, he makes no abstract statements, he follows no logical progression from verse to verse. The poem has no beginning, middle and end in a time-sequence. It would not really matter much if we read it starting from the last verse and went backward. Everything in it is happening at the same time. Wordsworth has a focal point, the daffodils: everything in the poem exists in relation to them. In the Auden scene no perspective emerges. A number of images are juxtaposed without logical order. Their *fusion* in the imagination of the poet produces a mood, but that mood is never defined. The poem is all about abstract qualities: loneliness, frustration, neurotic fears, paralysis of the will, lack of faith, the decay of tradition, despair; but not a single one of these conditions is mentioned by name. We feel them solely through the concrete images which awaken emotional and sensuous associations in our minds.

Wordsworth of course is working with sense impressions too, but he interprets their significance as he goes along—making *statements* about them. His method is direct, Auden's oblique. Auden simply leaves the reader to find the "meaning" for himself, and different readers may find different interpretations. Moreover, although his pictures are most vivid, they don't belong to any actuality. His landscape is an inner psychological, symbolic one, a landscape of the mind. The various figures, the leafless wood, the waterfall and the mountain are chosen because they suggest inward states of feeling, and so blend to create the mood in which he writes. André Gide calls the method that of "creative incoherence," and perhaps the two poems together illustrate a remark of Hopkins, in a letter to Robert Bridges: "One of two kinds of clearness one shd. have—either the meaning to be felt without effort as fast as one reads or else, if dark at first reading, when once made out *to explode*."

The poems by Wordsworth and Auden employ two very different kinds of poetic architecture which illustrate another distinction in design found all through the history of poetry. Much print has been used to discriminate between the classical and the romantic modes of writing. The terms, though, are confusing, since they're also used to label historical periods in literature. A simpler and clearer opposition is to call them the objective and the subjective forms, or the impersonal and the personal. "Daffodils" is an intensely personal poem, though its emotion has been "recollected in tranquillity" and distanced from the immediate impact of its rawness. Still, it creates a purely subjective experience. It is directly autobiographical: the poet tells us about the daffodils in order to tell us something about himself. Auden, on the other hand, is not in his poem as an "I" at all. The poet ostensibly projects a communal vision, though we feel strongly that he is himself deeply involved in it. Hence neither poem is a "pure" example of one form or the other, and we must go elsewhere for that.

The best example of purely objective poetry, where the poet seems entirely independent of the poem, are the old ballads. The names of their makers are lost, though it seems most unlikely that they had any kind of "group" authorship, as some experts believe. At the same time no doubt they were written in a long-established tradition with its own strict stylistic laws. The best of them are tragic and passionate, but without any moral conclusions or personal comment. "The Twa Corbies" is a good one.

As I was walking all alane,
I heard two corbies [1] making a mane [2]   [1] *ravens* [2] *moan*
The tane [3] unto the t'other say,   [3] *one*
"Where sall we gang and dine today?"

"In behint yon auld fail dyke [4]   [4] *old turf wall*
I wot there lies a new-slain knight;
And naebody kens that he lies there,
But his hawk, his hound, and lady fair."

"His hound is to the hunting gane
His hawk to fetch the wild-fowl hame,
His lady's ta'en another mate,
So we may mak our dinner sweet."

"Ye'll sit on his white hause-bane [5]   [5] *neck-bone*
And I'll pick out his bonny blue een;
Wi ae lock o' his gowden hair
We'll theek [6] our nest when it grows bare."   [6] *thatch*

"Mony a one for him makes mane,
But nane sall ken where he is gane;
O'er his white banes when they are bare,
The wind sall blaw for evermair."

This stark little conversation tells a complete story of murder, desertion and treachery. It is pure poetry of statement with no ornament or imagery. It rouses in us both an emotional and physical response of horror and repulsion, and we see vividly the desolate scene with the dead man, and imagine the fleeing hawk and hound, the faithless woman and the mourning friends. But the "I" who relates it is disembodied, just an impersonal voice reporting the facts, and giving them an added dramatic value by making the talk that of the ravens. Without that we wouldn't get the extra ironical twist that the murder not only rids the false lady of her mate, but provides food and soft bedding for the birds. It's the work of a fine artist in the macabre, but it would be impossible to say "what kind of a guy" the author was in any psychological sense.

Against this bare drama put Shelley's "The Indian Serenade," where the whole thing is a prolonged cry of subjective, swooning sentiment.

> I arise from dreams of thee
> In the first sweet sleep of night,
> When the winds are breathing low,
> And the stars are shining bright:
> I arise from dreams of thee,
> And a spirit in my feet
> Hath led me—who knows how?
> To thy chamber window, Sweet!
>
> The wandering airs they faint
> On the dark, the silent stream—
> The Champak odors fail
> Like sweet thoughts in a dream;
> The nightingale's complaint,
> It dies upon her heart;—
> As I must on thine,
> Oh! belovèd as thou art!
>
> Oh lift me from the grass!
> I die! I faint! I fail!
> Let thy love in kisses rain
> On my lips and eyelids pale.
> My cheek is cold and white, alas!
> My heart beats loud and fast;—
> Oh! press it to thine own again,
> Where it will break at last.

These poems present two extreme positions from which the poet can write: the completely impersonal and the completely personal. No one nowadays would hesitate about which is the finer poem. The design of "The Twa Corbies" is full of sinewy, spare strength, and vigorous energy; not a word is wasted in telling the story, sketching the scenes, creating the atmosphere. "The Indian Serenade," though it was very popular in the late nine-

teenth century, seems to our modern taste feeble in senti-
ment and sloppy in vocabulary. It purports to create in-
tensity of feeling and succeeds only in being vague. The
poet gives us no context for the situation, so that we
don't know why the lover is in this lamentable state. Why
should he die and faint and fail; and especially in that
order? Why should his heart break if his beloved comes
and takes him in her arms? He seems just a romantic
sentimentalist, and his language, though it is flowing and
melodious, is repetitive and commonplace.

Our modern age has been particularly barren in fine
love poetry, and one reason for it is certainly the fear of
expressing too much direct personal feeling in poetry.
This is no doubt partly a general rebellion against the
subjective ideal of the Romantic and Victorian poets
(which is seen at its worst in the Shelley poem), but
partly also a result of the stern critical creed of the im-
personality of the poet, insisted upon by Eliot in his early
essays. He preached the doctrine that poetry was an es-
cape from personality into a medium, and again that one
is prepared for art when one has ceased to be interested
in one's own emotions except as material: "Not our feel-
ings, but the pattern we make of our feelings is the centre
of value." Or again he speaks of "the struggle—which
alone constitutes life for the poet—to transmute his per-
sonal and private agonies into something rich and strange,
something universal and impersonal"; and declares that
the more perfect the poet the more completely separate
in him will be the man who suffers and the mind that
creates.

It is characteristic of Eliot that he doesn't mention per-
sonal and private joys as well as agonies, as poetic ma-
terial, but his whole position seems a denial that good
poetry can ever be the expression of direct personal emo-
tion. Somehow we rebel against that. Of course it is true
that it isn't the emotion itself but the pattern that gives
the value to the poem. The feeling in Tennyson's "Now
sleeps the crimson petal, now the white" is very similar
to that in "The Indian Serenade," but whereas one seems
mawkish, the other is beautifully controlled. Both use

night, nature and love as materials, but whereas Tenny-
son weaves something "rich and strange" out of them,
Shelley's poetry, like his lover, faints and fails.

> Now sleeps the crimson petal, now the white;
> Nor waves the cypress in the palace walk;
> Nor winks the gold fin in the porphyry font: —
> The firefly wakens: waken thou with me.

> Now droops the milk-white peacock like a ghost,
> And like a ghost she glimmers on to me.

> Now lies the Earth all Danaë to the stars,
> And all thy heart lies open unto me.

> Now slides the silent meteor on, and leaves
> A shining furrow, as thy thought in me.

> Now folds the lily all her sweetness up,
> And slips into the bosom of the lake:
> So fold thyself, my dearest, thou, and slip
> Into my bosom and be lost in me.

This is rich and strange, but surely not impersonal, and
Eliot's creed seems to push the separation between the
"verbal contraption" and the guy who inhabits it too far.
Moreover poetry need not even be rich and strange to be
profound and moving. An anonymous sixteenth-century
poet put the same grouping of night, nature and longing
for love into a bare quatrain:

> Western wind, when will thou blow,
> The small rain down can rain?
> Christ, if my love were in my arms
> And I in my bed again!

The first two lines give the lover's plight the parallel of
the universal longing for the coming of spring, the last
two focus suddenly on realistic human need. Only two
words in the poem are of more than one syllable, but the
passionate personal hunger for warmth, comfort, close-
ness, is far more intense than in either of the longer
poems. And here surely we feel very little gap between
the man who suffers and the mind that creates.

[*The Poetic Process*]   96

It is dangerous to make *any* flat dogmatic statements about poetry, or to enclose it in any rules. The personal and the impersonal are two different modes of presenting a theme and are neither good nor bad in themselves: good poems and bad poems have been written with both methods. Certain poets involve their personalities directly, others "distance" their material. It's no crime to be subjective in art; it's merely not a classical virtue. A single poet may write sometimes in one mode, sometimes in another; sometimes we feel he is outside the poem, sometimes inside it. Or we might call the distinction that between "closed" and "open" poems. Obviously the poem is always a closed verbal unit, but some poems seem to absorb all their emotion completely into the pattern. "The Twa Corbies" does that, or Donne's "Batter my heart, three personed God . . ." But sometimes the emotion seems to flow on unresolved though the poem has ended, as in "Leda and the Swan" and as in these last love lyrics.

PART II

Poetry and the Human Condition

7. Time

"The woods decay, the woods decay, and fall. . . ."
Alfred Tennyson

In the analysis of the elements of poetic form in Part I, it has been obvious that form in itself has no worth apart from function. The two are indivisible. Poetry is a special use of language, but the value of any use of language is to say something; it is a medium of communication between human beings. Auden declares that the creative artist has three wishes: to make something; to perceive something, either in the external world of sense or the internal world of feeling; and to transmit these perceptions to others. In poetry the transmission of the perceptions is done through the uses of language, hence it is important to be as much alive as possible to the ingenuities and varieties, the strengths and subtleties of the poet's craft, his "making," for by so being we increase our power of response. But technical skill for its own sake will never satisfy, nor is novelty the same thing as originality. As Dr. Johnson says with his immense solid wisdom:

> Nothing can please many and please long, but just representations of human nature . . . The irregular combinations of fanciful invention may delight awhile, by that novelty of which the satiety of life sends us all in quest; but the pleasures of sudden wonder are soon exhausted, and the mind can repose only on the stability of truth.

The poet's "truth" may not be as solemn as this sounds. The perception he wants to communicate may be as airy and fanciful as Herrick's "Delight in Disorder" (p. 78), a graceful trifle like Campion's "Rose-Cheeked Laura" (p. 38), an intimate personal portrait like Frost's "A Silken Tent" (p. 54). The pleasures of "sudden wonder," too, may not be exhausted as quickly as Johnson thinks, yet it is surely true that no serious interest and pleasure in verse stops at versification.

Wordsworth declared that the aim of his poetry was "to teach the young and the gracious of every age, to see, to think and feel, and therefore to become more actively and securely virtuous." He uses "virtuous" in its old sense of "possessing power." The stimulus of poetry to seeing, thinking and feeling does not make us any more morally virtuous; it makes us more *conscious*. It intensifies and extends our faculties, and therefore gives us more understanding and illumination of our own lives and the lives of others. It takes us beyond the surface of our own responses by its fresh apprehension and expression of the commonplace, and by the satisfaction it brings to our own inadequate insights and words. For fine poetry never deals with any thoughts, sensations or emotions that we haven't all felt in *some* degree. A new poetic technique may block our perception of this until the unfamiliar form is understood; but once understood, the result will always be a new vision of old truth or old mystery. As the English poet-critic Donald Davie says: "For Poetry to be great, it must reek of the human, as Wordsworth's poetry does. This is not a novel contention, but perhaps one of those things that cannot be said too often." Or Yeats, in one of his last poems, lamenting the failure of his imagination to provide the "ladders" of myth, symbol and dream which had earlier embodied his themes, concludes:

I must lie down where all the ladders start,
In the foul rag-and-bone shop of the heart.

We read poetry because the poets, like ourselves, have been haunted by the inescapable tyranny of time and death; have suffered the pain of loss, and the more wearing, continuous pain of frustration and failure; and have had moods of unlooked-for release and peace. They have known and watched in themselves and others what Hopkins calls "dear and dogged man" and what Yeats calls "passionate fragmentary man," and how he struggles to make himself whole, and to transcend his slavery to time by completion in something beyond his own ego—in love, in nature, in art, in religion—seeking eagerly a "still point in a turning world." Or how, in default of that, man has contented himself with a serene or a wry acceptance of "things as they are."

"The unexamined life is not worth living" said Socrates, and no poet has ever lived such a life. Sympathy and empathy, feeling with and feeling into, are the basis for his search for the true embodiment in words of his perceptions, great or small. What he presents will appeal to some readers and may repel others, for the relationship between writer and reader must always be a personal one. On the one side is the poet, a man alive in a certain time and place, influenced by a particular social, intellectual and physical environment, writing out of a particular life situation, endowed by nature with an individual temperament, creating his poem, maybe, in one mood among the many he has lived through. On the other side is the reader, who is equally particularized, conditioned by his own age and circumstances, by his own psychological make-up and his own idiosyncrasies of taste. What is really surprising, perhaps, is not that wide varieties of opinions exist about the enjoyment of poems, but the amount of ground on which readers can find agreement. The chief reason for that is that poets seldom demand intellectual beliefs in readers or try to persuade us of their validity. What they ask is emotional assent. As we shall see in the later discussions of various beliefs, we may not agree with the faith a poet holds but we can nevertheless enter into the feeling with which he holds it and that is enough. What we take is "the wonderfully full, new and intimate sense of things" which is the poet's gift.

A "sense of things" is human experience in its widest aspects, and since the poet is "a man speaking to men" he shares the limitations of the human condition with all his fellows. Of these the foremost is the tyranny of time and the knowledge of mortality. Poetry can be immortal, but man himself is doomed to a time world. Transience is the law of his being, as it is of the civilization he creates and even of "the great globe itself." No one has suggested the great sweep of impermanence better than Archibald MacLeish in "You, Andrew Marvell."

And here face down beneath the sun
And here upon earth's noonward height
To feel the always coming on
The always rising of the night

To feel creep up the curving east
The earthy chill of dusk and slow
Upon those under lands the vast
And ever climbing shadow grow

And strange at Ecbatan the trees
Take leaf by leaf the evening strange
The flooding dark about their knees
The mountains over Persia change

And now at Kermanshah the gate
Dark empty and the withered grass
And through the twilight now the late
Few travelers in the westward pass

And Baghdad darken and the bridge
Across the silent river gone
And through Arabia the edge
Of evening widen and steal on

And deepen on Palmyra's street
The wheel rut in the ruined stone
And Lebanon fade out and Crete
High through the clouds and overblown

And over Sicily the air
Still flashing with the landward gulls
And loom and slowly disappear
The sails above the shadowy hulls

And Spain go under and the shore
Of Africa the gilded sand

[Poetry and the Human Condition] 104

And evening vanish and no more
The low pale light across that land

Nor now the long light on the sea
And here face downward in the sun
To feel how swift how secretly
The shadow of the night comes on . . .

Andrew Marvell is not mentioned in the poem, and to understand its title we must have in mind the lines from his poem "To His Coy Mistress":

But at my back I always hear
Time's wingèd chariot hurrying near:
And yonder all before us lie
Deserts of vast eternity.

The poet, lying in the midday sunshine, feels, instead of the light and warmth around him, "the always rising of the night." We speak of night-*fall*, but the metaphor MacLeish has chosen combines time and tide that wait for no man. "The flooding dark" engulfs the "under lands" on the other side of the globe as he basks in high noontide. He imagines the ever-climbing shadow creeping from Persia and Mesopotamia (now Iran and Iraq), to Syria and Lebanon and westward across the Mediterranean to the Atlantic on its way to America. The device of omitting punctuation, and the slow, even flow of the lines and rhymes enforces the feeling of Time's remorseless continuity. But beyond the surface level of meaning is all that is suggested by the regions and the places he names: the birthplaces of great civilizations now extinct, or great ancient cities now ruined, or remembered only through history or archeology. The poet himself is a son of the latest civilization, now basking in its "noonward height," but Time will deal with that as it has with all the past cultures and empires of the world.

Andrew Marvell, the man who wrote the immortal poem, passed inevitably into "the flooding dark," and the man who writes this poem, though he writes it in his own noontime of age, knows only too well "how swift how secretly / The shadow of the night comes on . . ."

No wonder that this great commonplace is an ever-recurring theme in poetry, though the poets manage to transform the clichés about it into something deathless.

> The glories of our blood and state
>> Are shadows, not substantial things;
> There is no armour against fate;
>> Death lays his icy hand on Kings:
>>> Sceptre and crown
>>> Must tumble down,
> And in the dust be equal made
> With the poor crooked scythe and spade.
>
> (James Shirley)

The facts are a truism: rank gives no protection against death; it comes inevitably to kings and farm workers. But Shirley (1596–1666) turns this platitude into a verse full of power through its rhythmical movement and its concrete imagery. We are inclined to think of living figures as reality and death as an abstraction, but the poet makes death the actuality, with his "icy hand" against which man-made glories and armor are mere shadows. Man is reduced to the lifeless objects that symbolize his calling, and the stately crown and scepter have the indignity of "tumbling down" as helplessly as the lowly scythe and spade. Shirley sustains this tone of forceful inevitability for the first two stanzas and into the third, but the weak moral conclusion of the final couplet seems somehow anticlimactic.

> Only the actions of the just
> Smell sweet and blossom in the dust.

Shakespeare had already contradicted that pious hope in part of Ulysses's great speech on Time in *Troilus and Cressida*.

> O! let not virtue seek
> Remuneration for the thing it was;
> For beauty, wit,
> High birth, vigour of bone, desert in service,
> Love, friendship, charity, are subject all
> To envious and calumniating time.

[*Poetry and the Human Condition*]   106

The orthodox religious poets can point to a future immortality as the final escape, and urge men to hasten toward it:

> Heaven is our heritage,
> Earth but a player's stage;
> Mount we unto the sky
> I am sick, I must die.
>> Lord, have mercy on us!

So Thomas Nashe concluded his famous lament "Adieu, Farewell Earth's Bliss," written when the plague was raging in London in 1593. But the lines we all remember from the poem are not the conclusion, but

> Beauty is but a flower
> Which wrinkles will devour;
> Brightness falls from the air,
> Queens have died young and fair,
> Dust hath closed Helen's eye.

Again Time's ravages are made concrete and active in the series of pictures. It doesn't matter much if, as some critics suggest, Nashe wrote "hair" for "air" in the third line. One reading gives a specific image, the other leaves a mistier suggestion, but it's the "falling" of the brightness that saddens us, as in George Herbert's "Virtue."

> Sweet day, so cool, so calm, so bright,
> The bridal of the earth and sky:
> The dew shall weep thy fall tonight;
>> For thou must die.

Herbert, like Shirley and Nashe, solaces himself with the belief that "a sweet and virtuous soul" lives on, but again it is the inexorable passing of the beautiful that remains with the reader.

Gerard Manley Hopkins mourns the same inescapable doom in a much more concentrated and odder little poem, "Spring and Fall: To a Young Child," written two centuries later.

> Márgarét, are you gríeving
> Over Goldengrove unleaving?

Leáves, líke the things of man, you
With your fresh thoughts care for, can you?
Ah! ás the heart grows older
It will come to such sights colder
By and by, nor spare a sigh
Though worlds of wanwood leafmeal lie;
And yet you wíll weep and know why.
Now no matter, child, the name:
Sórrow's spríngs áre the same.
Nor mouth had, no nor mind, expressed
What heart heard of, ghost guessed:
It ís the blight man was born for,
It is Margaret you mourn for.

Hopkins's metrics are highly individual and part of the fascination of his rhythms. Here, the only "regular" four-beat line is the centrally placed eighth, "Though worlds of wanwood leafmeal lie." This line illustrates too Hopkins's characteristic inventions of new words: *wanwood* for pale deserted woodlands and *leafmeal* for littered with fallen leaves—on the analogy of "piecemeal." In the other lines the stresses run from two to five, and though we may not agree in our own reading with the way in which Hopkins accents some of the lines, the whole gives the effect of very personal, compressed, rhythmical speech. Alliteration too adds much to the music, both in the use of vowels and consonants: "By and by, nor spare a sigh" creates the dying fall of a sigh itself. The first eight lines are straightforward in meaning, though unusual in movement, but the ninth, "And yet you will weep and know why," is ambiguous, and can be read in two ways. We can interpret it: "You will weep later, and then it will not be for such things as fallen leaves. You will weep because you will have learnt that all life, including your own, is transient." But with Hopkins's own accent coming on *will*, the sense seems changed. The poet has already told the child that age will cure this particular grief; now he continues: "Yet you persist in weeping and demand that I tell you why you grieve over fallen leaves." This seems, perhaps, a better transition to the rest of the poem, which is the answer. There's no need to name any particular aspect of the ravages of time, for the springs of all our sorrows are the fact of our own mortality. Neither in thought nor in speech has Margaret yet formulated any idea of death, yet intuitively the "unleaving" has brought the pang to heart and spirit (ghost) which is that knowledge. The last couplet sums it up with telling finality.

The more usual expression of the theme is that of age regretting the past it can never recover. A. E. Housman puts it in question and answer of melodious nostalgia.

> Into my heart an air that kills
>> From yon far country blows:
> What are those blue remembered hills,
>> What spires, what farms are those?
>
> That is the land of lost content,
>> I see it shining plain,
> The happy highways where I went
>> And cannot come again.

He gets great emotional intensity into the simplicity with the contrasts of his two symbolic landscapes: the land of lost content (though shouldn't it be the lost land of content?) with its hills and spires and aspiration, its fertile creative "farms," its adventurous highways of happy youth; and the world of his own heart, blighted by the loss and pierced by the inexorable negative, "where I went / And cannot come again."

The forbidding negatives create some of the most mournful cadences in English poetry. Lear, facing the fact of Cordelia's death:

> No, no, no life!
> Why should a dog, a horse, a rat, have life,
> And thou no breath at all? Thou'lt come no more,
> Never, never, never, never, never!

Wordsworth summing up life without Lucy:

> She died and left to me
> This heath, this calm and quiet scene,
> The memory of what has been,

And never more will be. . . .

Byron's farewell:

> So we'll go no more a-roving
>   So late into the night,
> Though the heart be still as loving,
>   And the moon be still as bright.
>
> For the sword outwears its sheath,
>   And the soul wears out the breast,
> And the heart must pause to breathe,
>   And Love itself have rest.
>
> Though the night was made for loving,
>   And the day returns too soon,
> Yet we'll go no more a-roving
>   By the light of the moon.

Shelley's lament:

> O world! O life! O time!
> On whose last step I climb,
>   Trembling at that where I had stood before;
> When will return the glory of your prime?
>   No more— Oh never more.
>
> Out of the day and night
> A joy has taken flight
>   Fresh spring, and summer, and winter hoar,
> Move my faint heart with grief, but with delight
>   No more— Oh never more!

This plaintive music about the brevity of life and love
sounds through the ages. It is the theme of all Shake-
speare's earlier sonnets:

> When I consider everything that grows
> Holds in perfection but a little moment . . .
>
> (XV)

or

> Since brass, nor stone, nor earth, nor boundless sea,
> But sad mortality o'er-sways their power,

How with this rage shall beauty hold a plea
Whose action is no stronger than a flower?

(LXV)

Shakespeare's answers to it are, first, to urge his beloved
youth to marry, for

> nothing 'gainst Time's scythe can make defence
> Save breed to brave him when he takes thee hence,

and then the thought that he, as poet, may outwit Time:

> in hope my verse shall stand
> Praising thy worth, despite his cruel hand;

and finally the assurance that "To me, fair friend, you
never can be old" (CIV), and the brave insistence:

> Love's not Time's fool, though rosy lips and cheeks
> Within his bending sickle's compass come;
> Love alters not with his brief hours and weeks,
> But bears it out even to the edge of doom.

(CXVI)

Shakespeare, I think, never uses what is perhaps the
most popular argument in poetry, that of *carpe diem,*
"enjoy the day." The words are taken from the first Ode
of Horace, though we find it in *Ecclesiastes;* and way back
before that in the *Epic of Gilgamesh,* dating from four
thousand years ago:

> For when the Gods created man, They let
> Death be his share, and life
> Withheld in their own hands.
> Gilgamesh, fill your belly—
> Day and night make merry,
> Dance and make music day and night . . .
> Look at the child that is holding your hand,
> And let your wife delight in your embraces.
> These things alone are the concern of men.

So Spenser's Sir Guyon, in *The Faerie Queen,* when he
comes to the Bower of Bliss, listens to the temptation of
"this lovely lay."

So passeth in the passing of a day,
Of mortal life the leaf, the bud, the flower;
No more doth flourish after first decay
That erst was sought to deck both bed and bower
Of many a lady, and many a paramour.
Gather therefore the rose while yet is prime,
For soon comes age, that will her pride devour:
Gather the rose of love whilst yet is time,
Whilst loving thou mayest lovèd be with equal crime.

Herrick is famous for his graceful lyrics on this theme: "Gather ye rosebuds while ye may," "To Daffodils," "To Blossoms," but my own favorite is the last verse of "Corinna's Going A-Maying."

Come, let us go, while we are in our prime,
And take the harmless folly of the time!
  We shall grow old apace, and die
  Before we know our liberty.
  Our life is short, and our days run
  As fast away as does the sun.
And, as a vapor or a drop of rain,
Once lost, can ne'er be found again,
  So when or you or I are made
  A fable, song, or fleeting shade,
  All love, all liking, all delight
  Lies drowned with us in endless night.
Then, while time serves, and we are but decaying,
Come, my Corinna, come, let's go a-Maying.

A modern version, with a touch of the macabre at the end, is John Crowe Ransom's "Blue Girls."

Twirling your blue skirts, travelling the sward
Under the towers of your seminary,
Go listen to your teachers old and contrary
Without believing a word.

Tie the white fillets then about your hair
And think no more of what will come to pass
Than bluebirds that go walking on the grass
And chattering on the air.

Practise your beauty, blue girls, before it fail;
And I will cry with my loud lips and publish
Beauty which all our power shall never establish,
It is so frail.

For I could tell you a story which is true;
I know a lady with a terrible tongue,
Blear eyes fallen from blue,
All her perfections tarnished—yet it is not long
Since she was lovelier than any of you.

Ransom reminds us grimly of the final condition in Time's wastage, old age, and not many poets have had much to say in favor of that. Shakespeare's Macbeth tells us what should accompany it, "honour, love, obedience, troops of friends," but Shakespeare's own pictures of its tragedy in Lear and its pathetic comedy in Justice Shallow give us very different feelings. Browning welcomes it, declaring "the best is yet to be," rather a hollow and over-optimistic affirmation for anyone who observes life at all. In "Soliloquy" the contemporary Scottish poet, Edwin Muir, is truer in his description of the downward slope past the watershed of the individual life.

Oh the air is different on this side of the hill,
The sunset side. And when I breathed it first
I felt dismay so deep and yet so quiet
It was silence rather, a sea of silence.
This is my trouble, the common trouble.

Matthew Arnold wrote "Growing Old" when he was forty-five, so that presumably it is the result of observation rather than experience.

What is it to grow old?
Is it to lose the glory of the form,
The lustre of the eye?
Is it for beauty to forgo her wreath?
Yes, but not this alone.

Is it to feel our strength—
Not our bloom only, but our strength—decay?

[*Time*] 113

Is it to feel each limb
Grow stiffer, every function less exact,
Each nerve more weakly strung?

        *   *   *   *

It is to suffer this,
And feel but half, and feebly, what we feel.
Deep in our hidden heart
Festers the dull remembrance of a change,
But no emotion—none.

It is—last stage of all—
When we are frozen up within, and quite
The phantom of ourselves,
To hear the world applaud the hollow ghost
Which blamed the living man.

This is an accurate description of some symptoms but not one of Arnold's most successful poems. The unrhymed stanzas lack any vigor of movement; the language is true but weak. "He thinks justly, but he thinks faintly," as Johnson said of Gray. It's as if the loss of faculty he is describing had communicated itself to the poetry.

Thomas Hardy's complaint, and he had first-hand knowledge of the subject, is the opposite of Arnold's: not the loss of the power to feel, but the keeping of it.

I look into my glass,
And view my wasting skin,
And say, "Would God it came to pass
My heart had shrunk as thin!"

For then I, undistrest
By hearts grown cold to me,
Could lonely wait my endless rest
With equanimity.

But Time, to make me grieve,
Part steals, lets part abide;
And shakes this fragile frame at eve
With throbbings of noontide.

Eliot's "familiar compound ghost," who visits the poet in "Little Gidding," gives what is perhaps the most brilliant poetic account of the horrors of old age. Like Arnold's poem it is unrhymed, but the lines are very carefully patterned in alternating accented and unaccented end syllables, which creates a peculiar rhythm of its own. Every word is precise, and the whole has a clarity and austerity which is searching and deeply disturbing.

> First, the cold friction of expiring sense
> Without enchantment, offering no promise
> But bitter tastelessness of shadow fruit
> As body and soul begin to fall asunder.
> Second, the conscious impotence of rage
> At human folly, and the laceration
> Of laughter at what ceases to amuse.
> And last, the rending pain of re-enactment
> Of all that you have done, and been; the shame
> Of motives late revealed, and the awareness
> Of things ill done and done to others' harm
> Which once you took for exercise of virtue.

Eliot's "ghost" has come to remind the poet, with withering irony, that these are the "gifts" which crown a lifetime's effort, unless the soul chooses the "refining fire" of the purgatorial discipline, and re-creates itself in a new pattern. The other great poet of our age, Yeats, agrees on the need to re-create, but not on the means. He found no answers in Christian theology, and Eliot declared in one of his lectures that Yeats's world was not one of "spiritual significance, not a world of real good and evil, of holiness and sin." This is as unfair to Yeats as Yeats was unfair to Eliot when he described his art as "gray, cold, dry" and "essentially prosaic." Temperamentally, the two poets are at opposite poles: Yeats the unabashed individualist, with his unique vitality of spirit which insists on the essential goodness of life in the face of time and change; Eliot with his doctrine of humility and suffering, his repudiation of the sensuous and the sensual world except as a faint analogy of the realities of an eternal one. Yeats simply did not see the central conflict as between good and evil, holiness and sin, but as between energy and apathy, between wholeness of living and poverty of heart. He knew very well the mood of the last five lines in the passage from Eliot's "Little Gidding."

> Things said and done long years ago,
> Or things I did not do or say
> But thought that I might say or do,
> Weigh me down, and not a day
> But something is recalled,
> My conscience or my vanity appalled.

But he put aside such remorse as futile and negative, and in "An Acre of Grass," written when he was over seventy, his prayer is only for that spiritual fire and vision which he describes as "frenzy." I think he had in mind here a letter of William Blake, which he quotes elsewhere as "the most beautiful of all the letters."

> I have been very near the gates of death, and have returned very weak and an old man, feeble and tottering, but not in spirits and life, not in the real man, the imagination, which liveth forever. In that I am stronger and stronger as this foolish body decays.

So Yeats prays that "the real man" may triumph in him too.

> Picture and book remain,
> An acre of green grass
> For air and exercise
> Now strength of body goes;
> Midnight, an old house
> Where nothing stirs but a mouse.

> My temptation is quiet.
> Here at life's end
> Neither loose imagination,
> Nor the mill of the mind
> Consuming its rag and bone,
> Can make the truth known.

> Grant me an old man's frenzy,
> Myself must I remake

Till I am Timon and Lear
Or that William Blake
Who beat upon the wall
Till Truth obeyed his call.

A mind Michael Angelo knew
That can pierce the clouds,
Or inspired by frenzy
Shake the dead in their shrouds;
Forgotten else by mankind,
An old man's eagle mind.

The tranquil opening stanza sets the physical scene, as if
for a poem of serene acceptance, but the first line of the
second stanza announces this quiet as temptation. He
defines the "quiet" further in two ways: "loose imagina-
tion," which perhaps means daydreams or fantasies that
might comfort physical decay, and "the mill of the mind /
Consuming its rag and bone." This may well be the mill-
ing over the past in nagging, negative regret—what Eliot
in "Ash Wednesday" calls

Those matters that with myself I too much discuss
Too much explain.

Instead of these he prays to push further into spiritual
apprehension. He calls it "frenzy," repeating the word,
but removing it from its usual connotation of hysterical
lack of control by the suggestions surrounding it. In-
stead of being anything in the way of "loose imagination,"
it carries the sense of an intensity of inner vision that
can "pierce the clouds" and be worthy of an "eagle mind"
like that of Shakespeare, Blake and Michelangelo. In the
mouths of Timon and Lear, Shakespeare put that piercing
perception which, out of frantic disillusion and hatred of
mankind, came to have insights into the deepest nature of
truth. Blake, as always to Yeats, is the prototype of the
poet and prophet who distrusted all mere intellect, saying:
"Passions, because most living, are most holy . . . and
man shall enter eternity borne upon their wings." It is
upon such eagle wings that the old poet prays to rise from

his earthbound acre of grass. His prayer seems to have been granted; he wrote poetry until a few weeks before his death, and in his last letter, after saying that he knew for certain his time would not be long, he added, "I am happy, and I think full of an energy I had despaired of."

8. Death

"If it is not now, yet it will come."

William Shakespeare

Yeats did not dread death, for he was convinced that "death is but passing from one room to another." Yet its finality as the end of life, of the physical being, of the known and recognizable, invests it with overwhelming significance. It remains forever unchangeable. It may be made transcendent and magnificent, as when Cleopatra decks herself to meet her dead Antony, kisses her woman, and puts the asp to her breast.

> Give me my robe, put on my crown. I have
> Immortal longings in me. . . . Methinks I hear
> Antony call. I see him rouse himself
> To praise my noble act. . . .
> I am fire and air; my other elements
> I give to baser life. So, have you done?
> Come then and take the last warmth of my lips . . .
> The stroke of death is as a lover's pinch,
> Which hurts, and is desir'd. . . . Peace, peace!
> Dost thou not see my baby at my breast,
> That sucks the nurse asleep?

Or it may fill the mind with images of shuddering horror, as with Claudio in *Measure for Measure,* when he hears in his prison that the price of his life is to be his sister's honor.

> Ay, but to die, and go we know not where;
> To lie in cold obstruction and to rot;
> This sensible warm motion to become

A kneaded clod; and the delighted spirit
To bathe in fiery floods, or to reside
In thrilling region of thick-ribbed ice;
To be imprison'd in the viewless winds
And blown with restless violence round about
The pendent world . . . 'tis too horrible!

Confronted with death the poet may feel simply that there's nothing to say either of hope or dread. This feeling comes through very strongly in the slow, sorrowful cadences of Robert Bridges's "On a Dead Child," a memory of the days when he practiced medicine.

Perfect little body, without fault or stain on thee,
  With promise of strength and manhood full and
      fair!
    Though cold and stark and bare,
The bloom and the charm of life doth awhile remain
  on thee.

Thy mother's treasure wert thou;—alas, no longer
  To visit her heart with wondrous joy; to be
    Thy father's pride;—ah, he
Must gather his faith together, and his strength make
  stronger.

To me, as I move thee now in the last duty,
  Dost thou with a turn or gesture anon respond;
    Startling my fancy fond
With a chance attitude of the head, a freak of beauty.

Thy hand clasps, as 'twas wont, my finger, and holds
  it;
  But the grasp is the clasp of Death, heartbreaking
      and stiff;
    Yet feels to my hand as if
'Twas still thy will, thy pleasure and trust that en-
  folds it.

So I lay thee, thy sunken eyelids closing,—
  Go lie thou there in thy coffin, thy last little bed!—
    Propping thy wise, sad head,
Thy firm, pale hands across thy chest disposing.

[*Poetry and the Human Condition*]   120

So quiet! doth the change content thee?--Death,
    whither hath he taken thee?
  To a world, do I think, that rights the disaster of
    this?
  The vision of which I miss,
Who weep for the body, and wish but to warm thee
  and awaken thee?

Ah! little at best can all our hopes avail us
  To lift this sorrow, or cheer us, when in the dark,
    Unwilling, alone we embark,
And the things we have seen and have known and
  have heard of fail us.

Wilfred Owen, killed just a week before the Armistice
in 1918, when he was twenty-five, responds in his poem,
"Futility," to a fellow-soldier's death first with quiet sor-
row, and then with angry exasperation at man's helpless-
ness.

Move him into the sun—
Gently its touch awoke him once,
At home, whispering of fields unsown.
Always it woke him, even in France,
Until this morning and this snow.
If anything might rouse him now
The kind old sun will know.

Think how it wakes the seeds,—
Woke, once, the clays of a cold star.
Are limbs, so dear-achieved, are sides,
Full-nerved—still warm—too hard to stir?
Was it for this the clay grew tall?
—O what made fatuous sunbeams toil
To break earth's sleep at all?

Death can be accepted as a "quiet consummation."

Fear no more the heat o' the sun,
  Nor the furious winter's rages;
Thou thy worldly task hast done,
  Home art gone, and ta'en thy wages;
Golden lads and girls all must,
  As chimney-sweepers, come to dust.

That is a dirge in a play (Shakespeare's *Cymbeline*): it doesn't carry the accents of piercing personal loss, nor speak to anyone who has suffered one. Yet poems that do tell of such loss differ very widely in their tone. They can be as tender and muted as "The Exequy" by Bishop Henry King, written on the death of "his matchless, never-to-be-forgotten friend," his wife, who died in 1624.

> Sleep on, my Love, in thy cold bed,
> Never to be disquieted!
> My last good night! Thou wilt not wake
> Till I thy fate shall overtake:
> Till age, or grief, or sickness must
> Marry my body to that dust
> It so much loves; and fill the room
> My heart keeps empty in thy tomb.
> Stay for me there; I will not fail
> To meet thee in that hollow vale.
> And think not much of my delay;
> I am already on the way,
> And follow thee with all the speed
> Desire can make, or sorrows breed.
> Each minute is a short degree,
> And ev'ry hour a step towards thee.
> At night when I betake a rest,
> Next morn I rise nearer my West
> Of life, almost by eight hours' sail,
> Than when sleep breathed his drowsy gale.
>
>   *   *   *   *
>
> 'Tis true, with shame and grief I yield,
> Thou like the van first took'st the field,
> And gotten hast the victory
> In thus adventuring to die
> Before me, whose more years might crave
> A just precedence in the grave.
> But hark! My pulse, like a soft drum
> Beats my approach, tells thee I come;
> And slow howe'er my marches be,
> I shall at last sit down by thee.

It is all conceived in metaphors: of the marriage bed and

of travel, which extends into marching and ritual warfare; but the carefully constructed embroidery does not interfere at all with the simple, loving personal voice that comes through it. This is not true, I think, of the epitaph that Ben Jonson (who was a friend of King) wrote "On My First Son."

> Farewell, thou child of my right hand, and joy;
>   My sin was too much hope of thee, lov'd boy.
> Seven years thou wert lent to me, and I thee pay,
>   Exacted by thy fate, on the just day.
> O, could I lose all father, now! For why
>   Will man lament the state he should envy—
> To have so soon scap'd world's, and flesh's rage,
>   And, if no other misery, yet age?
> Rest in soft peace, and, ask'd, say here doth lie
>   Ben Jonson his best piece of *poetry*.
> For whose sake, henceforth, all his vows be such
>   As what he loves may never like too much.

This pointed epigrammatic series of couplets is very skillful and concentrated, and we do feel emotion behind it. Yet somehow the emotion is weakened by the obvious artfulness of it. The poet can think too cleverly about the situation to carry conviction. We stay too much on the surface of the words, and are too much occupied with the intellectual intricacy of verbal meaning.

How different in feeling is Wordsworth's sonnet as he remembers his little girl, Catherine, who died when she was four.

> Surprised by joy—impatient as the wind
> I turned to share the transport—Oh! with whom
> But Thee, deep buried in the silent tomb,
> That spot which no viscissitude can find?
> Love, faithful love, recalled thee to my mind—
> But how could I forget thee? Through what power,
> Even for the least division of an hour,
> Have I been so beguiled as to be blind
> To my most grievous loss?—That thought's return
> Was the worst pang that sorrow ever bore,

Save one, one only, when I stood forlorn,
Knowing my heart's best treasure was no more;
That neither present time, nor years unborn
Could to my sight that heavenly face restore.

In contrast with Jonson's terse couplets, this seems to flow in simple passionate speech without ornament or poetical ingenuity. But its rhythmical variety carries subtle changes of emotional mood. It starts on a sudden full note of gladness, that is checked almost at once by a pause, as the poet recognizes that the "Thee" who could share his rapture is "deep buried in the silent tomb / That spot which no viscissitude can find" where no sudden living visitation of joy, impatience or transport can ever reach. He follows this with a rush of perplexed questioning of how the love that prompted his longing to share the joy, could have allowed such a "vicissitude" to break his grief. But to such questioning the "silent tomb" can give no answer, and the rhythm breaks again as the poet takes us back heavily to the moment when he first acknowledged that death is changeless and partakes of no vicissitudes. All the swift darting delight of the opening sentences is quenched in the "no more" and the steady regular beat of the last couplet, the irrevocable sentence "That neither present time, nor years unborn / Could to my sight that heavenly face restore."

Wordsworth's language is simple, except for the one unexpected key-word "vicissitude," and it contains no metaphors at all. The poet may, however, use a startling and obtrusive imagery provided the effect is not contrived and artificial. Take Emily Dickinson's "After great pain a formal feeling comes." It seems at first just "a heap of broken images," with very little arrangement.

After great pain a formal feeling comes—
The nerves sit ceremonious like tombs;
The stiff Heart questions—was it He that bore?
And yesterday—or centuries before?

The feet mechanical go round
A wooden way

[*Poetry and the Human Condition*]   124

Of ground or air or Ought,
Regardless grown,
A quartz contentment like a stone.

This is the hour of lead
Remembered if outlived
As freezing persons recollect
The snow—
First chill, then stupor, then
The letting go.

At first reading it appears a confused jumble; yet every strange analogy adds to the sense of lifeless rigidity and dazed torpor. From the last verse we know that this has been a death of the heart, outlived, but remembered in all its sensations. These sensations transform themselves into grotesque pictures of mental and physical fixity and movement. The living flesh goes through its "ceremonies," but as if it were stone or wood or lead. The "stiff Heart" cannot orient itself in time or identity, nor can the feet. Whether they carry the body indoors or out, or perform some duty (Ought), they are "regardless" of what they do. But what is "a quartz contentment like a stone"? Since there's no "contentment" in its usual meaning in the poem, does she mean *containing* a hard, stony quality? The suggestion matches that of the nerves sitting "ceremonious like tombs" and carries the same feeling of numb acquiescence, and the weight of great grief.

Another poem that creates the sensation of stunned misery is "The Woodspurge" by Dante Gabriel Rossetti.

The wind flapped loose, the wind was still,
Shaken out dead from tree and hill:
I had walked on at the wind's will,—
I sat now, for the wind was still.

Between my knees my forehead was,—
My lips, drawn in, said not Alas!
My hair was over in the grass,
My naked ears heard the day pass.

My eyes, wide open, had the run
Of some ten weeds to fix upon;

Among those few, out of the sun,
The woodspurge flowered, three cups in one.

From perfect grief there need not be
Wisdom or even memory:
One thing then learnt remains to me,—
The woodspurge has a cup of three.

Rossetti's method is very different from that of Emily Dickinson. He doesn't state the subject matter directly. The title gives no hint of it: the word "dead" in the first verse has no human association until the last verse. Not the poet's emotions, but simply his posture, is described— its paralyzed immobility and silence. The chance happening arising from that frozen attitude, the impress of the flower on his sight, becomes a symbol for the total experience of grief. The climax of emotional intensity in the last verse then colors all that has gone before.

Another poet whose voice speaks directly to any grieving heart is Thomas Hardy. We know nothing of his first marriage beyond what his poetry tells us. It lasted nearly forty years, and perhaps it is just the very usual story of a happy romance that was not "kept in constant repair," as Dr. Johnson said friendships must be, and that cooled into indifference, at least on the woman's side. In "Wessex Heights" he comments:

As for one rare fair woman, I am now but a thought
of hers,
I enter her mind and another thought succeeds me
that she prefers,
Yet my love for her in its fulness she herself even
did not know;
Well, time cures hearts of tenderness, and now I can
let her go.

But he couldn't let her go, and after her sudden death in 1912, when he was an old man in his seventies, he wrote many poems of love and longing, speaking to her of the past and the present. In "The Voice":

Woman much missed, how you call to me, call to me,
Saying that now you are not as you were

[*Poetry and the Human Condition*]   126

When you changed from the one who was all to me,
But as at first, when our day was fair . . .

In "After a Journey" her early self, with her "nut-coloured
hair / And gray eyes, and rose-flush coming and going,"
summons him to places alive with memories:

Yes: I have re-entered your olden haunts at last;
   Through the years, through the dead scenes I have
      tracked you;
What have you now found to say of our past—
   Scanned across the dark space wherein I have
      lacked you?
Summer gave us sweets, but autumn wrought di-
   vision?
   Things were not lastly as firstly well
      Between us twain, you tell?
But all's closed now, despite Time's derision.

The last words seem to say that Hardy's experience has
contradicted Shakespeare's assurance about "the marriage
of true minds," that "Love's not Time's fool." But he ends
the poem:

Trust me, I mind not, though Life lowers,
   The bringing me here; nay, bring me here again!
      I am just the same as when
Our days were a joy, and our paths through flowers.

"The Going" tells of her sudden death when he was not
with her, and again he sees her as a girl in Cornwall,
where they first met.

You were she who abode
   By those red-veined rocks far West,
You were the swan-necked one who rode
Along the beetling Beeny Crest,
   And reining nigh me
   Would muse and eye me
While Life unrolled us its very best.

Why then, latterly did we not speak,
Did we not think of those days long dead,
And ere your vanishing strive to seek

That time's renewal? We might have said,
    In this bright spring weather
    We'll visit together
Those places that once we visited.

    Well, well! All's past amend,
    Unchangeable. It must go . . .

The lines are often strangely bumpy and lumbering and
the vocabulary clumsy. Walter de la Mare said that Hardy
"forces, hammers poetry into his words; not, like most
poets charms it out of them," and Eliot declares that he
reaches "sublimity without ever having passed through
the stage of being good." No fine poet, indeed, except per-
haps Wordsworth, wrote more that is plain bad. Of the
eight hundred pages of Hardy's collected poems, the really
memorable ones would fit into about twenty-five. But in
those the "felt life" is so intense, the poet's voice so per-
sonal and so deeply true, that the prosy, matter-of-fact
language, the awkward inversions and rough metrics
seem only to add to the absolute integrity of vision and to
his power to move us. The forms express perfectly the
atmosphere of love-starved, stumbling, bleak honesty be-
hind the poems, and whether that was the cause or the
effect of his life-experience who can say?

    Wintertime nights;
But my bereavement-pain
It cannot bring again;
    Twice no one dies.

    Flower-petals flee;
But, since it once hath been,
No more that severing scene
    Can harrow me.

    Birds faint in dread:
I shall not loose old strength
In the lone frost's black length;
    Strength long since fled!

    Leaves freeze to dun;
But friends can not turn cold

> This season as of old
> > For him with none.
>
> > Tempests may scath;
> But love can not make smart
> Again this year his heart
> > Who no heart hath.
>
> > Black is night's cope;
> But death will not appal
> One who, past doubtings all,
> > Waits in unhope.

In these examples of poems of loss, none illustrates the pure straightforward love lament, pouring itself out in all its subjective pain. Poets feel as other people feel, but they are artists, *making* something from their grief. We may be sure no first-rate poem on this theme was ever composed in the actual shock and agony of bereavement. One of the miseries of that sorrow is that the mind cannot detach itself from its suffering; escape into concentration elsewhere is impossible. Moreover what Thomas Mann says in his story *Tonio Kröger* is probably largely true:

> If you care too much about what you have to say, if your heart is too much in it, you can be pretty sure of making a mess. Feeling, warm heartfelt feeling, is always banal and futile; only the irritations and icy ecstasies of the artist's corrupted nervous system are artistic.

The emotion need not be recollected in *tranquillity,* but it is recollected before the poem is written, even in poetry giving such a feeling of immediate truth as some of Hardy's. But the difference in tone between the degrees and kinds of "esthetic distance" is very marked, though not in itself a standard of merit or of the emotion communicated. For instance, the method of Emily Brontë's "Cold in the earth" is at the opposite extreme from Hardy's realistic reticence. It would not be exact to call this an illustration of direct subjective passion, since in recent years discoveries have proved that many of her poems, including this one, were written as part of the "Gondal" romance the Brontë sisters constructed among themselves, in which they dramatized an imaginary world peopled with characters of their own invention. The poem is supposed to be the utterance of one of these characters. It is most unlikely that the situation had any basis in Emily's factual life, and yet no one could doubt that it is a dramatization of her own passions, her own loneliness and her own self discipline. It has been called "one of the greatest personal lyrics in the language." That must be a matter of opinion, but it is a fine creation of the wild longings of a stormy heart, of its desolation, and of its self-mastery.

Cold in the earth—and the deep snow piled above thee,
　　Far, far removed, cold in the dreary grave!
Have I forgot, my only Love, to love thee,
　　Sever'd at last by Time's all-severing wave?

Now, when alone, do my thoughts no longer hover
　　Over the mountains, on that northern shore,
Resting their wings where heath and fern-leaves cover
　　Thy noble heart for ever, ever more?

Cold in the earth—and fifteen wild Decembers
　　From these brown hills have melted into spring:
Faithful, indeed, is the spirit that remembers
　　After such years of change and suffering!

Sweet Love of youth, forgive, if I forget thee,
　　While the world's tide is bearing me along;
Other desires and other hopes beset me,
　　Hopes which obscure, but cannot do thee wrong!

No later light has lighten'd up my heaven,
　　No second morn has ever shone for me;
All my life's bliss from thy dear life was given,
　　All my life's bliss is in the grave with thee.

But when the days of golden dreams had perish'd,
　　And even Despair was powerless to destroy;

[*Poetry and the Human Condition*]　130

Then did I learn how existence could be cherish'd,
  Strengthen'd and fed without the aid of joy.

Then did I check the tears of useless passion—
  Wean'd my young soul from yearning after thine;
Sternly denied its burning wish to hasten
  Down to that tomb already more than mine.

And even yet, I dare not let it languish,
  Dare not indulge in memory's rapturous pain;
Once drinking deep of that divinest anguish,
  How could I seek the empty world again?

This lacks the verbal precision found in the other poems quoted in this chapter. Lines such as "Sever'd at last by Time's all-severing wave," or "While the world's tide is bearing me along," are close to cliché. Put beside Hardy's exact use of speech rhythms and physical detail, this seems generalized rhetoric, and the situation betrays itself as part of a dream world. Yet it strengthens into true poetic utterance in the last three verses. The movement remains the same, a stanza with a throb in it that suits the tone of romantic yearning and regret, but now the context becomes symbolic of Emily Brontë's own real daily struggles to avoid retreat into fantasy, and to find fulfillment in illusion. She becomes the woman who loved the moors, and did the cooking in the Haworth parsonage, who disciplined her genius to write *Wuthering Heights* and who wrote elsewhere of herself:

Few hearts to mortals given
On earth so wildly pine,
Yet none would ask a heaven
More like the earth than thine.

As "Cold in the earth" contrasts interestingly with Hardy's poems as a different form of personal intensity, so it contrasts with another poem by Wordsworth that is a perfect example of *im*personal intensity. "Surprised by joy" (p. 123) is a directly subjective reverie, whereas Hardy and Emily Brontë seem to be speaking out of immediate emotion to the lost loved figure and to themselves. In "A slumber did my spirit seal," one of the so-called "Lucy" poems, the feeling is no less powerful, but it is "distanced" so that the effect is one of controlled serenity. We know nothing at all about Lucy beyond the group of five simple poems that Wordsworth added to the second edition of the *Lyrical Ballads* in 1800, telling of a love and a sense of overwhelming loss: "She is in her grave and Oh / The difference to me!"

> A slumber did my spirit seal;
>   I had no human fears;
> She seemed a thing that could not feel
>   The touch of earthly years.
>
> No motion has she now, no force;
>   She neither hears nor sees;
> Rolled round in earth's diurnal course,
>   With rocks, and stones, and trees.

The poem's simplicity is deceptive. It seems a series of direct statements in the plainest language, but they are so cunningly interrelated that each part depends upon every other part for its full significance. The two verses are not a mere sequence of thought and feeling. They balance the past with the present, the individual with the cosmic, illusion with reality, and interweave them all into a unity. The slumber of the first line, and the sealing of the poet's spirit in total human unawareness, matches Lucy's sleep of death and the sealing of her body in the vast indifference of the earth. In her living movements she *seemed* a thing—a living spirit—too vital to be touched by time, and then in stark reality she becomes a "thing" untouchable by time, without motion or force. She cannot feel "the touch of earthly years" because she is now absorbed into the perpetual punctual motion of the earth itself.

The pause between the two verses is made to contain all that is unspoken. The past becomes the present without further explanation: time turns to eternity for Lucy; seeming is now fact for the poet.

The language shows what can be done by apparent complete lack of any elaboration. The only metaphor is the opening line, and that is followed by the same idea expressed in statement. The first six lines announce negative positions, first in the past, then in the present, but in spite of the negation of human life and love, the last couplet takes on a majestic affirmation. The third line of the verse lengthens in cadence as well as surprising us with the one long formal word in the poem, "rolled round in earth's diurnal course," as the dead are identified forever with the life of nature and the order of the cosmos.

Whereas Emily Brontë in "Cold in the earth" is carried along on the stream of her turbulent emotions, Wordsworth here possesses his in a still pattern of deep calm. Profound personal feeling is beneath the reserve and understatement, but at the same time the poem is impersonal and universal. Moreover, while even at first reading we recognize it as a rare piece of simple formal beauty, the more familiar we are with it the more we see it as a masterpiece of poetic structure.

9. Frustration and Loneliness

"O wearisome condition of humanity!"
Fulke Greville

In finite terms, death is the end of the individual sentient
creature. The poet who writes of it or who mourns the
pain of personal loss continues to experience life in all its
myriad experiences in the body-mind. The pain of loss,
moreover, however agonizing, however haunting in mem-
ory, quiets imperceptibly into acceptance as the currents
of active living and of fresh emotions flow over it. Worse,
perhaps, than the sufferings of grief are the torments that
man endures from the conflicts within his own being.
What Yeats dreads in "An Acre of Grass" (p. 116) is not
death but the loss of spirit, the fire that burns only so
long as the continual process of self-creation continues.
Man, says Auden, is "the only animal aware of lack of
finish": the only animal aware of the difference between
what things are and what they ought to be. Something
drives him to find meaning in his life; to regard it as a
venture to be fulfilled and himself as an instrument which
should be used for some purpose beyond himself. Hence
his miseries; for not only is he inevitably vanquished by
time, but the complexities of his own nature thwart him
in his efforts to find his true path.

> Oh wearisome condition of humanity!
> Born under one law, to another bound:
> Vainly begot, and yet forbidden vanity;
> Created sick, commanded to be sound:
> What meaneth nature by these diverse laws?
> Passion and reason, self-division cause.

[*Poetry and the Human Condition*] 134

So writes one of the Elizabethans, Fulke Greville, Lord Brooke, and a contemporary of his, Sir John Davies, makes the same lament. He is writing in the great age of exploration and discovery, and contrasts man's exploits in those physical realms with his ignorance of self.

> All things without, which round about we see,
>   We seek to know, and how therewith to do;
> But that whereby we reason, live, and be,
>   Within ourselves, we strangers are thereto.
>
> We seek to know the moving of each sphere,
>   And the strange cause of th' ebbs and floods
>   of Nile;
> But of that clock within our breasts we bear
>   The subtle motions we forget the while.
>
> We that acquaint ourselves with every zone
>   And pass both tropics, and behold the poles,
> When we come home, are to ourselves unknown,
>   And unacquainted with our own souls.

Moreover, the poets feel that man's lot is made harder by a God who ordains these penalties. The next verse of Greville's poem opens:

> Is it a mark of majesty or power
> To make offences that it may forgive?

And Henry Vaughan, in the next century, implies in "Man" the same arbitrary and unjust behavior of man's creator, as he compares the homing instincts given to birds and bees (and according to him, to stones!) with the denial of rest to man.

> Weighing the stedfastness and state
> Of some mean things which here below reside,
> Where birds like watchful clocks the noiseless date
>   And intercourse of times divide,
> Where bees at night get home and hive, and flowers
>   Early, as well as late,
> Rise with the sun, and set in the same bowers;

I would (said I) my God would give
The staidness of these things to man! for these
To his divine appointments ever cleave,
    And no new business breaks their peace;
The birds nor sow, nor reap, yet sup and dine,
      The flowers without clothes live,
Yet Solomon was never dressed so fine.

    Man hath still either toys, or care,
He hath no root, nor to one place is tied,
But ever restless and irregular
    About this earth doth run and ride,
He knows he hath a home, but scarce knows where,
      He says it is so far
That he hath quite forgot how to go there.

    He knocks at all doors, strays and roams,
Nay, hath not so much wit as some stones have
Which in the darkest nights point to their homes,
    By some hid sense their Maker gave;
Man is the shuttle, to whose winding quest
      And passage through these looms
God ordered motion, but ordained no rest.

Many people speak today as if this sense of frustration
and restlessness were something new. It is true that no age
has ever been so self-conscious as ours about its plight, or
has analyzed, diagnosed and discussed itself so fully. In
part because it feels spiritually sick, this age is perpetually
taking its own emotional pulse and temperature, but the
real extension of self-knowledge and perception in the last
half century is also a fact. Psychological exploration may
still be in its pre-Columbus age, and future travelers may
prove its present maps distorted and its information mis-
construed, but nevertheless psychology has added an enor-
mous territory to human awareness. The darkness of self-
ignorance need not be quite so baffling as it was to Sir
John Davies: man can be helped to recognize and resolve
some of his conflicts. Yet his civil war continues, and his
habit of behaving like the hero of D. H. Lawrence's novel,

Kangaroo: "Richard Lovat wearied himself to death struggling with the problem of himself and calling it Australia." And the poets, since those of Greece, Rome, China, India and the Hebrews, illustrate how at all times man's spirit has been "restless and irregular," consuming its rag and bone, seeking peace of mind, and finding it the hardest of all quests. As Housman says:

> The stars have not dealt me the worst they could do:
> My pleasures are plenty, my troubles are two.
> But oh, my two troubles they reave me of rest,
> The brains in my head and the heart in my breast.

Man's brains and his heart, his mind and his passions, both crave satisfaction, and it is the failure of vital activity in them and between them that causes much of his soul-sickness. His "proud and angry dust" suffers in many other rebellious ways, but the negative sense of restless impotence is a central situation forbidding fulfillment. Any positive emotion is better than this muffled, dreary misery.

Poetry all down the ages is full of advice on how to avoid it. It urges withdrawal from the outer stress of a competitive society, with its goals of wealth, success, court favor or business ambitions. One could make an anthology of minor poets stretching from Biblical and Classical times to the present day, giving recipes for the attainment of "sweet content." They all recommend the same things:

> I like the plain, I climb no hill,
> In greatest storms I sit on shore;

while "My mind to me a Kingdom is." They prescribe a small house, a few friends and good books; bird-watching, gardening, fishing, hunting; the cultivation of repose, humility, and a taste for solitude. The poets, like any modern manual on How to Relax, assure us repeatedly that these things will produce the answer. But as other poets know very well, the brains in the head and the heart in the breast are not so easily calmed and comforted. As we have seen from Auden's "Now the leaves are falling fast" (p. 88) if solitude is isolation, it is not tranquillity but torture.

Withdrawal, indeed, is often no antidote, since it is the sense of inaction that is the source of suffering. Matthew Arnold, in his preface to the first edition of his poems, gave what now seems a very strange reason for the exclusion of his verse-drama *Empedocles on Etna*. He declared that poetry must give enjoyment and add to the happiness of men, and that true tragic poetry did this, but he goes on:

> What then are the situations, for the representations of which, though accurate, no poetical enjoyment can be derived? They are those in which the suffering finds no vent in action; in which a continuous state of mental distress is prolonged, unrelieved by incident, hope or resistance. . . . In such situations there is inevitably something morbid, in the description of them something monotonous. When they occur in actual life they are painful, not tragic; the representation of them in poetry is painful also.

It would be strange if the sufferers from this all-too-common condition could take no pleasure in the poetry that reveals their own dilemma, or if they did not find some small comfort in the knowledge of the poet's fellow-feeling and understanding.

William Empson has created this atmosphere of blight very well in "Missing Dates," together with the sad recognition of how much the sense of withered emotions is the result of our own apathy: of things we have left undone, of experiences we have refused, of relationships we have rejected or allowed to lapse. The title can mean either missing specific opportunities for fulfillment, or the failure to create such opportunities. Empson's poetry is often obscure because, as he says, "a sort of puzzle interest is part of the pleasure that you are meant to get from the verse." He is often likened to Donne, from his habit of drawing references and metaphors from unlikely fields as analogies to his central idea. Here, in one short poem on the theme of lost chances, he uses as illustrative metaphors: toxins in the blood stream, the grinding of grain, blood transfusions, Chinese tombs, mining operations, land erosion, body metabolism and the double-edged title of missing dates. He uses a difficult Old French verse form, the *villanelle*, a poem of nineteen lines, based on only two rhymes, with two recurrent refrains, and divided into three-line stanzas and a final quatrain. But whereas the *villanelle* was generally used for light lyrics, Empson lengthens the lines and slows the pace to that of a sorrowful lament. The sluggish rhythm and the throbbing refrains themselves create a sense of the poisonous wastes clogging the emotional bloodstream. Empson himself commented, "The poem, I think, consists of true statements, but I suppose what they add up to is a mood rather than an assertion, anyway not something you can feel all the time."

Slowly the poison the whole blood stream fills.
It is not the effort nor the failure tires.
The waste remains, the waste remains and kills.

It is not your system or clear sight that mills
Down small to the consequence a life requires;
Slowly the poison the whole blood stream fills.

They bled an old dog dry yet the exchange rills
Of young dog blood gave but a month's desires;
The waste remains, the waste remains and kills.

It is the Chinese tombs and the slag hills
Usurp the soil, and not the soil retires.
Slowly the poison the whole blood stream fills.

Not to have fire is to be a skin that shrills.
The complete fire is death. From partial fires
The waste remains, the waste remains and kills.

It is the poems you have lost, the ills
From missing dates, at which the heart expires,
Slowly the poison the whole blood stream fills.
The waste remains, the waste remains and kills.

The theme doesn't emerge fully until the first two lines of the final quatrain, when we learn that the poem is about the slow death of the heart from our own inertia. The argument in the earlier verses is very compressed, and the technical difficulties of the rhymes seem to interfere sometimes with the meaning. I read it that active efforts do not exhaust us, even if they end in failure, nor does intellectual effort (system and clear sight) grind the life of the heart beneath the upper and the nether millstone. "The consequence a life requires" is, I suppose, the time-sequence ending in death. That must come finally, but the heart should not die before the body is consumed. No transfusions from outside can revive dwindling emotional vitality. Life gets cumbered with useless regrets for our dead past, waste products, when it could still be productive. (China is alleged to have extravagant quantities of ancestral tombs.) I could make nothing of "Not to have fire is to be a skin that shrills," until a friend pointed out that a skin that shrills is a bagpipe, with "shrills" suggesting the "skirling" of the pipes. The "fire" is the emotional parallel to the process of combustion in the body.

Many readers find that the "puzzle interest" destroys the emotional impact of this poem, and indeed I feel that it comes through strongly only in the last four lines where the metaphysical ingenuities are dropped. But the refrains are very haunting.

More powerful and moving, and closer to the condition of sustained spiritual drought and sterility Arnold describes is a sonnet of Hopkins. Hopkins was a convert to the Catholic faith, a Jesuit priest, who died in 1889 at the age of forty-five. His poetry was unknown in his lifetime, and was first published in 1918 when its fineness was at once recognized. Not only was its quality so deeply human in its joys and sorrows, but technically Hopkins had been practicing the compression, the speech rhythms and the fondness for concrete images introduced by Pound and Eliot, before either of those poets were born. His poetry is very dramatic. We can *hear* the speaking voice as we read it, with its varied rhythms breaking up the even flow of the sonnet form and the regular rhyme-scheme, and changing its tone several times in this very small compass.

> *Justus quidem tu es, Domine, si disputem tecum:*
> *verumtamen justa loquar ad te: Quare via impiorum*
> *prosperatur? etc.*

Thou art indeed just, Lord, if I contend
With thee; but, sir, so what I plead is just.
Why do sinners' ways prosper? and why must
Disappointment all I endeavour end?
Wert thou my enemy, O thou my friend,
How wouldst thou worse, I wonder, than thou dost
Defeat, thwart me? Oh, the sots and thralls of lust
Do in spare hours more thrive than I that spend,
Sir, life upon thy cause. See, banks and brakes
Now, leavèd how thick! lacèd they are again
With fretty chervil, look, and fresh wind shakes
Them; birds build—but not I build; no, but strain,
Time's eunuch, and not breed one work that wakes.
Mine, O thou lord of life, send my roots rain.

He starts with the appeal of Jeremiah: "Righteous art thou, O Lord, when I plead with thee: yet let me talk with thee of thy judgments: Wherefore doth the way of the wicked prosper?" He is arguing with a powerful opponent, but is sure of the strength of his own case, challenging the divine justice (in which he believes) with the obvious injustice of his own situation. After the first four lines, the tone shifts to a more personal pleading as he points to the ironic paradoxes of alleged divine love and his own unmerited failure; to the easy success of the lazy and the sensual in the face of his own honest, patient, frustrated service. In another dramatic contrast and change of voice, he looks at the external world of lush fertility and of movement and action—of growth and fresh wind and nesting birds—and at his own strain, impotence and aridity. Then in the last line, his rebellion spent, the simple submission and agonized prayer for help.

In spite of his despairing sense of failure, Hokpins's faith remains alive, and the hope of spiritual rebirth (though it never came). But as he writes he yearns for the response that George Herbert describes in his beautifully tender poem "The Flower." Herbert, after a youth at the court of James I, took orders in the Anglican Church in 1630 and retired to a country parish in Wiltshire. He died three years later when he was only thirty-nine.

> How fresh, O Lord, how sweet and clean
> Are thy returns! Ev'n as the flowers in spring,
> To which, besides their own demean,
> The late-past frosts tributes of pleasure bring.
> Grief melts away
> Like snow in May,
> As if there were no such cold thing.
>
> Who would have thought my shrivel'd heart
> Could have recover'd greenness? It was gone
> Quite under ground, as flowers depart
> To see their mother-root when they have blown;
> Where they together
> All the hard weather,
> Dead to the world, keep house unknown.
>
>   *   *   *   *
>
> And now in age I bud again,
> After so many deaths I live and write;
> I once more smell the dew and rain,
> And relish versing. O my only light,
> It cannot be
> That I am he
> On whom thy tempests fell all night.

Shakespeare's twenty-ninth sonnet is a similar pattern in a secular setting.

> When in disgrace with fortune and men's eyes
> I all alone beweep my outcast state,
> And trouble deaf heaven with my bootless cries,
> And look upon myself, and curse my fate,
> Wishing me like to one more rich in hope,
> Featured like him, like him with friends possess'd,
> Desiring this man's art, and that man's scope,
> With what I most enjoy contented least:

[*Poetry and the Human Condition*]   142

Yet in these thoughts myself almost despising,
Haply I think on thee,—and then my state,
Like to the lark at break of day arising
From sullen earth, sings hymns at heaven's gate;
    For thy sweet love remember'd such wealth
      brings
    That then I scorn to change my state with kings.

The first eight lines are another version of the condition of Hopkins, the sense of restless frustration and barrenness of spirit. The last six lines announce—rather too glibly perhaps—the sudden change at the remembrance of his beloved. The joyous image of the lark rising in the dawn from the "sullen earth," and singing its song of praise in the heavens, contrasts perfectly with the troubled, envious discontent of the opening picture. It carries the "rebirth" effect so fully indeed that the last couplet seems anticlimax—tagged on to fill out the sonnet form, but really adding nothing.

These poems give the clue to the cause of man's visitations of spiritual flatness, when, as Auden puts it, "vaguely life leaks away." It's a sense of unfulfillment, and fulfillment means fruitful relationship, with God or nature or other men and women or the Muse. Lacking that, the human soul wilts. John Clare in the early nineteenth century, writing (in a lucid period) from the insane asylum in which he was confined for twenty-seven years, expresses the worst torment of all; not only the loss of others, but the loss of self.

I am: yet what I am who cares or knows?
    My friends forsake me like a memory lost.
I am the self-consumer of my woes;
    They rise and vanish, an oblivious host,
Shadows of life, whose very soul is lost,
    And yet I am, I live, though I am tossed

Into the nothingness of scorn and noise,
    Into the living sea of waking dream
Where there is neither sense of life, nor joys,

But the huge shipwreck of my own esteem
And all that's dear. Even those I love the best
Are strange; nay, they are stranger than the rest.

To Coleridge, in his ode "Dejection," the loss of the
capacity for joy, the "strong music of the soul," is the
worst of his afflictions.

A grief without a pang, void, dark, and drear,
   A stifled, drowsy, unimpassioned grief,
   Which finds no natural outlet, no relief,
      In word, or sigh, or tear—
O Lady! in this wan and heartless mood,
To other thoughts by yonder throstle woo'd,
   All this long eve, so balmy and serene,
Have I been gazing on the western sky,
   And its peculiar tint of yellow green:
And still I gaze—and with how blank an eye!
And those thin clouds above, in flakes and bars,
That give away their motion to the stars;
Those stars, that glide behind them or between,
Now sparkling, now bedimmed, but always seen:
Yon crescent Moon, as fixed as if it grew
In its own cloudless, starless lake of blue;
I see them all so excellently fair,
I see, not feel, how beautiful they are!

The union between himself and the natural universe, so
vital to the Romantic poets, has been shattered, and "the
passion and the life, whose fountains are within" have
dried up.

This too, however, is a mood. These "viper thoughts,
that coil around the mind" have loosened their stifling
folds before the end of the poem, the wind of inspiration
has awakened the poet's shriveled heart from its torpor of
apathy, and he shifts from his own miseries to a prayer
for the happiness of the "Lady" to whom the poem is ad-
dressed. In earlier form, before the coolness between the
two close friends, the Lady had been "Wordsworth."

Another mood of blackness, arising from the sense of
isolation, without Coleridge's romantic trappings and

[*Poetry and the Human Condition*] 144

without any resolution into rebirth, is poignantly created in Frost's "Acquainted with the Night."

> I have been one acquainted with the night.
> I have walked out in rain—and back in rain.
> I have outwalked the furthest city light.
>
> I have looked down the saddest city lane.
> I have passed by the watchman on his beat
> And dropped my eyes, unwilling to explain.
>
> I have stood still and stopped the sound of feet
> When far away an interrupted cry
> Came over houses from another street,
>
> But not to call me back or say good-bye;
> And further still at an unearthly height,
> One luminary clock against the sky
>
> Proclaimed the time was neither wrong nor right.
> I have been one acquainted with the night.

This is a sonnet, but the poet has intensified the atmosphere of unrelatedness by breaking up the close-knit form into triplets. Every detail adds to the feeling of alienation from the daylight world of fellowship: the rain, the walk beyond "the furthest city light," the looking down the empty lane, the denial of a greeting to the watchman, the listening to the cry which is not to him—each increases the desolation. Cut off from either giving or receiving human sympathy, the final image sets the solitary soul against the vast indifference of the firmament, utterly removed from the earthly moral and emotional problems of the human race.

This loneliness, felt as the inescapable mortal condition, is the theme of Matthew Arnold's "Isolation." It is one of a group of poems addressed to "Marguerite," about whom we know nothing except that she was a girl he met in Thun, Switzerland, when he was twenty-five, and again on his return there two years later. From the poems it appears that she had then ceased to love him. The parting was very bitter to him and the poem is full of its pain, though its theme is made universal as well as personal.

Yes! in the sea of life enisled,
With echoing straits between us thrown,
Dotting the shoreless watery wild,
We mortal millions live *alone*.
The islands feel the enclasping flow
And then their endless bounds they know.

But when the moon their hollows lights,
And they are swept by balms of spring,
And in their glens, on starry nights,
The nightingales divinely sing;
And lovely notes, from shore to shore,
Across the sounds and channels pour—

Oh! then a longing like despair
Is to their farthest caverns sent;
For surely once, they feel, we were
Parts of a single continent!
Now round us spreads the watery plain—
Oh might our marges meet again!

Who ordered that their longing's fire
Should be, as soon as kindled, cooled?
Who renders vain their deep desire?—
A God, a God their severance ruled!
And bade between their shores to be
The unplumbed, salt, estranging sea.

The symbolism of the poem is simple. The islands are
individuals; the hollows, glens and caverns their hearts;
the sea the flux of life and time around them; the moon,
the spring, the nightingales, the joys and beauties of na-
ture in which all can share. The theme of human isola-
tion is expressed, ironically enough, in a formal esthetic
pattern beautifully organized in balance and contrast,
statement and resolution. "Yes!" implies that the poet has
pondered on the question and acquiesces in the inexorable
answer of the last lines. The emotion of the statement,
"we mortal millions live *alone*" is translated into the con-
crete image of the islands embraced only by the ocean—
an embrace that brings no sense of union, but only the
knowledge of "endless bounds" (where "endless" must be

read as "everlasting"). The next two stanzas contrast the loneliness with the moments of longing for relatedness and the intuitive instinct that at some time union existed. The universal and the personal blend in the use of the pronouns. "For surely once, *they* feel, *we* were . . . ," and the third verse ends with a cry for companionship in the present. The last verse drops the personal altogether in the question of the responsibility for the conflict between desire and destiny. That a supernatural being is made accountable for the human condition may seem an evasion that weakens the poem, but poetically the translation of the statement "A God, a God their severance ruled" into the specific symbol of severance, the depth and distance of "the unplumbed, salt, estranging sea," is a satisfying conclusion.

Enclosed within the "enclasping" first and last lines, which make the theme into the form of a circle from which no escape is possible, the images of longing and loneliness, of rebellion and bitter acceptance, of past and present, the general and the particular, play out their drama, and reach the relentless conclusion.

10. Social Satire

"O sacred weapon! left for truth's defence."

Alexander Pope

The poet is first and foremost an individual with a personal vision. His poem is not an event in social history nor a symptom of a literary movement; it is an assertion of the poet's singular identity. Implicitly he is saying to the reader: "This is how I have seen and shaped a moment of living or a view of life. Come and feel it through my senses and emotions and perceptions." But at the same time no writer lives and writes in isolation. He is a personality alive in a particular period of time, in a particular place, in a particular social environment. He is an individual *and* a member of society, and society will inevitably play its part in his poetry. He may be in sympathy with his social environment, or in rebellion against it; he may try to reject it, but its influence will be there. He knows this himself. As Eliot said (p. 25), when the poet is at work, he is abstracted from any thought of social consequences, but without the context of use to society or to other individuals, present or future, he could not have the conviction that sustains him.

The poet's concern with his audience, however, varies very much from poet to poet and from age to age. Poetry may be divided roughly into private and public. On the one hand poetry that springs from the great personal affairs of the human spirit: religion and love, communion with nature or meditative contemplation; on the other, poetry that aims at immediate social entertainment or influence: the ancient epics, poetic drama, narrative poetry, or what we shall be concerned with here, satiric verse. Though there may be all the difference in the world between the atmosphere and expression of religious feeling in a sonnet by Donne (p. 58) and one by Hopkins (p. 141), both poets are in the midst of individual emotional experience, alone with it, creating the living moment in all its intimacy and immediacy. In Pope's "Essay on Man," however, the poet aims directly at a public audience. Though he may have wrestled with doubt before reaching his conclusions, as far as the poem goes he is himself detached and assured. His findings are general, not particular. His arguments survey all objections, but reach the solution satisfactory to the general thinking of his age and class.

> All Nature is but art, unknown to thee;
> All chance, direction, which thou canst not see:
> All discord, harmony not understood;
> All partial evil, universal good:
> And, spite of pride, in erring reason's spite,
> One truth is clear, Whatever is, is right.

Private poetry is not necessarily superior to public. The function of each is different, and each appeals to different tastes and faculties in the reader.

Propaganda has a bad name, but its root meaning is simply to disseminate through a medium, and all writing therefore is propaganda for *something*. It's a seeding of the self in the consciousness of others. But social poetry has a deliberate moral purpose. In it the poet speaks directly to his society and holds up its shortcomings for general recognition. Yeats said of poets that out of their quarrel with others they make rhetoric, and out of their quarrel with themselves, poetry. But surely that's too rigid a distinction. Yeats himself is not uttering mere rhetoric when he declares:

> Things fall apart; the centre cannot hold;
> Mere anarchy is loosed upon the world,
> The blood-dimmed tide is loosed, and everywhere

The ceremony of innocence is drowned;
The best lack all conviction, while the worst
Are full of passionate intensity.

He is giving memorable expression to a vision of his own
times that his readers recognize as true. Criticism of others
is easier than self-criticism, but its insights may be quite
as piercing and its expression quite as powerful. All indi-
viduals, all societies and all eras are full of offenses, and
the poet would not be human if he did not sometimes use
his art to protest. Louis MacNeice says the poet "is not
the loud-speaker of society, but something much more
like its still, small voice. . . . He can be its conscience, its
critical faculty." Pope gave satire more importance.

O sacred weapon! left for truth's defence,
Sole dread of folly, vice and insolence!
To all but Heaven-directed hands denied,
The Muse may give thee, but the Gods must guide.

The satiric poet may like to believe he is taking a God's-eye
view and is heaven-directed, but satire is in fact the most
mundane form of poetry and comes closest to our com-
mon judgments as social beings. We welcome the satiric
poet because he expresses with wit and force, and some-
times with deep feeling, our own disapproval of the
human race in general and specific vices or persons in
particular.

We can agree with the seventeenth-century Earl of
Rochester in "A Satire Against Mankind":

Which is the basest creature, man, or beast?
Birds feed on birds, beasts on each other prey;
But savage man alone does man betray.
Press'd by necessity, *they* kill for food;
Man undoes man, to do himself no good.
With teeth and claws, by nature arm'd, *they* hunt
Nature's allowance, to supply their want:
But man with smiles, embraces, friendship, praise,
Inhumanly his fellow's life betrays,
With voluntary pains, works his distress:
Not through necessity, but wantonness.

[*Poetry and the Human Condition*]   150

For hunger, or for love, *they* bite or tear,
Whilst wretched man is still in arms for fear:
For fear he arms, and is of arms afraid;
From fear, to fear, successively betray'd.

We can echo Arthur Hugh Clough (a close friend of Matthew Arnold), in "The Latest Decalogue":

Thou shalt have one God only; who
Would be at the expense of two?

No graven images may be
Worshipped, except the currency:

Swear not at all; for by thy curse
Thine enemy is none the worse:

At church on Sunday to attend
Will serve to keep the world thy friend:

Honour thy parents; that is all
From whom advancement may befall:

Thou shalt not kill; but need'st not strive
Officiously to keep alive:

Do not adultery commit;
Advantage rarely comes of it:

Thou shalt not steal; an empty feat,
When it's so lucrative to cheat:

Bear not false witness; let the lie
Have time on its own wings to fly:

Thou shalt not covet, but tradition
Approves all forms of competition.

We accept, with reluctant cynicism, the truth of Swift's clear-sighted "Verses on the Death of Dr. Swift":

Here shift the scene, to represent
How those I love, my death lament.
Poor *Pope* will grieve a month; and *Gay*
A week; and *Arbuthnot* a day.

*　　*　　*　　*

[*Social Satire*]　151

My female friends, whose tender hearts,
Have better learned to act their parts,
Receive the news in doleful dumps,
"The Dean is dead (*and what is trumps?*)
Then Lord have mercy on his soul.
(Ladies I'll venture for the *vole.*)
Six Deans they say must bear the pall.
(I wish I knew which King to call.)
Madam, your husband will attend
The funeral of so good a friend.
No madam, 'tis a shocking sight,
And he's engaged tomorrow night!"

We acknowledge the fact that a once popular writer can be
allowed by his friends to die in poverty, as commemorated
by Samuel Wesley (elder brother of John Wesley) in "On
the setting up of Mr. Butler's monument in Westminster
Abbey." "Mr. Butler" is Samuel Butler, author of *Hudibras*,
a political satire on Presbyterianism, much admired by
Charles II and his court. Butler died in 1680, and the bust
was put up in 1721.

While Butler, needy wretch! was yet alive,
No generous patron would a dinner give:
See him, when starved to death and turned to dust,
Presented with a monumental bust!
The poet's fate is here in emblem shown;
He asked for bread, and he received a stone.

Lear, blind to his own abuse of power when he was him-
self king, sees clearly in his outcast misery the relativity
of virtue, expressing it in strong prose, rising into rich
visual poetic metaphor.

See how yond justice rails upon yon simple thief.
Hark in thine ear: change places, and, handy-dandy,
which is the justice, which is the thief? Thou hast
seen a farmer's dog bark at a beggar? . . . And the
creature run from the cur? Then thou mightest be-
hold the great image of authority: a dog's obeyed in
office . . .

[*Poetry and the Human Condition*]   152

Through tatter'd clothes small vices do appear;
Robes and furr'd gowns hide all. Plate sin with gold,
And the strong lance of justice hurtless breaks;
Arm it in rags, a pigmy's straw does pierce it.

These are large and bitter generalizations about the
cruelty, egotism and callousness of ordinary human na-
ture in all ages. They are all colored by the same atmos-
phere. But the tones of satiric attack can be varied, as we
can see from a few poems on the same theme: the ever-
popular one of the weaknesses of women. Swift is sardonic
on the responses of the card-playing ladies to the news of
his death, but Pope is far more savage in his Moral Essay
"Of the Characters of Women."

Beauties, like tyrants, old and friendless grown,
Yet hate repose, and dread to be alone. . . .
As hags hold Sabbaths, less for joy than spite,
So these their merry, miserable night;
Still round and round the ghosts of beauty glide,
And haunt the places where their honour died.
See how the world its veterans rewards!
A youth of frolics, an old age of cards;
Fair to no purpose, artful to no end,
Young without lovers, old without a friend;
A fop their passion, but their prize a sot;
Alive ridiculous, and dead, forgot!

These horrible old society women, whom we meet so often
in Restoration drama, have never been analyzed with
more brutal precision. Their gatherings are likened to the
orgies of the medieval Witches' Sabbath, but without any
of the positive evil that gave the Walpurgis Night its ter-
ror. Instead it's the negative aimlessness and emptiness of
the "merry, miserable night" that provokes the poet's con-
tempt. These women have made the world of fashion their
only existence, and the epithet "veterans" is heavily ironic.
In English usage the word doesn't refer to one who has
done military service: it connotes long and distinguished
service in any field. This is how dedication to fashion is

rewarded. The final couplet is distilled hatred and disgust of a whole way of life, created chiefly by the coupling of the honorable words "passion" and "prize" with the base and mean ones "fop" and "sot."

Pope had little good to say of women, but his tone is lighter, though no less barbed, in the description of the heroine of "The Rape of the Lock," Belinda.

> And now, unveil'd, the Toilet stands display'd,
> Each silver Vase in mystic order laid.
> First, rob'd in white, the Nymph intent adores,
> With head uncover'd, the Cosmetic powers.
> A heavenly image in the glass appears,
> To that she bends, to that her eyes she rears;
> The inferior Priestess, at her altar's side,
> Trembling begins the sacred rites of Pride.
> Unnumbered treasures ope at once, and here
> The various offerings of the world appear;
> From each she nicely culls with curious toil,
> And decks the Goddess with the glittering spoil.
> This casket India's glowing gems unlocks,
> And all Arabia breathes from yonder box.
> The Tortoise here and Elephant unite,
> Transformed to combs, the speckled and the white.
> Here files of pins extend their shining rows,
> Puffs, Powders, Patches, Bibles, Billet-doux.

This is the mock-heroic style, the deliberate application of dignified language to a trivial occasion. It is more malicious than savage about feminine fakes and follies. From the opening picture we see at once that the object of reverent worship is Belinda herself, while her bureau becomes an altar, her maid a priestess, and her cosmetics and toilet articles objects in a sacred ritual. Everything stands out in bright clarity, suffused at first with a tone of semi-indulgent mockery. This shifts slightly and becomes more biting as we read on. The "glittering spoil" with which she decks herself represents "the various offerings of the world" used solely to minister to her vanity. The "curious toil" with which she chooses her adornments is set by implication against the labors of others in far places which have gone into producing her jewels, her perfumes, her combs. Finally the character of her empty, undiscriminating little mind is summed up in the assorted articles littered on her "altar," with Bibles sandwiched between patches and love-letters. Belinda will certainly end as one of the beldames of the earlier passage.

In contrast to all the concentrated brilliance of Pope, here is a satire, "In Westminster Abbey," by the modern English poet, John Betjeman. Like Belinda, the lady is also performing a religious ritual, but this is no heroic burlesque. It has no adornments of language; in fact the lady might have used just the same vocabulary, without the rhyme-scheme, in her actual prayer—though perhaps it would be better to call it an internal monologue rather than a prayer. Betjeman presents it without comment, in all its naïve snobbery and self-absorption. He leaves the picture of the kneeling figure and her absurd yet chilling egotism to make its effect against the suggestions of all that Westminster Abbey stands for in the history of the English people.

> Let me take this other glove off
>   As the *vox humana* swells,
> And the beauteous fields of Eden
>   Bask beneath the Abbey bells.
> Here where England's statesmen lie,
> Listen to a lady's cry.
>
> Gracious Lord, oh bomb the Germans.
>   Spare their women for Thy sake,
> And if that is not too easy
>   We will pardon Thy mistake.
> But, gracious Lord, whate'er shall be
> Don't let anyone bomb me.
>
> Keep our Empire undismembered
>   Guide our Forces by Thy Hand,
> Gallant blacks from far Jamaica,
>   Honduras and Togoland;
> Protect them, Lord, in all their fights
> And, even more, protect the whites.

Think of what our Nation stands for,
  Books from Boots' and country lanes,
Free speech, free passes, class distinction,
  Democracy and proper drains.
Lord, put beneath thy special care
One eighty-nine Cadogan Square.

Although, dear Lord, I am a sinner,
  I have done no major crime;
Now I'll come to Evening Service
  Whensoever I have time.
So, Lord, reserve for me a crown,
And do not let my shares go down.
        *   *   *   *
Now I feel a little better,
  What a treat to hear Thy Word,
Where the bones of leading statesmen,
  Have so often been interr'd.
And now, dear Lord, I cannot wait
Because I have a luncheon date.

These sketches of women are all satires against society.
They are as much indictments of a whole class as of the
individuals within it, merciless in the accuracy with which
they evoke types that we recognize immediately, just as
we recognize the universal failings of human nature in
the quotations earlier in this chapter. Another category in
which the general and the particular blend, again in tones
varying from light comedy to rage, is political satire. Poli-
tics is a natural subject for satire since venality, self-inter-
est and class interest play so large a part in it. Dryden and
Pope are the two great English poets whose political satire
survives in enduring works of art, but a large body of
popular literature in the form of ballads was written from
the seventeenth to the nineteenth centuries. These ballads
exploit political themes with direct shrewdness and irony,
aiming at the "man in the street" rather than the literary
world. Indeed many of them were sold in the streets as
"broadsides" and only later found their way into collec-
tions. The anonymous "Vicar of Bray" dates from the early

eighteenth century and is a light-hearted monologue on
the ethics of the clergy whose livings depended on political
patronage.

> In good King Charles's golden days,
>   When loyalty no harm meant,
> A furious High-Church man I was,
>   And so I gained preferment.
> Unto my flock I daily preached:
>   "Kings are by God appointed,
> And damned are those who dare resist,
>   Or touch the Lord's anointed."
>   And this is law, I will maintain
>   Unto my dying day, sir,
>   That whatsoever king shall reign,
>   I will be Vicar of Bray, sir!
>
> When royal James possessed the crown,
>   And Popery grew the fashion,
> The Penal Law I hunted down
>   And read the Declaration:
> The Church of Rome, I found, would fit
>   Full well my constitution,
> And I had been a Jesuit,
>   But for the Revolution.
>   And this is law . . . etc.

When Queen Anne comes to the throne, the vicar turns
Tory, but under George I switches to Whiggery and de-
cides to remain in that camp as long as necessary.

> The illustrious House of Hanover
>   And Protestant Succession,
> To these I lustily will swear
>   While they can keep possession:
> For in my faith and loyalty
>   I never once will falter,
> But George my lawful King shall be,
>   Except the times should alter.
>   And this is law . . . etc.

"A Ballad on the Taxes," that dates from a little earlier,
has a modern ring!

[Social Satire]   157

Good people, what, will you of all be bereft—
Will you never learn wit while a penny is left?
You are all like the dog in the fable betray'd,
To let go the substance and snatch at the shade;
With specious pretences, and foreign expenses,
   We war for Religion, and waste all our chink,
'Tis nipped, and 'tis clipped, 'tis lent, and 'tis spent,
   Till 'tis gone, 'tis gone to the Devil I think.

We pay for our new-born, we pay for our dead,
We pay if we're single, we pay if we're wed;
To show that our merciful senate don't fail,
They begin at our head and tax down to the tail.
   Yet for all our expenses get nothing but blows;
At home we are cheated, abroad we're defeated,
   But the end on't, the end on't—the Lord above
   knows!

In the nineteenth century, with the rise of the bourgeoisie, the class war comes into the picture. "The Song of the Lower Classes" (c. 1848) shows at least that the proletariat could be vocal with ironic sarcasm.

We plough and sow—we're so very, very low,
   That we delve in the dirty clay,
Till we bless the plain—with the golden grain,
   And the vale with the fragrant hay,
Our place we know,—we're so very low,
   'Tis down at the landlord's feet:
We're not too low—the bread to grow,
   But too low the bread to eat.

Down, down we go,—we're so very low,
   To the hell of the deep sunk mines,
But we gather the proudest gems that glow,
   When the crown of a despot shines.
And whenever he lacks—upon our backs
   Fresh loads he deigns to lay:
We're far too low to vote the tax,
   But not too low to pay.

The most vigorous and angry of these ballads was that by Byron, "An Ode on the Framers of the Frame Bill." In

1812 the Nottinghamshire weavers, goaded by the loss of their livelihood through the introduction of the new machine-looms, rose and smashed them in the factories. They used no violence against their employers, but the government punished the rioters with shootings, hanging and transportation. Byron, playing a role that we don't usually associate with him, made an impassioned speech in the House of Lords, defending the workmen and condemning the government, and published the poem in *The Morning Chronicle* the following month.

Oh well done Lord E[ldo]n! and better done R[yde]r!
    Britannia must prosper with councils like yours;
Hawkesbury, Harrowby, help you to guide her,
    Whose remedy only must *kill* ere it cures:
Those villains; the Weavers, are all grown refractory,
    Asking some succour for Charity's sake—
So hang them in clusters round each Manufactory,
    That will at once put an end to *mistake*.

The rascals, perhaps, may betake them to robbing,
    The dogs to be sure have got nothing to eat—
So if we can hang them for breaking a bobbin,
    'Twill save all the Government's money and meat:
Men are more easily made than machinery—
    Stockings fetch better prices than lives—
Gibbets on Sherwood will heighten the scenery,
    Shewing how Commerce, how Liberty thrives!

Justice is now in pursuit of the wretches,
    Grenadiers, Volunteers, Bow-street Police,
Twenty-two Regiments, a score of Jack Ketches,
    Three of the Quorum and two of the Peace;
Some Lords, to be sure, would have summoned
      the Judges,
    To take their opinion, but that they ne'er shall,
For Liverpool such a concession begrudges,
    So now they're condemned by *no Judges* at all.

Some folks for certain have thought it was shocking,
    When Famine appeals and when Poverty groans,
That Life should be valued at less than a stocking,

And breaking of frames lead to breaking of bones.
If it should prove so, I trust, by this token,
    (And who will refuse to partake in the hope?)
That the frames of the fools may be first to be *broken*,
    Who, when asked for a *remedy*, sent down a *rope*.

Byron is in a more familiar role as satirist in "The Vision of Judgment." In 1821 on the death of George III, Robert Southey, as Poet Laureate, had published an absurdly extravagant eulogy, called "A Vision of Judgment," in which he described the entry of the old king into the joys of the Lord. This was too much for Byron, who disliked humbug in general and Southey in particular, and in the preface to his own "Vision" he declares that "the gross flattery, the dull impudence and impious cant" of Southey cannot go unanswered. In Byron's poem "an old man / With an old soul, and both extremely blind," is wafted on a cloud, accompanied by a troop of Tory angels, to the gates of Heaven. Here Satan and the Archangel Michael argue whether he shall be let into Heaven or be sent to Hell. Satan protests:

"Look to the earth, I said, and say again:
    When this old, blind, mad, helpless, weak poor
        worm
Began in youth's first bloom and flush to reign,
    The world and he both wore a different form,
And much of earth and all the watery plain
    Of ocean call'd him king: through many a storm
His isles had floated on the abyss of time;
For the rough virtues chose them for their clime.

He came to his sceptre young; he leaves it old:
    Look to the state in which he found his realm,
And left it; and his annals too behold,
    How to a minion first he gave the helm;
How grew upon his heart a thirst for gold,
    The beggar's vice, which can but overwhelm
The meanest hearts; and for the rest, but glance
Thine eye along America and France.

'Tis true, he was a tool from first to last
   (I have the workmen safe); but as a tool
So let him be consumed. From out the past
   Of ages, since mankind has known the rule
Of monarchs—from the bloody rolls amass'd
   Of sin and slaughter—from the Caesar's school,
Take the worst pupil; and produce a reign
More drench'd with gore, more cumber'd with the
    slain."

Michael interrupts, calling for individual witnesses against
the king. From a host who volunteer, he calls the political
reformer John Wilkes, but Wilkes is too large-minded to
vote for damnation.

                   "Why,"
Replied the spirit, "since old scores are past,
   Must I turn evidence? In faith, not I.
Besides, I beat him hollow at the last,
   With all his Lords and Commons: in the sky
I don't like ripping up old stories, since
His conduct was but natural in a prince."

Michael then calls Junius, the pseudonym of the author
of the famous series of Letters attacking the King and his
Government, whose identity has never been confirmed.

The shadow came—a tall, thin, grey-haired figure,
   That look'd as it had been a shade on earth;
Quick in its motions, with an air of vigour,
   But nought to mark its breeding or its birth;
Now it wax'd little, then again grew bigger,
   With now an air of gloom, or savage mirth;
But as you gazed upon its features, they
Changed every instant—to *what* none could say.

But Junius, too, refuses to give further evidence, saying,

"My charges upon record will outlast
   The brass of both his epitaph and tomb."

He melts away in "celestial smoke."
   Satan then suggests calling George Washington and

Franklin, but is interrupted by the arrival of the devil
Asmodeus, with so heavy a burden that it has strained his
left wing! Remarking that "one would think / Some of his
works about his neck were chained," he dumps Southey
in the midst of the gathering. The Laureate first describes
at great length the dignity and importance of his many
works in verse and prose, then,

> He ceased, and drew forth an MS; and no
> Persuasion on the part of devils, saints,
> Or angels, now could stop the torrent; so
>   He read the first three lines of the contents;
> But at the fourth, the whole spiritual show
>   Had vanished, with variety of scents,
> Ambrosial and sulphureous, as they sprang,
> Like lightning off from his "melodious twang."
>   *   *   *   *
> All I saw further, in the last confusion,
>   Was, that King George slipp'd into heaven for one;
> And when the tumult dwindled to a calm,
> I left him practising the hundredth psalm.

Byron splashes plenty of vitriol about in his poem, but
his fun and good spirits and the essential justice of his at-
tack remove his satire from the atmosphere of personal
spite. This is hardly true of Dryden in his portrait of
Thomas Shadwell in "MacFlecknoe" (1682). Politics and
personalities blend in the situation there too, for Shad-
well was a supporter of Dryden's arch-enemy, the Earl
of Shaftesbury (pilloried as Achitophel in Dryden's po-
litical satire "Absalom and Achitophel"). But though the
subtitle to "MacFlecknoe" was "A satire upon the true-
blue Protestant Poet T. S.," a hit at Shadwell's Whiggery,
the poem itself aims to blast his literary reputation. The
mockery of the portrait is full-blooded and devastating,
as Dryden describes how the King of the Realms of Non-
sense decides on his heir.

> This aged Prince, now flourishing in peace,
> And blest with issue of a large increase;
> Worn out with business, did at length debate

To settle the succession of the State;
And pond'ring which of all his sons was fit
To reign, and wage immortal war with wit,
Cried: " 'Tis resolved; for Nature pleads, that he
Should only rule, who most resembles me.
Sh—— alone my perfect image bears,
Mature in dulness from his tender years:
Sh—— alone, of all my sons, is he
Who stands confirm'd in full stupidity.
The rest to some faint meaning make pretense,
But Sh—— never deviates into sense.
Some beams of wit on other souls may fall,
Strike thro', and make a lucid interval;
But Sh——'s genuine night admits no ray,
His rising fogs prevail upon the day.

The supreme mastery of the satiric personal portrait, as of the social type, remains with Pope. Swift claimed that he himself was attempting "to cure the vices of mankind" in his satire, but adds:

Yet malice never was his aim;
He lashed the vice, but spared the name.

This is not strictly true; nothing could be more personal than Swift's "A Satirical Elegy," heaping insults on the Duke of Marlborough after his death. Pope, however, strews names wholesale. Not of course the actual names of his enemies, but classical pseudonyms which deluded no one, including the victims. The eighteenth century was the great age of satire, and with good reason. The worlds of the court and the coffee-houses and clubs of London were a small, closed, urban society where the poet could write for an audience divided in political opinions and personal relationships, but united in social assumptions and literary standards. Public men found poets useful agents for political propaganda, and the poets could regard themselves as the mouthpieces of the social conscience, its protest against greed, humbug, vanity, pedantry and corruption. The poet had no wish to be a mystical allegorist like Spenser, a prophet and seer like Milton,

[*Social Satire*] 163

an explorer of the inner life like Donne. He was content to measure human nature against a generally held canon of civilized and sophisticated morality, and to give it the witty and energetic expression which the average intelligent man would use if he could.

In Pope, the age found the genius most perfectly suited to its tastes and needs. He had a set of dramatic fictions about himself which he modified to fit the various occasions of his satire. He could appear as the graceful mocker of feminine follies and absurdities, as in "The Rape of the Lock"; or the urbane man of good will, forced into the unwilling exposure of shallowness, envy and complacency. Such is his pose in the portrait of Addison in the "Epistle to Dr. Arbuthnot" (1735). After the damning description of the talented man ruined by his petty-mindedness and self-importance, Pope concludes as if so *saddened* by it all!

> Who but must laugh if such a man there be?
> Who would not weep, if *Atticus* were he!

His third mask is that of the fearless fighter for truth; the man who must speak out courageously against evil, using his "sacred weapon" to protect society from its enemies by giving the utmost force to his invective. Lytton Strachey gives a somewhat different angle to this attitude, calling Pope's attacks "spoonfuls of boiling oil, ladled out by a fiendish monkey at an upstairs window upon such of the passers-by the wretch had a grudge against." The most searing and spiteful of all the personal portraits is that of Sporus, also in the "Epistle to Dr. Arbuthnot." Lord Hervey, the victim, was a friend of the King, and especially of the Queen (the "Eve" in the verse). He was Vice-Chamberlain at the Court, and is given the name of a favorite eunuch of the Emperor Nero. Pope had already ridiculed Hervey as a versifier, and Hervey, a vain man, had replied in some scurrilous lines, accusing Pope of plagiarism in his translations of Homer, and linking Pope's deformity of body to a similar deformity of mind. Hence, no doubt, Pope's insistence on Hervey's effeminacy of face and feebleness of intelligence. The passage opens with Pope announcing "Let Sporus tremble"—on which

Arbuthnot is supposed to break in, taking a tone of light contempt and dismissal:

> What? that thing of silk,
> *Sporus*, that mere white curd of Ass's milk?
> Satire or sense, alas! can *Sporus* feel?
> Who breaks a butterfly upon a wheel?

On which Pope sweeps in with his own direct venom.

> Yet let me flap this bug with gilded wings,
> This painted child of dirt, that stinks and stings;
> Whose buzz the witty and the fair annoys,
> Yet Wit ne'er tastes, and Beauty ne'er enjoys;
> So well-bred spaniels civilly delight
> In mumbling of the game they dare not bite.
> Eternal smiles his emptiness betray,
> As shallow streams run dimpling all the way,
> Whether in florid impotence he speaks,
> And, as the prompter breathes, the puppet squeaks,
> Or at the ear of Eve, familiar Toad,
> Half froth, half venom, spits himself abroad,
> In puns, or politics, or tales, or lies,
> Or spite, or smut, or rhymes, or blasphemies;
> His wit all see-saw between *that* and *this*,
> Now high, now low, now master up, now miss,
> And he himself one vile Antithesis.
> Amphibious thing! that acting either part,
> The trifling head, or the corrupted heart;
> Fop at the toilet, flatt'rer at the board,
> Now trips a Lady, and now struts a Lord.
> Eve's tempter thus the Rabbins have exprest,
> A cherub's face, a reptile all the rest;
> Beauty that shocks you, Parts that none will trust,
> Wit that can creep, and Pride that licks the dust.

It would be difficult to get more variety of vituperation and loathing into the lines. Every couplet is packed with poison. First the play on the idea of crushing the bug, the insect that stinks and stings; then the images of the shoddy mind, the inane smiles, the rhetoric, the toadying to royalty. Then the pursuit of the "vile Antithesis," every

[*Social Satire*] 165

verse spitting out a contrast, each side of which is in itself an insult.

Lord Hervey didn't attempt any reply, and Pope surely spoke the truth in his comment on himself:

> Yes, I am proud; I must be proud to see
> Men not afraid of God, afraid of me.

None of the satire quoted thus far, whether general, social or personal, has had any room for pity. Hatred, malice and all uncharitableness are its elements. But social satire can communicate deep human feeling if the poet's bitterness against the conditions he portrays can be infused with real compassion for the victims of those conditions. Blake's "London," for instance, is such a poem.

> I wander thro' each chartered street,
> Near where the chartered Thames does flow,
> And mark in every face I meet
> Marks of weakness, marks of woe.
>
> In every cry of every Man,
> In every Infant's cry of fear,
> In every voice, in every ban,
> The mind-forged manacles I hear.
>
> How the Chimney-sweeper's cry
> Every black'ning Church appalls;
> And the hapless Soldier's sigh
> Runs in blood down Palace walls.
>
> But most thro' midnight streets I hear
> How the youthful Harlot's curse
> Blasts the new born Infant's tear,
> And blights with plagues the Marriage hearse.

At one level this is an appalling blanket indictment of society. The "mind-forged manacles" shackle everything that should be free to grow into spontaneous living. Everything and everyone is "chartered," that is, regimented along lines for financial profit. Weakness, woe, fear "blight" every face, and sound through street, church and palace. The plight of the child chimney-sweepers, the grown soldier, the young harlot, outrages the ideals of Christianity, of good government, of humane personal relationships. The final "marriage hearse" sums up the idea of the death-in-life of the picture.

Yet behind it all is not only hatred of the callousness of the human heart, and compassion for suffering, but a passionate sense of the positive values that these evil things dishonor: freedom, strength, joy, community; in a word, love.

Today, Auden's "The Shield of Achilles" presents a similar social comment, with all of Blake's pity, but without his passion. The title refers to Homer's description in the *Iliad* (Book XVIII) of the shield that Hephaestos, the Olympian smith, makes for Achilles when he is to go into battle against Hector. Homer puts scenes of war and the brutalities of war on the shield, which Auden omits, but the peaceful scenes depict all that never appears in the *Iliad* itself; the ordered life of cities, pastoral tranquillity, country farms and fields and vineyards, country games and the dances of the men and girls with the older people watching: all the shared work and play that makes a living community. Auden's criticism of the modern world is to suggest this background, and to contrast it with the regimentation and aridity of mass civilization— Blake's "mind-forged manacles"—and like Blake too, to point to the cruelty of man to man, and to the crimes and the sufferings of loveless childhood.

> She looked over his shoulder
>   For vines and olive trees,
> Marble, well-governed cities
>   And ships upon wine-dark seas;
> But there on the shining metal
>   His hands had put instead
> An artificial wilderness
>   And a sky like lead.

A plain without a feature, bare and brown,
    No blade of grass, no sign of neighborhood,
Nothing to eat and nowhere to sit down;

Yet, congregated on that blankness, stood
  An unintelligible multitude,
A million eyes, a million boots, in line,
Without expression, waiting for a sign.

Out of the air a voice without a face
  Proved by statistics that some cause was just
In tones as dry and level as the place;
  No one was cheered and nothing was discussed,
  Column by column, in a cloud of dust,
They marched away, enduring a belief
Whose logic brought them, somewhere else, to grief.

    She looked over his shoulder
      For ritual pieties,
    White flower-garlanded heifers,
      Libation and sacrifice:
    But there on the shining metal
      Where the altar should have been
    She saw by his flickering forge-light
      Quite another scene.

Barbed wire enclosed an arbitrary spot
  Where bored officials lounged (one cracked a joke)
And sentries sweated for the day was hot;
  A crowd of ordinary decent folk
  Watched from outside and neither moved nor spoke
As three pale figures were led forth and bound
To three posts driven upright in the ground.

The mass and majesty of this world, all
  That carries weight and always weighs the same,
Lay in the hands of others; they were small
  And could not hope for help, and no help came;
  What their foes liked to do was done; their shame
Was all the worst could wish: they lost their pride
And died as men before their bodies died.

    She looked over his shoulder
      For athletes at their games,
    Men and women in a dance
      Moving their sweet limbs,

Quick, quick, to music;
    But there on the shining shield
His hands had set no dancing-floor
    But a weed-choked field.

A ragged urchin, aimless and alone,
    Loitered about that vacancy; a bird
Flew up to safety from his well-aimed stone:
    That girls are raped, that two boys knife a third,
    Were axioms to him, who'd never heard
Of any world where promises were kept
Or one could weep because another wept.

        The thin-lipped armorer
    Hephaestos hobbled away;
        Thetis of the shining breasts
            Cried out in dismay
        At what the God had wrought
            To please her son, the strong
        Iron-hearted man-slaying Achilles
            Who would not live long.

11. Nature

"In our life alone does Nature live."

S. T. Coleridge

Virginia Woolf entered in her diary, May 5, 1935: "The more complex the vision, the less it lends itself to satire; the more it understands the less it is able to sum up and make linear." This accounts for the ascendancy of satire in the Augustan age. Its poets refused to look into any emotional depths below the social surface; they were determined to subjugate all mystery to rational discernment. The individual must neither lament nor criticize the limits of the human condition, nor presume to try to transcend them. As Pope put it:

> Know thy own point: This kind, this due degree
> Of blindness, weakness, Heaven bestows on thee.

Against this we might put Wordsworth's impassioned romantic aspiration:

> Whether we be young or old,
> Our destiny, our being's heart and home,
> Is with infinitude and only there;
> With hope it is, hope that can never die,
> Effort and expectation and desire,
> And something evermore about to be.

To the Augustans all such spiritual or imaginative longings were suspect. They dismissed them as "enthusiasm," a definitely derogatory term in their vocabulary. Civilization meant an ideal as orderly and compact as their own heroic couplets. But Dryden, even in the late seventeenth century, before that ideal had fully established it-self, saw its limitations, in both living and writing:

> Our age was cultivated thus at length,
> But what we gain'd in skill we lost in strength.

The irrational, spontaneous elements in man's nature cannot be ignored, and it was inevitable that artificial repression should be followed by the romantic revolt.

The "Romantic Revival," which is usually dated from the publication of the *Lyrical Ballads* by Wordsworth and Coleridge in 1798, is sometimes called the "Return to Na-ture," and is particularly associated with nature poetry. But poetry about nature has been written in all ages, though its character and quality change according to the tastes of the age and the sensibilities of the individual poets. Plenty of nature poetry was written in the eight-eenth century, though few now read it. The conventional "pastoral," imitated from the classical poets, was popular, clothed in the conventional "poetic diction" that spoke of vernal airs and blushing dawns, the bloomy spray, the swelling clusters of the vine, the sun's mild luster, the gentle gales, and the sounding main. The "return to na-ture" in the sense of discarding this pure stylization and mixing accurate description with the formal vocabulary, came with James Thomson's *The Seasons* (published 1726–1730), and at the end of the century in the poetry of William Cowper and George Crabbe. But there's noth-ing quite so dull as descriptions of nature in undistin-guished verse. They seem to send the Muse packing. They need some special qualities of workmanship or emotion to make them live, and the eighteenth-century poets who possessed those qualities used them for special subjects. We go to the poets before and after the Augustans to be stirred and delighted with the reminder of natural beau-ties and their effects on the mind of man; with descrip-tions of outer and inner weather. The medieval poets, Chaucer, Langland, the author of "Sir Gawain and the Green Knight," and the lyric writers, take us into the real

countryside at all seasons, as the natural background for
the figures of men and women. The language is difficult
though, and makes quotation from them unrewarding for
the common reader. Elizabethan poets had the same tastes,
but the revival of interest in the Greek and Latin poets
made them love to imitate and adapt the pastoral, though
with far more individuality and charm than their eight-
eenth-century successors. Here is a verse from Spenser's
"Prothalamion," where the description of the classical
nymphs, preparing to crown their "paramours," almost
creates in words the sensuous flowing movement and color
of Botticelli's "Primavera," while the rhythm adds its
graceful melody.

> There, in a meadow, by the river's side,
> A flock of nymphs I chancèd to espy,
> All lovely daughters of the flood thereby,
> With goodly greenish locks all loose untied,
> As each had been a bride;
> And each one had a little wicker basket,
> Made of fine twigs entrailèd curiously,
> In which they gathered flowers to fill their flasket,
> And with fine fingers cropped full featously
> The tender stalks on high.
> Of every sort, which in that meadow grew,
> They gathered some; the violet pallid blue,
> The little daisy, that at evening closes,
> The virgin lily, and the primrose true,
> With store of vermeil roses,
> To deck their bridegrooms' posies,
> Against the bridal day, which was not long:
>   Sweet Thames, run softly, till I end my song.

The Elizabethans, too, wrote innumerable songs about
the joys of spring that still keep their freshness. This, for
instance, by Thomas Nashe, makes a complete contrast
with his verses in the time of plague (p. 107).

> Spring, the sweet spring, is the year's pleasant king;
>   Then blooms each thing, then maids dance in a
>   ring,

Cold doth not sting, the pretty birds do sing—
    Cuckoo, jug-jug, pu-we, to-witta-woo!

The palm and may make country houses gay,
Lambs frisk and play, the shepherds pipe all day,
And we hear aye birds tune this merry lay—
    Cuckoo, jug-jug, pu-we, to-witta-woo!

The fields breathe sweet, the daisies kiss our feet,
Young lovers meet, old wives a-sunning sit,
In every street these tunes our ears do greet—
    Cuckoo, jug-jug, pu-we, to-witta-woo!
        Spring, the sweet Spring!

Shakespeare's plays, songs and sonnets are filled with realistic touches that seem to mark him as a countryman. In his first poem, "Venus and Adonis," he describes poor Wat, the hare, pursued by the hunters:

How he outruns the winds, and with what care
He cranks and crosses with a thousand doubles;

and then:

              far off upon a hill,
Stands on his hinder legs with listening ear,
To hearken if his foes pursue him still:

And late in his career, Perdita in *The Winter's Tale*, tells of the daffodils,

That come before the swallow dares, and take
The winds of March with beauty.

(I read recently that "take" at that time had the additional meaning of "cast a spell on," which adds to the lines.)

Milton, like Spenser, put the flowers of the English meadows and hedgerows into a classical setting, but to deck a burial, not a wedding.

Bring the rathe primrose that forsaken dies,
The tufted crow-toe, and pale jessamine,
The white pink, and the pansy freaked with jet,
The glowing violet,

The musk-rose, and the well-attired woodbine,
With cowslips wan that hang the pensive head,
And every flower that sad embroidery wears;
Bid Amaranthus all his beauty shed,
And daffadillies fill their cups with tears,
To strew the laureat hearse where Lycid lies.

Wordsworth gives us a vivid picture of a happy, instead of a frightened hare:

The hare is running races in her mirth;
And with her feet she from the plashy earth
Raises a mist, that, glittering in the sun,
Runs with her all the way, wherever she doth run.

Shelley creates desolation in two stark stanzas:

A widow bird sat mourning for her love
  Upon a wintry bough;
The frozen wind crept on above,
  The freezing stream below.

There was no leaf upon the forest bare,
  No flower upon the ground,
And little motion in the air
  Except the mill-wheel's sound.

Among the moderns two poets are specially distinguished for unusual descriptive methods: D. H. Lawrence and Marianne Moore. Lawrence's birds, beasts and flowers (one of his volumes of poetry bears that title) have a glowing vigor. He addresses the turkey:

Your wattles are the colour of steel-slag which has
    been red-hot
And is going cold,
Cooling to a powdery, pale oxydized sky-blue.

And then creates the bird's sudden demonic rush:

All the bronze gloss of all his myriad petals
Each one apart and instant . . .
So delicate
Yet the bronze windbell suddenly clashing.

[*Poetry and the Human Condition*]   174

Or he sketches the kangaroo, with "her little loose hands and drooping Victorian shoulders," or the she-goat "smiling with goaty munch-mouth, Mona Lisa."

Lawrence makes us feel the intensity of life in the natural world, each creature living from its own center of being, but Marianne Moore's animals live in a world of precisely patterned movements. The jerboa, for instance, seeking its food:

> By fifths and sevenths,
> in leaps of two lengths,
>   like the uneven notes
>   of the Bedouin flute, it stops its gleaning
>   on little wheel castors, and makes fern-seed
>   foot-prints with kangaroo speed.

Or the British coat of arms, with

> the lion civilly rampant
> the unicorn also on its hind legs in reciprocity.

Charming or brilliant descriptive passages about the natural world could fill an anthology, but that subject soon palls. It's the deeper and more complex relationships between the external world and the mind of man that inspires the best nature poetry. Of this, we can distinguish two main modes: the intensely subjective identification with natural forces, which we associate particularly with Wordsworth and the other romantic poets of the early nineteenth century; and the "parable" or "fable," where nature never appears in the poem for its own sake only, but becomes part of a much larger and more general vision of moral or emotional truth.

Wordsworth is out of fashion nowadays. One reason, no doubt, is because of the extreme unevenness of his own writing, a fact wittily stressed in a comment by J. K. Stephen. Starting with the opening of Wordsworth's own sonnet "Thoughts of a Briton on the Subjugation of Switzerland": "Two voices are there; one is of the Sea / One of the mountains . . ." Stephen turns it into:

> Two voices are there: one is of the deep;

It learns the storm-clouds thunderous melody,
Now roars, now murmurs with the changing sea,
Now bird-like pipes, now closes soft in sleep:
And one is of an old half-witted sheep
Which bleats articulate monotony,
And indicates that two and two are three,
That grass is green, lakes damp, and mountains
  steep:
And, Wordsworth, both are thine. . . .

But even his best poetry lacks appeal for another reason. Wordsworth is a particularly personal poet, speaking directly to the reader of his most inward experiences, and the character of those experiences doesn't communicate itself to the majority of modern readers. A mystical relationship with nature is a rarity today. People live in the country to escape the rush, the noise, the dirt and smells of city life. They work in their gardens and take trips in their cars over scenic routes between one Howard Johnson and another. They spend the summer by the ocean and make the same round of cocktail parties as they do at home. All life has become so urbanized that the intensities of the romantic poets over mountains and nightingales and skylarks and cuckoos and clouds and west winds and the lesser celandine seem alien and remote. The poems are read in courses in a period of English literature, and an old joke from *Punch* has a certain pertinence. A professor, with examination questions running in his head, and a poet are walking in the woods in springtime. The poet quotes:

O cuckoo, shall I call thee bird,
Or but a wandering voice?

which the professor caps by finishing the verse:

State the alternative preferred,
With reasons for your choice.

Yet Wordsworth and his disciples are revealing the mysteries of man, not of nature. As Jacques Barzun says of the romantic poet: "He is in effect a dramatist using his

[*Poetry and the Human Condition*] 176

own self as a sensitive plate to catch whatever molecular or spiritual motion the outer world may supply." Whether or not we respond to the particular emotional stimuli of such a poet, or to different stimuli in our own lives, we can enter imaginatively into the experience, for the emotions aroused are human ones, which we too can share. In "Daffodils" (p. 87) we shared an incident where a mood of apathy and loneliness was miraculously changed, by a vision of the flowers and the lake, into the assurance of universal harmony. But though this assurance is the final faith that Wordsworth held, he by no means always held it. In Book I of *The Prelude* he tells us:

> Fair seed-time had my Soul, and I grew up
> Fostered alike by beauty and by fear. . . .

With extraordinary vividness he evokes some of the episodes of fear, such as the night in a boat on the moonlit lake, when by some accident of perspective, a formerly hidden peak suddenly looms up and seems to be pursuing him as he rows.

> a huge Cliff,
> As if with voluntary power instinct,
> Uprear'd its head. I struck and struck again,
> And, growing still in stature, the huge Cliff
> Rose up between me and the stars, and still
> With measured motion, like a living thing,
> Strode after me.

These terrors brought "a dim and undetermined sense / Of unknown modes of being," darkness and solitude and "blank desertion." But they are balanced by other feelings of a "presence" that encloses him safely. In the ice skating scene, first the hills seem to spin along with himself. Then he stops short,

> Yet still the solitary Cliffs
> Wheel'd by me, even as if the earth had roll'd
> With visible motion her diurnal round. . . .
> And I stood and watched
> Till all was tranquil as a dreamless sleep.

[*Nature*]   177

These and many other differing phases of consciousness gradually convinced him that

> The mind of man is fram'd even like the breath
> And harmony of music. There is a dark
> Invisible workmanship that reconciles
> Discordant elements and makes them move
> In one society.

The music includes, and must include, the experiences of vexation, misery, regrets and pain, all "the still, sad music of humanity," which must be "reconciled" in the living soul. In the "Lines Written above Tintern Abbey" Wordsworth states his belief that through this sense of final harmony "we see into the life of things." He questions whether this "be but a vain belief," yet affirms his faith that it has proved true for him, and for his sister Dorothy, whom he is addressing. He rests finally in the assurance that quietness and beauty and joy so fill them,

> that neither evil tongues,
> Rash judgments, nor the sneers of selfish men,
> Nor greetings where no kindness is, nor all
> The dreary intercourse of daily life,
> Shall e'er prevail against us.

This is not an "escape into nature" but a revelation that through the conviction of the unity of man with nature, the mind can discover itself in fullness and disciplined calm, and escape that "dizzy perturbation" which meets it in the world's ways.

Too much of Wordsworth's poetry talks *about* his beliefs instead of creating them in "moments of vision"; but in many scenes in "The Prelude" his own figure becomes symbolic like the single figures of the solitary reaper, or Michael, or the old leech-gatherer, moving through each experience toward some new perception into "the life of things," against the background of lake or river, moor or vale.

None of the other romantic poets attains the serenity of Wordsworth, but their insights are arrived at in the same way. In Keats's famous "Ode to a Nightingale," for instance, through a vision of a timeless world roused by the bird's song, the poet attains Wordsworth's sense of complex harmony and peace. But he can hold it only for an instant, and the end carries no assurance of its truth. The method is the complete opposite of Wordsworth's. Instead of bare narrative statement, every stanza is loaded with rich, sensuous imagery and description. The poet first listens to the song where the "light-winged Dryad of the trees"

> In some melodious plot
> Of beechen green and shadows numberless
> Singest of summer in full-throated ease.

The song acts as an opiate to free him from the sad memories of

> The weariness, the fever, and the fret
> Here, where men sit and hear each other groan.

First he longs to match the song with "a beaker full of the warm South," and the whole atmosphere of a summer feast,

> Tasting of Flora and the country green
> Dance, and Provençal song, and sunburnt mirth.

Then the world of the imagination replaces that sunny picture, and he will pursue the bird's song into a vision of the glade where it is singing:

> I cannot see what flowers are at my feet,
> Nor what soft incense hangs upon the boughs,
> But, in embalmed darkness, guess each sweet
> Wherewith the seasonable month endows
> The grass, the thicket, and the fruit-tree wild;
> White hawthorn, and the pastoral eglantine;
>   Fast fading violets cover'd up in leaves;
>   And mid-May's eldest child,
> The coming musk-rose, full of dewy wine,
>   The murmurous haunt of flies on summer
>   eves.

[Nature]   179

The sensuous beauty of the imagined scene in the "embalmed darkness" dissolves into a voluptuous longing for death itself. Not the death of the third verse, "where youth grows pale, and spectre-thin, and dies," but an "easeful death" where the song of the nightingale would become his requiem, and he would be folded into the world of the flowers, passing into the cycle of renewed fertility.

He is brought back from this by a new perception of an immortal aspect of the nightingale's song. The poet is no longer alone as he listens, but passes in imagination to the long history of the human beings who have responded with his own mingled joy and sorrow to that "self-same song," in pagan times of "emperor and clown"; in Jewish history with Ruth "amid the alien corn"; or in the world of medieval romance, those

> magic casements, opening on the foam
> Of perilous seas, in faery lands forlorn.

For the moment he is both inside and outside time, one with the whole sweep of nature and of man. But the moment of transcendence passes:

> Forlorn! the very word is like a bell
> To toll me back from thee to my sole self!

"Fled is that music"—the music that to Wordsworth reconciled all discordant elements—and the poet is left with his own conflicting feelings and the question of what is reality, what illusion? "Do I wake or sleep?"

Out of the same blended sadness and rapture, Shelley addresses the West Wind. In the first section of his ode he calls it both destroyer and preserver, the wild being that drives the flying dead leaves and carries "to their dark wintry bed / The winged seeds"; but only so that the same wind in spring shall blow a clarion call of resurrection, call forth the buds and fill "with living hues and odours plain and hill." But Shelley resolves the poem into a prayer for the identification of himself, in the autumnal sadness of his spirit, with the wind itself:

[*Poetry and the Human Condition*]   180

> Be thou, spirit fierce,
> My spirit! Be thou me, impetuous one!

and he creates an association between the awakening
earth in springtime, the reawakening of his own spirit
to inspiration, and the hope that his poetry may bring a
resurrection to human kind.

> Drive my dead thoughts over the universe
> Like withered leaves, to quicken a new birth!
> And, by the incantation of this verse,
>
> Scatter, as from an unextinguished hearth
> Ashes and sparks, my words among mankind!
> Be through my lips to unawakened earth
>
> The trumpet of a prophecy! O, wind,
> If Winter comes, can Spring be far behind?

Dylan Thomas is the only modern poet who has some-
thing of the same sense of "oneness" with nature that
possessed the romantics, but the identification is on a dif-
ferent plane. It has no spiritual or moral feeling in it, but
dwells in the inescapable knowledge that man is one with
nature as part of the life-death cycle. Nature is not a
spirit through whose contemplation he can transcend
earthly limitations; it is a force, a process, in whose in-
exorable laws he is caught, and which holds for him far
more terror than beauty. His poetry has none of the clarity
of Wordsworth or the decoration of Keats or Shelley. It
is powerful, packed with interfused metaphors, and very
obscure.

> The force that through the green fuse drives the
>   flower
> Drives my green age; that blasts the roots of trees
> Is my destroyer.
> And I am dumb to tell the crooked rose
> My youth is bent by the same wintry fever.
>
> The force that drives the water through the rocks
> Drives my red blood; that dries the mouthing streams

Turns mine to wax.
And I am dumb to mouth unto my veins
How at the mountain spring the same mouth sucks.

The hand that whirls the water in the pool
Stirs the quicksand; that ropes the blowing wind
Hauls my shroud sail.
And I am dumb to tell the hanging man
How of my clay is made the hangman's lime.

The lips of time leech to the fountain head;
Love drips and gathers, but the fallen blood
Shall calm her sores.
And I am dumb to tell a weather's wind
How time has ticked a heaven round the stars.

And I am dumb to tell the lover's tomb
How at my sheet goes the same crooked worm.

The poet feels simultaneously both the impelling drive
of the life-force and its inseparable complement, the in-
evitability of the death-force. The refrain "I am dumb"
suggests that no mere words can express this apprehen-
sion: it is lodged in every cell of his being. The statement
starts at once in a compressed metaphor. The green fuse of
the flower-stem fuses his own life with that of nature; but
it is also the fuse that will blast his green age as it does
the trees. It is a creator and consumer; the inseparable
warmth and cold (wintry fever) that bends the glowing
rose on its stalk when the frost strikes.

In the second verse the opposition is that of liquid driv-
ing and drying, and the metaphor that of a mouth that
can both suck in and pour out. Again the statement of
creation is interfused with that of destruction.

The pattern repeats itself in the third verse. The force
becomes personified into a hand, which has all the
strength of the hand of God in the Book of Job: "He
stirreth up the sea with his power." But no religious feel-
ing of awe informs this poem, as it does Thomas's later
writings. The hand here controls the water, the air, the
earth, and it controls the ship of the poet's own life, voy-
aging through the elements. The "shroud sail" telescopes

the meaning of the shroud that wraps the dead and the ropes that support the mast-head. Then he passes to a completely different image. I suppose the ropes have suggested the "hanging man," and that he is saying that he, though still living "clay," produces continually waste products that go to make the quick-lime in which the bodies of the hanged are destroyed.

The final verse is even more complicated. The force becomes time, that "leeches" to the life-source, here sex, and sucks its vitality, just as a leech sucks blood from the body. Love drips and gathers, like the blood from the wound of a leech, which was regarded as a healing process and is here associated with the calming effect of the sexual act. But the "fallen blood" must mean also the final failing blood, the act of dying, bringing its final "calm." The last two lines defeat me entirely. Is he describing love as a *seeming* absolute, "a heaven round the stars," and telling lovers that time and the seasons really control it too? It, too, is nothing but *process*? The final couplet condenses what the rest of the poem has said.

It's impossible not to feel the intensity and vigor of the language, its dynamic violence and energy; but also impossible not to wonder if such a simple thought need be made quite so complex. The metaphors are so piled up and so closely woven that they end by stifling the free flow of the meaning.

The parable taken from nature, with its moral lesson or some fresh insight into human truth, has been popular in all ages. This is the first verse of "A Palinode" by the Elizabethan poet, Edmund Bolton. The title means a verse form which depends upon the reversal and recurrence of the words creating the theme. Here the words dance and dissolve and reappear in a most musical and graceful pattern of repetition.

> As withereth the primrose by the river,
>   As fadeth summer's sun from gliding fountains,
> As vanishes the light-blown bubble ever,
>   As melteth snow upon the mossy mountains:

So melts, so vanishes, so fades, so withers
   The rose, the shine, the bubble and the snow
Of praise, pomp, glory, joy (which short life gathers),
   Fair praise, vain pomp, sweet glory, brittle joy.
The withered primrose by the mourning river,
   The faded summer's sun by weeping fountains,
The light-blown bubble vanishèd for ever,
   The molten snow upon the naked mountains,
Are emblems that the treasure we up-lay
   Soon wither, vanish, fade, and melt away.

Henry King, author of "The Exequy" (p. 122), in "A Contemplation upon Flowers" moralizes about them and himself with charming simplicity.

Brave flowers, that I could gallant it like you
And be as little vain,
You come abroad, and make a harmless show,
And to your beds of earth again;
You are not proud, you know your birth
For your embroidered garments are from earth:

You do obey your months and times, but I
Would have it ever spring,
My fate would know no winter, never die
Nor think of such a thing;
Oh that I could my bed of earth but view
And smile, and look as cheerfully as you:

Oh teach me to see Death and not to fear
But rather to take truce;
How often have I seen you at a bier,
And there look fresh and spruce;
You fragrant flowers, then teach me that my breath
Like yours may sweeten, and perfume my death.

Thomas Hardy finds a gleam of hope for the new century in "The Darkling Thrush," written in December, 1900.

I leant upon a coppice gate
   When Frost was spectre-gray,
And Winter's dregs made desolate

The weakening eye of day.
The tangled bine-stems scored the sky
    Like strings of broken lyres,
And all mankind that haunted nigh
    Had sought their household fires.

The land's sharp features seemed to be
    The Century's corpse outleant,
His crypt the cloudy canopy,
    The wind his death-lament.
The ancient pulse of germ and birth
    Was shrunken hard and dry,
And every spirit upon the earth
    Seemed fervourless as I.

At once a voice arose among
    The bleak twigs overhead
In a full-hearted evensong
    Of joy illimited;
An agèd thrush, frail, gaunt, and small,
    In blast-beruffled plume,
Had chosen thus to fling his soul
    Upon the growing gloom.

So little cause for carolings
    Of such ecstatic sound
Was written on terrestrial things
    Afar or nigh around,
That I could think there trembled through
    His happy good-night air
Some blessed Hope, whereof he knew
    And I was unaware.

The nature poetry of the twentieth century is almost all
of this kind. Modern poets rarely write purely descriptive
poems, nor do they find strength in escaping to what
Coleridge called "some quiet spirit-healing nook," as the
minor romantics did. Implicitly they say with Auden:

To me art's subject is the human clay
And landscape but the background for a torso.

Yeats and Eliot use natural symbols, a swan or a chestnut tree, a desert or a rose garden, but these are in no sense part of the natural world: they are there to objectify an inner world of human feeling. It used to be thought that Frost was a "nature poet," and it must have surprised many of his admirers when he declared publicly that he'd written only one "nature poem" in his life—a very early lyric. He is associated so much with birches and birds and colts and running brooks and the whole New England countryside that readers often forget that he's "saying one thing in terms of another." His subject may seem to be nature, but his theme is man. Nature is never in the poems for its own sake, but is part of a general vision in which homely details take on metaphysical values. It's the same with Frost's simplicity of surface. Because the poems usually communicate easily at one level, readers go no further and think of his content as quite different from that of the difficult symbolic poets. But no fine poetry is really simple and no "regional" poetry lasts unless it is at the same time universal. Frost seems simple because he manages, as Wordsworth did, to reduce profound experiences to simple language.

His sonnet "Design" makes an interesting contrast to the mood of "Daffodils" (p. 87). He starts from a parallel happening. The poet is out for a country walk and sees a certain grouping of natural things in his physical surroundings. To Wordsworth these brought a revelation of the sense of joyous organic harmony and beneficent order within nature herself and between nature and man. In "Design" a chance assemblage of "death and blight" in the natural world brings a sense of horror, and questions if perhaps any design there is evil, or even whether moral design of any kind exists.

> I found a dimpled spider, fat and white,
> On a white heal-all, holding up a moth
> Like a white piece of rigid satin cloth—
> Assorted characters of death and blight
> Mixed ready to begin the morning right,
> Like the ingredients of a witches' broth—

A snow-drop spider, a flower like froth,
And dead wings carried like a paper kite.
What had that flower to do with being white,
The wayside blue and innocent heal-all?
What brought the kindred spider to that height,
That steered the white moth thither in the night?
What but design of darkness to appall?—
If design govern in a thing so small.

The poem in an earlier form was called "In White,"
and the irony starts with the fact that the "design" is all
in the color we associate with innocence and purity, some-
thing radiant and unsullied. *Dimpled* and *fat* are adjec-
tives which bring to mind healthy babies; the flower
heal-all brings ideas of a universal panacea, while the
white satin suggests the soft shimmering folds of a bridal
gown. These, however, are "assorted characters of death
and blight," and maybe "characters" are meant to have
a double meaning: that of *signs* and of *personalities.*
Without any difficulty we can think of human situations
paralleling the horrible spider, the blighted flower and the
dead moth—victimized innocence, promise thwarted, in-
explicable disease and so on.

The irony continues as he describes these "assorted
characters" as "mixed ready to begin the morning right,"
and we hear overtones of cheery radio programs with
various recipes to insure beginning the morning right in
physical or emotional ways: perhaps too recommenda-
tions for ready-made "mixes" that solve the cook's prob-
lems. Here the result is a "witches' broth" of horror. The
spider is *not* a snowdrop, the flower is like the scum on
some deadly brew, the wings that should fly are help-
lessly "carried."

The factual material has been presented in vivid de-
scription. Now comes the questioning. What directive has
brought these things together in the night? If we believe
that some design operates in the universe, doesn't this
prove that such cosmic laws are as much evil as good,
as much destructive as creative? What is this whiteness
but "design of darkness" to appall us, and also to put a

pall of death and blight over our easy assumptions of a divine providence?

Frost gives the poem a final sardonic twist in the last lines with the apparently offhand remark, "If design govern in a thing so small." At first he seems to be dismissing the matter, as if such a trifling catastrophe as a repulsive spider and an anemic flower and a dead moth were hardly worth mentioning at all. But the dismissal opens up a further dark possibility. We may be willing to accept that destructive forces exist, as part of a larger creative design that is beyond human comprehension. Supposing, though, there's no design at all, either in nature or in human fate? We think of Gloucester's words in *King Lear:*

> As flies to wanton boys are we to the gods.
> They kill us for their sport.

Man himself is perhaps "a thing so small" that his life is a matter of pure haphazard chance.

> . . . we receive but what we give,
> And in our life alone does Nature live:
> Ours is her wedding garment, ours her shroud!

Coleridge is surely right as far as poets are concerned. Nature herself remains the same; it's the poet who finds reflections in her of his own varying moods and perceptions. It is his particular senses that respond to the sight, sound, touch, taste and perfume of natural objects; it is his heart that finds comfort, or feels desolation, or exults in the natural forces of creation and destruction; it is his mind that contemplates her, and through the thoughts and insights she arouses, leads him to penetrate further into the mysteries of his own being. It may even intensify his sense of fellowship with other men, a truth beautifully suggested in another poem of Frost, "The Tuft of Flowers."

The poet goes out to turn the grass that the mower has cut in the dawn, but the mower has gone and the poet is alone:

"As all must be," I said within my heart,
"Whether they work together or apart."

A butterfly passes, seeking flowers and finding them all
cut down, until it comes upon a tuft blooming by the
brook, left by the mower out of love and joy in their
beauty. The poet feels "a message from the dawn."

That made me hear the wakening birds around,
And hear his long scythe whispering to the ground,

And feel a spirit kindred to my own;
So that henceforth I worked no more alone. . . .

"Men work together," I told him from the heart,
"Whether they work together or apart."

12. Love

"O spirit of love, how quick and fresh art thou."

William Shakespeare

"Love is only one among the passions, and it has no great influence upon the sum of life." So said Dr. Johnson, but there's no question of the influence love has had upon the sum of poetry. It must be far and away the most popular stimulus to verse. Floods of love poetry have poured out, each age having its own conventions for expression, and each poet giving his own personal stamp to those conventions, or breaking them for a poetic effect of his own. We can move from a very minor eighteenth-century versifier announcing placidly:

> For that which makes our lives delightful prove
> Is, a genteel sufficiency, and love.

to Sir Walter Raleigh's exultation:

> But love is a durable fire
>   In the mind ever burning;
> Never sick, never old, never dead,
>   From itself never turning.

From Donne's impatient declamation: "For God's sake hold your tongue and let me love," to Christina Rossetti's pure singing voice:

> My heart is like a singing bird
>   Whose nest is in a water'd shoot;
> My heart is like an apple-tree
>   Whose boughs are bent with thickset fruit;

My heart is like a rainbow shell
　　That paddles in a halcyon sea;
My heart is gladder than all these,
　　Because my love is come to me.

The differences in tone in which the poets speak of love are perhaps wider than on any other topic. We would hardly guess that the same subject is being talked about when Chaucer's Wife of Bath looks back on her adventures in matrimony and when Tennyson mourns lost love. The Wife of Bath has no regrets:

But, Lord Christ, whan that it remembreth me
Upon my youthe, and on my jolitee,
It tickleth me aboute myn herte rote.[1]　　　　[1] *root*
Unto this day it doth myn herte bote[2]　　　　　[2]*good*
That I have had my world as in my tyme.

This is very different from the romantic anguish.

　　　　　Dear as remembr'd kisses after death,
And sweet as those by hopeless fancy feign'd
On lips that are for others; deep as love,
Deep as first love, and wild with all regret;
O Death in Life, the days that are no more.

Love may be seen as an aspect of nature which is as eternal as the renewal of the seasons. Hardy in the little lyric written on the outbreak of the first World War, "In Time of the Breaking of Nations," sees "a man harrowing clods" with a sleepy old horse, "thin smoke without flame" from the heap of weeds, and finally:

Yonder a maid and her wight
　　Come whispering by:
War's annals will cloud into night
　　Ere their story die.

Or love may be the light froth on the life of a court wit:

Out upon it, I have lov'd
Three whole days together;
And am like to love three more,
If it prove fair weather. . . .

Or this same poet, Sir John Suckling, may put himself in the position of a commonsense third person addressing some young Restoration gallant going through the same emotions as Shelley in "The Indian Serenade" (p. 94).

> Why so pale and wan, fond lover?
>   Prithee, why so pale?
> Will, when looking well can't move her,
>   Looking ill prevail?
>   Prithee, why so pale?
>
> Why so dull and mute, young sinner?
>   Prithee, why so mute?
> Will, when speaking well can't win her,
>   Saying nothing do't?
>   Prithee, why so mute?
>
> Quit, quit for shame! This will not move;
>   This cannot take her.
> If of herself she will not love,
>   Nothing can make her:
>   The devil take her!

The bantering mockery turns the lover's position from tragedy to comedy; and to be lovelorn, pale and mute becomes absurd instead of romantic. Suckling too, with dramatic skill, changes the sound pattern to suit a shift in attitude. The first two verses are half sympathetic and follow the same intonation, but he loses patience in the third and changes the beat of the lines to a movement of abrupt and robust dismissal.

In fact the different kinds of love are legion and so are the attitudes and formal designs in which poets express them. The sixteenth and seventeenth centuries are the great ages of the love lyric, including the many hundreds of sonnets to Stella or Delia or Phyllis or Diana and so on. The sonnet was a fashion—really a craze—for a while, and most of them now seem unbearably artificial and insipid. Hair like gold wires, lips of coral, cheeks of red and white roses, "globy fronts" (which means foreheads) like marble, and snowy breasts repeat themselves over and over, and the lovers all "fry" in the flames of their passion as they vainly court these aloof ladies. Against all this inane frippery, Shakespeare's realistic comment gains force:

> My mistress' eyes are nothing like the sun;
> Coral is far more red than her lips' red:
> If snow be white, why then her breasts are dun;
> If hairs be wires, black wires grow on her head. . . .

Extravagance was in vogue, and indeed some lovely poems were made out of it. Many of them are anonymous, and come down to us in the song-books of the time. This is from *John Dowland's First Book of Songs and Airs,* 1597:

> Dear, if you change, I'll never choose again;
> Sweet, if you shrink, I'll never think of love;
> Fair, if you fail, I'll judge all beauty vain;
> Wise, if too weak, more wits I'll never prove.
>> Dear, sweet, fair, wise, change, shrink, nor be
>>   not weak;
>> And, on my faith, my faith shall never break.

> Earth with her flowers shall sooner heaven adorn;
> Heaven her bright stars, through earth's dim globe
>   shall move.
> Fire, heat shall lose; and frosts of flames be born;
> Air made to shine, as black as hell shall prove:
>> Earth, heaven, fire, air, the world transformed
>>   shall view,
>> Ere I prove false to faith, or strange to you.

Or this, called "A Girdle," by Edmund Waller.

> That which her slender waist confined,
> Shall now my joyful temples bind;
> No monarch but would give his crown
> His arms might do what this has done.

> It is my Heaven's extremest sphere,
> The pale which held the lovely dear,
> My joy, my grief, my hope, my love,
> Do all within this circle move.

A narrow compass, and yet there
Dwells all that's good, and all that's fair:
Give me but what this ribbon tied,
Take all the sun goes round beside.

Spontaneous love poetry seems to flow from the minor
Elizabethans more easily and melodiously than from the
poets of any other period. They make their absurdities
sound natural, and take us into a world of verbal enchant-
ment in their fantasy and freshness. This is "A Nosegay,"
by John Reynolds.

Say, crimson rose and dainty daffodil,
    With violet blue;
Since you have seen the beauty of my saint,
    And eke her view;
Did not her sight (fair sight!) you lonely fill,
    With sweet delight
Of goddess', grace and angels' sacred teint,
    In fine, most bright?

Say, golden primrose, sanguine cowslip fair,
    With pink most fine;
Since you beheld the visage of my dear,
    And eyes divine;
Did not her globy front, and glistering hair,
    With cheeks most sweet,
So gloriously like damask flowers appear,
    The gods to greet?

Say, snow-white lily, speckled gilliflower,
    With daisy gay;
Since you have viewed the queen of my desire,
    In her array;
Did not her ivory paps, fair Venus' bower,
    With heavenly glee,
A Juno's grace, conjure you to require
    Her face to see?

Say rose, say daffodil, and violet blue,
    With primrose fair,
Since ye have seen my nymph's sweet dainty face
    And gesture rare,

Did not (bright cowslip, blooming pink) her view
   (White lily) shine—
(Ah, gilliflower, ah, daisy!) with a grace
   Like stars divine?

Or this evocation of voluptuous delight, both in its images and its undulating melody, which has all the sensual effect that "A Nosegay" innocently lacks. It is by Bartholomew Griffin.

Fair is my love that feeds among the lilies,
 The lilies growing in that pleasant garden,
Where Cupid's mount, that well-belovèd hill is,
 And where the little god himself is warden.
See where my love sits in the bed of spices,
 Beset all round with camphor, myrrh and roses,
And interlaced with curious devices,
 Which her from all the world about incloses.

Or as a change in tone, this wry commentary by Barnaby Googe, which depends for its momentum on the semi-comic repetitions and logical sequences.

The oftener seen, the more I lust,
 The more I lust, the more I smart,
The more I smart, the more I trust,
 The more I trust, the heavier heart,
The heavy heart breeds mine unrest,
Thy absence therefore like I best.

The rarer seen, the less in mind,
 The less in mind, the lesser pain,
The lesser pain, less grief I find,
 The lesser grief, the greater gain,
The greater gain, the merrier I,
Therefore I wish thy sight to fly.

The further off, the more I joy,
 The more I joy, the happier life,
The happier life, less hurts annoy,
 The lesser hurts, pleasure most rife,
Such pleasures rife shall I obtain
When distance doth depart us twain.

The popular ballads were, as one would expect, rather more earthy than the literary songs and sonnets. They often keep to the pastoral tradition, but set it in the English countryside and lace it with common sense and sensibility. This is called "The Happy Husbandman."

My young Mary does mind the dairy,
While I go hoeing and mowing each morn;
Then hey the little spinning wheel
Merrily round does reel,
   While I am singing amidst the corn:
Cream and kisses both are my delight,
She gives me them, and the joys of night;
She's soft as the air, as morning fair,
Is not such a maid a most pleasing sight?

While I whistle, she from the thistle
Does gather down for to make us a bed,
And then my little love does lie
All the night long, and die
   In the kind arms of her own dear Ned;
There I taste of a delicate spring,
But I must not tell you, nor name the thing,
To put you a-wishing, and think of kissing,
For kisses cause sighs, and young men should sing.

* * * *

No youth here need willow wear,
No beauteous maid will her lover destroy:
The gentle little lass will yield
In the soft daisy field,
   Freely our pleasures we here enjoy:
No great Juno we boldly defy,
With young Cloris' cheeks or fair Celia's eye;
We let those things alone, and enjoy our own,
Every night with our beauties lie.

But the ballads can be realistic and unexpected too. In one, the milkmaid declares her unkindness to her shepherd was only to prove his love. Then the poem concludes:

I then did give her a kiss or two,
   Which she return'd with interest still;

I thought I had now no more to do,
　　But that with her I might have my will.
But she, being taught by her crafty Dad,
　　Began to be cautious and wary;
And told me, When I my will had had,
　　The Divell a bit I would marry.

So marry'd we were, and when it was o'er,
　　I told her plain, in the Parsonage Hall,
That if she had gi'en me my will before,
　　The Divell a bit I'de a marry'd at all.
She smil'd, and presently told me her mind:
　　She had vow'd she'd never do more so,
Because she was cozen'd (in being too kind)
　　By three of four men before so.

The seventeenth century brought more sophistication to their courtly lyrics, as we have seen in the poems of Suckling already quoted. He also wrote a cynical parody of Ben Jonson's "The Triumph of Love" (p. 27).

Hast thou seen the down in the air,
　　When wanton blasts have tost it?
Or the ships on the sea
　　When ruder waves have crost it?
Hast thou marked the crocodile's weeping,
　　Or the Fox's sleeping?
Or hast thou viewed the peacock in his pride,
　　Or the dove by his bride,
When he courts for his lechery?
Oh! so fickle, Oh! so vain, Oh! so false, so false is
　　she!

He ignores, too, all the conventional aspects of beauty or fantasy with which the Elizabethans loaded their lady-loves.

Of thee (kind boy) I ask no red and white
　　To make up my delight,
　　No odd becoming graces,
Black eyes, or little know-not-whats, in faces;
Make me but mad enough, give me good store

Of love, for her I court,
                    I ask no more,
'Tis love in love that makes the sport.
                *   *   *   *
'Tis not the meat, but 'tis the appetite
        Makes eating a delight,
            And if I like one dish
More than another, that a pheasant is;
What in our watches, that in us is found,
        So to the height and nick
                    We up be wound,
No matter by what hand or trick.

In this last verse, in the image of the watch, comes a hint of the "metaphysical" method that we now almost identify with the seventeenth century. It was no wonder Donne rebelled from the usual kind of love poetry in his own day. It can be very cloying to the palate, and his own inventive, intellectual and intensely personal self needed some quite different language and movement to express its identity. Instead of the smooth, melodious surface texture of the contemporary lyrists he brings a new colloquial intimacy and a sudden challenging address: "Go and catch a falling star, / Get with child a mandrake root . . ." or "I wonder, by my troth, what thou and I / Did, till we loved," or "So, so, break off this last lamenting kiss." Coleridge calls Donne

Rhyme's sturdy cripple, fancy's maze and clue,
Wit's forge and fire-blast, meaning's press and screw,

but speaks also of his wonder-exciting vigor, and his peculiar intensity. Certainly no one ever "deeper digg'd love's mine" or brought stranger ore from it. Each of his best poems is a drama in little, played out in a variety of tones, but never simple or static. "The Sun Rising" is one of his happiest, in every sense of the word. Donne's effort to "wreathe iron pokers into true love's knots," is in abeyance. In some of his most famous poems, as in the much-quoted "The Ecstasy," so many notes are needed on his use of obsolete scientific ideas that the poetry shines only in parts. But "The Sun Rising," though full of novel quirks of thought and concentrated argument, is easy to follow. It has a sort of joyous playfulness, and moves with such sureness between that and the hyperboles of true passion. No doubt Donne is satirizing the exaggerations of the fashionable songsters and sonneteers, but in doing so he is declaring throughout that his love alone is worthy of extravagance, and doing it through a series of outrageous, witty paradoxes, alternating with the sense of his own happy wholeness.

> Busy old fool, unruly Sun,
>   Why dost thou thus,
> Through windows, and through curtains call on us?
> Must to thy motions lovers' seasons run?
>   Saucy pedantic wretch, go chide
>   Late schoolboys, and sour prentices,
>   Go tell court-huntsmen, that the King will ride,
>   Call country ants to harvest offices;
> Love, all alike, no season knows, nor clime,
> Nor hours, days, months, which are the rags of time.
>
>   Thy beams, so reverend, and strong
>   Why shouldst thou think?
> I could eclipse and cloud them with a wink,
> But that I would not lose her sight so long:
>   If her eyes have not blinded thine,
>   Look, and tomorrow late, tell me,
>   Whether both the Indias of spice and mine
>   Be where thou left'st them, or lie here with me.
> Ask for those kings whom thou saw'st yesterday,
> And thou shalt hear, all here in one bed lay.
>
>   She is all states, and all princes, I,
>   Nothing else is.
> Princes do but play us, compared to this,
> All honor's mimic; all wealth alchemy.
>   Thou sun art half as happy as we,
>   In that the world's constructed thus;
>   Thine age asks ease, and since thy duties be

To warm the world, that's done in warming us.
Shine here to us, and thou art everywhere;
This bed thy centre is; these walls, thy sphere.

He starts with an irreverent yet good-humored salute to the center of the universe, "Busy old fool, unruly Sun." The sun regulates time, but love has nothing to do with time, and the sun is proving itself merely meddlesome in disturbing the lovers. To come and remind *them* of the ordinary workaday coming of morning is to be a "saucy, pedantic wretch" interfering officiously like a schoolmaster. No doubt the ordering of education, business, the royal household and seasonal farming chores have *some* importance and must reckon with time, but the sun should know that love's seasons transcend his.

The second verse continues the tone of semi-patronizing geniality to the sun, and the poet draws his attention to the exquisite sight of his beloved. What are sunbeams to the light in her eyes? Let the sun go on his journey to the other side of the world, and come back tomorrow (late!) and own that anything of riches or beauty or dominion that he's seen are eclipsed: "all here in one bed lay."

Then, having scolded the sun, and harangued him, and shown him his limitations, the poet concludes by softening his tone into gentle solicitude for the sun, and by elaborating his hyperbole that the universe is contracted to himself and his beloved: "nothing else is." The sun, having to spend half his time traveling elsewhere, can be only half as happy as they. So the poet advises him to be "unruly," take the ease his age justifies, and stay with them, thus fulfilling his duty to "warm the world," since "that's done in warming us."

In spite of all the fun Donne has with his cosmic joke, that doesn't interfere with the communication of his real emotion of wholeness and triumph in his love. And it's done in perfectly simple language, charged with energy: "love, all alike, no season knows, nor clime"; "She is all states, and all princes, I"; "This bed thy centre is; these walls, thy sphere."

[*Poetry and the Human Condition*]   200

A very different kind of "metaphysical" love poem written some fifty years later than "The Sun Rising," perhaps also aimed at the easy, glib extravagances of the Elizabethans, is Andrew Marvell's "The Definition of Love." The Elizabethans seldom complicated their love poems with more than decorative similes and metaphors, but the metaphysicals loved to conceive and carry through complex parallels and analogies that added both concreteness and intensity to their subjects. Marvell's poem is built almost entirely out of personifications and metaphors, some of them scientific illustrations seemingly as far removed as possible from the subject of impassioned love. The mood is the opposite of that of Donne: despair instead of triumph; strict calm instead of jovial raillery and rapture.

> My love is of a birth as rare
> As 'tis for object strange and high:
> It was begotten by Despair
> Upon Impossibility.
>
> Magnanimous Despair alone
> Could show me so divine a thing,
> Where feeble Hope could ne'er have flown
> But vainly flapped its tinsel wing.
>
> And yet I quickly might arrive
> Where my extended soul is fixed,
> But Fate does iron wedges drive,
> And always crowds itself betwixt.
>
> For Fate with jealous eye does see
> Two perfect loves, nor lets them close:
> Their union would her ruin be,
> And her tyrannic power depose.
>
> And therefore her decrees of steel
> Us as the distant poles have placed,
> (Though love's whole world on us doth wheel)
> Not by themselves to be embraced,
>
> Unless the giddy heaven fall,
> And earth some new convulsion tear,

And, us to join, the world should all
Be cramped into a planisphere.

As lines, so loves oblique may well
Themselves in every angle greet;
But ours, so truly parallel,
Though infinite, can never meet.

Therefore the love which us doth bind,
But fate so enviously debars,
Is the conjunction of the mind,
And opposition of the stars.

The first two verses express the ironic situation. The poet's love springs from the union of despair and impossibility; but only through despair could he have learned how "strange and high" unsatisfied love—renunciation—can be; how much more rarefied a thing it is than hope could ever have achieved. Ironically, Despair becomes personified as a semi-divine "magnanimous" figure, while Hope, vainly flapping its tinsel wing, could never reach such heights.

The rest of the poem develops the situation. Fate, not unrequited love, is the poet's enemy. Fate is determined that she rules human life, and the strength of such a perfect union of lovers would depose her as arbiter. Therefore she drives iron wedges and decrees of steel between them, and the poet enforces these harsh analogies with a startling figure. Fate has placed the lovers "poles apart," but Marvell particularizes this conventional phrase. As the world rotates upon the physical poles, so the whole world of love wheels about the two lovers, but they themselves can never meet. Never, that is,

Unless the giddy heaven fall,
And earth some new convulsion tear,
And, us to join, the world should all
Be cramped into a planisphere.

The controlled violence of the image is very powerful. The miracle of their confounding Fate would have to be as great as if the round world were collapsed into a thin flat plate, so that the poles came together. He continues with another mathematical figure. The very straightness and trueness of the lines of their love makes meeting impossible. "Oblique" loves are like free lines which cross one another at an angle; but their loves are parallel lines that stretch to infinity.

His final image is from astrology. Stars in conjunction are close together and unite their influences; those in opposition are far apart and repel one another. But Marvell shifts the meaning in a play on the words. Their love is a conjunction of the mind, like stars in conjunction, and it binds them together in spirit. But they do not war between themselves, like stars in opposition. It's simply that "the stars are against them"; Fate alone is responsible for their distance.

This austerely tragic poem may serve as a transition to some others on the pains instead of the pleasures of love. The simplest theme is that of the forsaken maiden betrayed by her lover. It is popular in the old folk-songs, with their lamenting, lilting cadences.

> Balow, my babe, spare thou thy tears,
> Until thou come to wit and years;
> Thy griefs are gathering to a sum,
> Heaven grant thee patience till they come,
> A mother's fault, a father's shame,
> A hapless state, a bastard's name.
>
> Be still, my babe, and sleep awhile,
> And when thou wakes then sweetly smile!
> But smile not as thy father did
> To cusen maids: O heaven forbid
> And yet into thy face I see
> Thy father dear, which tempted me.

The sonneteers naturally have much to say about thwarted love, but perhaps it's only Sir Philip Sidney and Shakespeare who give it memorable expression. Sidney died of his wounds after the battle of Zutphen in 1586 when he was only thirty-two, but he was the most beloved and admired character of Elizabeth's court: soldier, statesman, scholar, courtier, dreamer, athlete, musician and poet. He was a model of courtesy, generosity and friendship; he loved passionately and died nobly.

How much of the story behind his sonnet sequence, "Astrophel and Stella," is founded on fact, and how much is a poetic convention, is uncertain. Stella was Penelope Devereux, daughter of the Earl of Essex, and it is said that her father favored a match between her and Sidney and that it was the poet who was cool to the idea. Later, when she was unhappily married to Lord Rich, he fell in love with her. As the poem tells us, she refused to be unfaithful to her husband, and Sidney realized that he had only himself to blame for his sufferings: "to myself, myself did give the blow." But he creates the "civil wars" that rage in his heart between desire and idealism with a genuinely personal voice.

> Thou blind man's mark, thou fool's self-chosen snare,
> Fond fancy's scum, and dregs of scattered thought;
> Band of all evils, cradle of causeless care;
> Thou web of will, whose end is never wrought;
> Desire, desire! I have too dearly bought,
> With price of mangled mind, thy worthless ware;
> Too long, too long, asleep thou hast me brought,
> Who should my mind to higher things prepare.
> But yet in vain thou hast my ruin sought;
> In vain thou madest me to vain things aspire;
> In vain thou kindlest all thy smoky fire;
> For virtue hath this better lesson taught,
> Within myself to seek my only hire,
> Desiring nought but how to kill desire.

In a series of metaphors, Sidney creates the nature of desire. The man who chooses it as his target (mark) is either blind to its reality or a deliberate fool. Desire is the scum that rises to the surface of foolish daydreams, and the dregs left if the reason is allowed to disperse itself in unorganized thinking. To the Elizabethans all evils arose from the wrong use of the passions and of the reason, and desire is all these evils banded together. It creates "causeless care," anxieties which should never have been called into being. It spins an endless web of broken resolutions, "mangled mind"; and the poem ends with a fresh resolve which may have the same fate.

We know even less about the story of the relationships behind Shakespeare's sonnets than we do of Sidney's. But allowing for the contemporary convention, anyone can recognize the emotional conditions out of which they were written, whether in times of satisfaction or of distress, for they create the moods of any lover.

> Then hate me when thou wilt; if ever, now;
> Now, while the world is bent my deeds to cross,
> Join with the spite of fortune, make me bow,
> And do not drop in for an after-loss:
> Ah, do not, when my heart hath 'scaped this sorrow,
> Come in the rearward of a conquer'd woe;
> Give not a windy night a rainy morrow,
> To linger out a purposed overthrow.
> If thou wilt leave me, do not leave me last,
> When other petty griefs have done their spite,
> But in the onset come: so shall I taste
> At first the very worst of fortune's might
> > And other strains of woe, which now seem woe,
> > Compared with loss of thee will not seem so.

Michael Drayton, in his one famous sonnet, "Since there's no help . . ." is the only Elizabethan who approaches Shakespeare in the sense of writing out of the center of a dramatic situation. His voice changes its tones as his feeling shifts from impatience to grave lyrical lament, and then, with a sudden pounce in the last couplet, reverses all that has gone before and leaves the solution open.

> Since there's no help, come let us kiss and part.
> Nay, I have done; you get no more of me,
> And I am glad, yea, glad with all my heart,
> That thus so cleanly I myself can free;
> Shake hands for ever, cancel all our vows,

And when we meet at any time again,
Be it not seen in either of our brows
That we one jot of former love retain.
Now at the last gasp of Love's latest breath,
When, his pulse failing, Passion speechless lies,
When Faith is kneeling by his bed of death,
And Innocence is closing up his eyes,
Now if thou wouldst, when all have given him over,
From death to life thou mightst him yet recover.

Written more than two centuries later, Browning's "The Lost Mistress" makes a good contrast to this. Not that the conclusion is the same, though the crisis at the opening is, and the tone of the man speaking. But what he says is different. The romantic age has intervened. The poet associates details of the natural background as an essential element in the scene. The language too has the easy colloquial flow, which Browning himself introduced.

All's over, then; does truth sound bitter
    As one at first believes?
Hark, 'tis the sparrows' good-night twitter
    About your cottage eaves!

And the leaf-buds on the vine are woolly,
    I noticed that, to-day;
One day more bursts them open fully
    —You know the red turns grey.

To-morrow we meet the same then, dearest?
    May I take your hand in mine?
Mere friends are we,—well, friends the merest
    Keep much that I'll resign:

For each glance of that eye so bright and black,
    Though I keep with heart's endeavour,—
Your voice, when you wish the snowdrops back,
    Though it stay in my soul for ever!—

Yet I will but say what mere friends say,
    Or only a thought stronger;
I will hold your hand but as long as all may,
    Or so very little longer!

[*Poetry and the Human Condition*]   206

Married unhappiness wasn't treated seriously in lyric poetry, I think, before George Meredith. Dryden has a light sophisticated song on it in his play *Marriage-à-la-Mode:*

> Why should a foolish marriage vow
>   Which long ago was made,
> Oblige us to each other now
>   When passion is decayed?
> We lov'd, and we lov'd, as long as we could,
>   Till our love was lov'd out in us both:
> But our marriage is dead, when the pleasure is fled:
>   'Twas pleasure first made it an oath.

But Meredith is involved in a drama of real life. He was married in 1849 to a daughter of the novelist Thomas Love Peacock. In 1858 she left him for another man and died three years later. In 1862 he published the sonnet sequence "Modern Love," describing the course of the estrangement in scenes by day and by night, and analyzing the emotional conflicts of dying passion and nervous stresses between a man and woman living together yet apart: the venomous silences, the vain regrets, the degrading "unblest kisses," the lying awake on their "marriage tomb," and the final acceptance of failure.

> I see no sin:
> The wrong is mixed. In tragic life, God wot,
> No villain need be! Passions spin the plot:
> We are betrayed by what is false within.

The sequence concludes:

> Thus piteously Love closed what he begat:
> The union of this ever-diverse pair!
> These two were rapid falcons in a snare,
> Condemned to do the flitting of the bat.
> Lovers beneath the singing sky of May,
> They wandered once; clear as the dew on flowers:
> But they fed not on the advancing hours:
> Their hearts held cravings for the buried day.
> Then each applied to each that fatal knife,

Deep questioning, which probes to endless dole.
Ah, what a dusty answer gets the soul
When hot for certainties in this our life!—
In tragic hints here see what evermore,
Moves dark as yonder midnight ocean's force,
Thundering like ramping hosts of warrior horse,
To throw that faint thin line upon the shore!

It is an uneven poem. "Clear as the dew on flowers" is
feeble, and surely it's not necessary that deep questioning,
if it be honest, should probe to endless dole. The last four
lines express rather confusedly the image of the original
ocean of passion thinning out like a spent wave. But the
subject was a new one in poetry and is finely explored in
some of the poems. Meredith doesn't perhaps deserve the
eclipse that has overtaken him as a poet.

These are all intimate personal experiences, describing
what Eliot speaks of as the "torment / Of love unsatisfied
/ The greater torment / Of love satisfied," and it is natu-
ral that most love poetry should be interpersonal, whether
it sings of joy or grief. Yet the nature of love itself, or its
various natures, physical, moral, spiritual, are the themes
of poetry too. Shakespeare's most savage sonnet is a
searching analysis of the slavery and self-disgust of com-
pulsive physical desire without affection, even with hatred.

The expense of spirit in a waste of shame
Is lust in action; and till action, lust
Is perjured, murderous, bloody, full of blame,
Savage, extreme, rude, cruel, not to trust;
Enjoyed no sooner but despisèd straight;
Past reason hunted; and no sooner had,
Past reason hated, as a swallowed bait,
On purpose laid to make the taker mad:
Mad in pursuit, and in possession so;
Had, having, and in quest to have, extreme;
A bliss in proof, and proved, a very woe;
Before, a joy proposed; behind, a dream.
All this the world well knows; yet none knows well
To shun the heaven that leads men to this hell.

[*Poetry and the Human Condition*] 208

At the opposite extreme we might put Edgar Allan Poe's "To Helen," where love becomes a spiritual mystery evoked by a series of associative images, and the "beauty" is hardly that of a physical woman at all. Perhaps he is comparing the traditional Helen, "the face that launched a thousand ships" into a ten-year war, with the vision of a woman whose beauty has given him peace and serenity of heart.

> Helen, thy beauty is to me
>   Like those Nicaean barks of yore,
> That gently, o'er a perfumed sea,
>   The weary, wayworn wanderer bore
>   To his own native shore.
>
> On desperate seas long wont to roam,
>   Thy hyacinth hair, thy classic face,
> Thy Naiad airs have brought me home
>   To the glory that was Greece
>   And the grandeur that was Rome.
>
> Lo! in yon brilliant window-niche
>   How statue-like I see thee stand,
> The agate lamp within thy hand!
>   Ah, Psyche, from the regions which
>   Are Holy Land!

Her beauty is a ship that has brought him "home" after long wandering, as if he were a Ulysses reaching his Penelope. The very music of the lines bears the theme along on soothing waves of sound. The seas of emotion that were "desperate" have become gentle and perfumed, fanned by "Naiad airs"; and he associates her with the sense of the calm nobility and dignity of the whole world of classical art.

But she remains remote and unreachable. The last verse seems to negate some of the assurance of the earlier ones. She becomes Psyche, the soul, standing, vividly lighted, but far off, aloof, and finally belonging to regions unattainable to mortals. "Holy Land" certainly has no suggestion of a biblical background, or even of an historical Greece, but rather of some ethereal ideal of the spirit only.

Mortal love can seldom live on such heights. At the end of "The Ecstasy," after the description of the mystical union of the lovers' souls, Donne writes:

To our bodies turn we then, that so
Weak men on love revealed may look;
Love's mysteries in souls do grow
But yet the body is his book.

This is the vision in one of Yeats's finest short poems, "Crazy Jane Talks with the Bishop." Yeats said Crazy Jane had an original in an old peasant woman he knew, but from the series of poems in which she plays a part it seems more likely that she is a mask through whom he could express certain aspects of his own nature which could not emerge in his highly sophisticated and personal poems of meditation. The Crazy Jane poems are anti-intellectual and anti-clerical, and combine universal, mystical wisdom with racy, sensual and primitive elements. After finishing this poem, however, Yeats wrote to his wife that he must really exorcise "that slut, Crazy Jane" whose language was becoming unendurable.

I met the Bishop on the road
And much said he and I.
'Those breasts are flat and fallen now,
Those veins must soon be dry;
Live in a heavenly mansion,
Not in some foul sty.'

'Fair and foul are near of kin,
And fair needs foul,' I cried.
'My friends are gone, but that's a truth
Nor grave nor bed denied,
Learned in bodily lowliness
And in the heart's pride.

'A woman can be proud and stiff
When on love intent;
But Love has pitched his mansion in
The place of excrement;
For nothing can be sole or whole
That has not been rent.'

[*Poetry and the Human Condition*]   210

Jane refuses the division of love and lust, a heavenly mansion and a foul sty. She argues that "fair needs foul," which is not denied by grave or bed; that is, death does not negate life, but completes it, and physical and spiritual love are equally indivisible. "Love has pitched his mansion in / The place of excrement," and the poet gets a double suggestion in the word *pitched*. Love has set up his heavenly mansion there, and has darkened and stained it with that apparent dishonor. But all unity depends on the presence of oppositions and their reconciliation: that's the *nature* of love and life; "nothing can be sole or whole / That has not been rent."

On the realistic and not the metaphysical level, the fair and foul of human marriage is inextricably mixed, however many lucky individual exceptions we may have in mind. "Sunday: Outskirts of Knoxville, Tenn." is a moving but little known poem by James Agee, who died in 1955. His creative gifts have been recognized posthumously by the award of the Pulitzer prize to his novel *A Death in the Family.* The poem projects a direct visual scene of young love, followed by an inventory of the inevitable future that slides by with kaleidoscopic changes. But it is a vision seen through the eyes of pity and tenderness, written by a poet who supports his outer and inner landscapes with an interweaving of skillful verbal patterns.

> There, in the earliest and chary spring, the dogwood
>   flowers.
>
> Unharnessed in the friendly sunday air
> By the red brambles, on the river bluffs,
> Clerks and their choices pair.
>
> Thrive by, not near, masked all away by shrub and
>   juniper
> The ford v eight, racing the chevrolet.
>
> They cannot trouble her:
>
> Her breasts, helped open from the afforded lace,
> Lie like a peaceful lake;
> And on his mouth she breaks her gentleness:

Oh, wave them awake!

They are not of the birds. Such innocence
Brings us to break us only.
Theirs are not happy words.

We that are human cannot hope.
Our tenderest joys oblige us most.
No chain so cuts the bone; and sweetest silk most
    shrewdly strangles.

How this must end, that now please love were ended,
In kitchens, bedfights, silences, women's pages,
Sickness of heart before goldlettered doors,
Stale flesh, hard collars, agony in antiseptic corridors,
Spankings, remonstrances, fishing trips, orange juice,
Policies, incapacities, a chevrolet,
Scorn of their children, kind contempt exchanged,
Recalls, tears, second honeymoons, pity,
Shouted corrections of missed syllables,
Hot water bags, gallstones, falls downstairs,
Oldfashioned christmases, suspicions of theft,
Arrangements with morticians taken care of by sons
    in law.
Small rooms beneath the gables of brick bungalow,
The tumbler smashed, the glance between daughter
    and husband,
The empty body in the lonely bed
And, in the empty concrete porch, blown ash
Grandchildren wandering the betraying sun

Now, on the winsome crumbling shelves of the horror
God show, God blind these children!

It opens with suggestions of hope and spring gladness;
the flowers, the pairs of lovers, the spinning cars; then
centers on the young couple making love in a dream of
bliss. "Oh, wave them awake!" cries the poet, and darkens
the scene with a reminder of the human condition and
how many of the hopes of these young hearts will be
broken and strangled. The future flashes past, unwinding
itself with cinematic vividness and speed to the end. In the

plea of the last two lines the poem is summarized. The moment of love in the opening passage is recalled by the word "winsome," and merged with the sordidness to follow by the "crumbling shelves of horror," an image reflecting the swift descent from glimpse to glimpse in which the inventory scenes have passed. The last line is the concentration of pity in a prayer torn by the twofold vision. A prayer that these "children" may not face the future totally unaware, and a prayer that the beauty of the "winsome" moment may still live in all that is to come.

The sound pattern varies according to the mood. Throughout the opening many soft internal and end rhymes give a lyrical lightness. This mood is broken by the sharp "Oh, wave them awake!" and the short meditative passage uses assonance (the matching of vowel sounds) and alliteration instead of rhyme, giving it a graver movement. This again contrasts with the tumbling variety of the catalogue of actualities, where the sound is a monotone broken by irregular rhymes shelving brokenly into the final abyss, "The empty body in the lonely bed / And, in the empty concrete porch, blown ash." The next line "Grandchildren wandering the betraying sun" reminds us that the pattern is eternal. In the face of that, the last line, in its quiet simple tenderness seems a prayer for all mankind at all times.

A final contrast to the sexual, the ideal, the mystical vision, the realistic acceptance, is Shakespeare's triumphant assertion in his best known sonnet, "Let me not to the marriage of true minds / Admit impediments." Shakespeare too knows that

> Our tenderest joys oblige us most
> No chain so cuts the bone; and sweetest silk most
>   shrewdly strangles.

He knows that love does alter and can be removed; that tempests can shake it; that it wanders off course; that its value can't be proved, however steady; that the bending sickle and the brief hours and weeks are actualities; that the end of all is doom. But he will not "admit" these impediments, and sweeps forward on the soaring strength of the ideal of constancy, the ever-fixèd mark, the pole-star, the unalterable steadfastness, staking his poetry and the whole experience of the human race on his proud faith.

Let me not to the marriage of true minds
Admit impediments. Love is not love
Which alters when it alteration finds,
Or bends with the remover to remove:
Or, no! it is an ever-fixèd mark
That looks on tempests and is never shaken;
It is the star to every wandering bark,
Whose worth's unknown, although his height be
    taken.
Love's not Time's fool, though rosy lips and cheeks
Within his bending sickle's compass come;
Love alters not with his brief hours and weeks,
But bears it out even to the edge of doom.
If this be error and upon me proved,
I never writ, nor no man ever loved.

13. Humanism

"Our only portion is the estate of man."

A. E. Housman

The torment of human frustration, whatever its immediate cause, is the knowledge that the self is imprisoned, its vital forces and "mangled mind" leaking away in lonely wasteful self-conflict. "We think of the key, each in his prison / Thinking of the key," as Eliot says. The poet who can create in memorable form the truth of such suffering has temporarily transcended his situation, for the very act of composition is a form of release. But as a human being he may remain in the bonds of his discord, finding liberation only in his art, unless he can accept man's inevitable fragmentariness and imperfections, and direct his energies toward some fulfillment outside his own disappointments. It may be true, as Thoreau said, that most men (including women) lead lives of quiet desperation. It has been recognized only in recent years how much of physical as well as mental sickness arises from sheer unhappiness. The thought of "mighty poets in their misery dead" haunted Wordsworth on the morning he met the leech-gatherer (p. 61), and the histories of Burns and Chatterton (of whom Wordsworth was thinking) and in our own day of Hart Crane and Dylan Thomas, are illustrations of those who ended in despair. Yet as Frost says in "Our Hold on the Planet," though we may doubt the just proportion of good and ill,

> it must be a little more in favor of man,
> Say a fraction of one per cent at the very least,
> Or our number living wouldn't be steadily more,
> Our hold on the planet wouldn't have so increased.

So with the poets: affirmation outweighs rejection. Empson said of his poem "Missing Dates" (p. 139) that the mood is not something that can be felt all the time; and so with the other wearisome conditions of humanity. The sick regret over lost opportunities may fall away in the joy of positive achievement; the sense of sterility may melt into a rush of renewed relish for life; loneliness may fade into unlooked-for companionship; the contemplation of nature may bring comfort and strength; the torments of love dissolve into its ecstasies or its steadfastness.

The source of all such escapes is freedom from negative introspection; from "those things that with myself I too much discuss / Too much explain," as Eliot again says; and the assertion of some faith that enables man to face the mingled fair and foul in his fate with some activity or serenity. Such a faith may be religious or humanistic. Religious faith presumes a supernatural world of values beyond the natural universe: humanism is rooted in the values man can discover in the world as he can know it. The word Humanism, however, has also an historical meaning. It is associated with the "new learning" that blossomed over Europe in the fifteenth century and had its root in the discovery and dissemination of the original texts of the great Greek writers. The study of all this new experience was called Humanism because it presented the classical writers for the first time as direct commentators on the living of life and not as they had been interpreted by Christian theologians; because too it increased man's sense of his human potentialities and all that enriches them in the apprehension of the worlds of the past. But the early Humanists, such as Erasmus or Sir Thomas More, were in no sense pagan. They were good churchmen who saw their new studies as an extension and not a contradiction of Christian doctrine. Many "Christian Humanists" in the present day are in the same position. But the term "humanist" is now generally used, and is so used here, to indicate those who have rejected any dogmatic theology as an answer to the mysteries and sufferings of human existence, and have reached such resolutions as they possess by a secular and not a religious approach.

The mysteries and sufferings remain and must be accepted. The humanist faith rests not on any explanations, but on experiences of value in the human tradition, and in individual relationships between man and nature, man and man, or man and woman, that seem answer enough to the goodness of life and to the creative energies of man's spirit.

One tenet of faith, of any humanist is in the words of the modern American poet Wallace Stevens: "The greatest poverty is not to live / In a physical world." It is the theme of his most beautiful and melodious poem "Sunday Morning." Rejecting Christian doctrine, it celebrates the actualities of human life and of the physical universe as fulfilling man's needs without any compensating hope of immortality. The structure creates the fluctuations of the consciousness as it alternates between thoughts of earth and heaven, between the secular and the religious attitudes.

> Complacencies of the peignoir, and late
> Coffee and oranges in a sunny chair,
> And the green freedom of a cockatoo
> Upon a rug mingle to dissipate
> The holy hush of ancient sacrifice.
> She dreams a little, and she feels the dark
> Encroachment of that old catastrophe,
> As a calm darkens among water-lights.
> The pungent oranges and bright, green wings
> Seem things in some procession of the dead,
> Winding across wide water, without sound.
> The day is like wide water, without sound,
> Stilled for the passing of her dreaming feet
> Over the seas, to silent Palestine,
> Dominion of the blood and sepulchre.

> Why should she give her bounty to the dead?
> What is divinity if it can come
> Only in silent shadows and in dreams?
> Shall she not find in comforts of the sun,
> In pungent fruit and bright, green wings, or else

In any balm or beauty of the earth,
Things to be cherished like the thought of heaven?
Divinity must live within herself:
Passions of rain, or moods in falling snow;
Grievings in loneliness, or unsubdued
Elations when the forest blooms; gusty
Emotions on wet roads on autumn nights;
All pleasures and all pains, remembering
The bough of summer and the winter branch.
These are the measure destined for her soul.

The first three lines build up the gay and relaxed atmosphere of the secular Sunday morning. "Complacencies of the peignoir" suggest the placid contentment and informality of the woman's mood over her late breakfast, and the sun, the oranges and the "green freedom" of the exotic cockatoo add color and lightness to the scene. But another mood, which these things had dispersed, a "dark encroachment," blots them out. The "holy hush" of her mind becomes the dark calm of water, across which the gay things of the senses wind silently as in some procession of the dead. The day becomes "like wide water, without sound"; the physical universe has been emptied of sun and life. Over this sea her dreaming feet pass to Palestine. Finally, the last line reverses everything called up at the opening of the poem: "dominion" instead of "freedom," "blood" instead of coffee and oranges, "sepulchre" instead of sun and color.

In the second verse, the poet challenges this vision of "divinity," centered in "silent shadows" and dreams, on the grounds of its limitations. Against the "thought" of heaven, he puts "things" which should be cherished; the comforts and beauties of the earth. But the divinity he feels to be latent in the human soul seems to dwell in wholeness and intensity of experience. To him, all the mysteries of our own sensuous and emotional apprehension are the only "measures" we have of the divine.

The woman can't accept this view that man is only a part of nature, and that just as summer implies winter in the cyclical pattern, so life implies death, without any fu-

ture paradise. The poet answers her to declare that none
of man's dreams of an after-life can compare with the
sense of rebirth experienced in the yearly return of spring.

> She says, "I am content when wakened birds,
> Before they fly, test the reality
> Of misty fields, by their sweet questionings;
> But when the birds are gone, and their warm fields
> Return no more, where, then, is paradise?"
> There is not any haunt of prophecy,
> Nor any old chimera of the grave,
> Neither the golden underground, nor isle
> Melodious, where spirits gat them home,
> Nor visionary south, nor cloudy palm
> Remote on heaven's hill, that has endured
> As April's green endures; or will endure
> Like her remembrance of awakened birds
> Or her desire for June and evening, tipped
> By the consummation of the swallow's wings.

"Death is the mother of beauty," he argues. Any idea of
the changeless beauty of the Christian paradise is unbear-
ably insipid. So the poet creates the idea of a secular re-
ligion whose central ritual is a chant to the sun as the
source of life.

> Supple and turbulent, a ring of men
> Shall chant in orgy on a summer morn
> Their boisterous devotion to the sun,
> Not as a god, but as a god might be,
> Naked among them, like a savage source.
> Their chant shall be a chant of paradise,
> Out of their blood, returning to the sky;
> And in their chant shall enter, voice by voice,
> The windy lake wherein their lord delights,
> The trees, like serafim, and echoing hills,
> That choir among themselves long afterward.
> They shall know well the heavenly fellowship
> Of men that perish and of summer morn.
> And whence they came and whither they shall go
> The dew upon their feet shall manifest.

[*Humanism*]   219

This is *like* a pagan chant, worshiping a mythic Sun-God, but the hymn is really in celebration of the fellowship of man and nature. Skillfully, Stevens weaves Biblical echoes into the lines, preserving the atmosphere of a hallowed ceremony, though it glorifies humanity.

The final verse loses this tone of exultation.

> She hears, upon that water without sound,
> A voice that cries, "The tomb in Palestine
> Is not the porch of spirits lingering.
> It is the grave of Jesus, where He lay."
> We live in an old chaos of the sun,
> Or old dependency of day and night,
> Or island solitude, unsponsored, free,
> Of that wide water, inescapable.
> Deer walk upon our mountains, and the quail
> Whistle about us their spontaneous cries;
> Sweet berries ripen in the wilderness;
> And, in the isolation of the sky,
> At evening, casual flocks of pigeons make
> Ambiguous undulations as they sink,
> Downward to darkness, on extended wings.

Stevens makes the woman hear a voice telling her that there *is* no divine revelation, only natural law. He then creates, in various sense images, the summing up of the union of nature and man. But in spite of the "heavenly fellowship" hymned in the verse before, the tone here loses its jubilance. What does "inescapable" in the eighth line refer to: the island solitude or the wide water? Either of them carries the idea of the individual human spirit inescapably isolated and questioning, even if it has rejected supernatural solutions. And the final lovely picture of the pigeons is touched with sadness. "Ambiguous undulations" are the key words: the human spirit extending its wings, but sinking inevitably "downward to darkness."

In spite of its rare melodic beauty, its wealth of sensuous suggestion, the poem is somehow unsatisfying as a conception of the human condition without religious hope, and this is perhaps because of its disregard of the mind and the spirit. It exists in the senses and the emotions only. Stevens doesn't deny the necessary pain along with the joys:

> Passions of rain, or moods in falling snow;
> Grievings in loneliness, or unsubdued
> Elations when the forest blooms; gusty
> Emotions on wet roads on autumn nights.

But these are lightly dismissed without any further examination. Stevens doesn't do what the Elizabethan Samuel Daniel tells us must be done, even with the joys.

> Glory is most bright and gay
> In a flash, and so away.
> Feed apace then, greedy eyes,
> On the wonder you behold.
> Take it sudden as it flies
> Though you take it not to hold:
> When your eyes have done their part,
> Thought must length it in the heart.

The worlds of the senses and the emotions are very satisfying in poetry, as in life. But it's an essential part of the human condition that we can't rest content in them; "thought" must "length it in the heart." Stevens's resolution is too easy; it leaves out too much of the human heritage.

In contrast let us put Matthew Arnold's "Dover Beach," another poem on the theme of the impossibility (for the poet) of holding any religious faith, yet utterly different in argument, in tone and mood and rhythmic movement.

> The sea is calm to-night.
> The tide is full, the moon lies fair
> Upon the straits;—on the French coast the light
> Gleams and is gone; the cliffs of England stand,
> Glimmering and vast, out in the tranquil bay.
> Come to the window, sweet is the night-air!
> Only, from the long line of spray
> Where the sea meets the moon-blanched land,
> Listen! you hear the grating roar
> Of pebbles which the waves draw back, and fling,

At their return, up the high strand,
Begin, and cease, and then again begin,
With tremulous cadence slow, and bring
The eternal note of sadness in.

Sophocles long ago
Heard it on the Aegaean, and it brought
Into his mind the turbid ebb and flow
Of human misery; we
Find also in the sound a thought,
Hearing it by this distant northern sea.

The Sea of Faith
Was once, too, at the full, and round earth's shore
Lay like the folds of a bright girdle furled.
But now I only hear
Its melancholy, long, withdrawing roar,
Retreating, to the breath
Of the night-wind, down the vast edges drear
And naked shingles of the world.

Ah, love, let us be true
To one another! for the world, which seems
To lie before us like a land of dreams,
So various, so beautiful, so new,
Hath really neither joy, nor love, nor light,
Nor certitude, nor peace, nor help for pain;
And we are here as on a darkling plain
Swept with confused alarms of struggle and flight,
Where ignorant armies clash by night.

Like "Sunday Morning," it opens with a scene bathed in light and ends "darkling"; but the application of the imagery is different. Instead of a reminder of the natural cyclical pattern of "the old dependency of day and night," the opposition in "Dover Beach" matches the underlying contrasts between men's hopes and dreams, "so various, so beautiful, so new," full of joy, love, certitude and peace, like the opening lines of the poem, and the reality of "the eternal note of sadness," the pain, the struggle, the clash of the ignorant armies, at the conclusion. As in "Sunday Morning," the poem grows out of a setting, but instead of the creation of a further series of imaginary scenes to carry the theme, here it's the sights and sounds in the opening picture that develops the lines of the dramatic monologue. These finally melt into symbols, and the actual scene becomes a metaphorical one of the human plight in a world without faith, redeemed only by human love and loyalty.

It opens with the emphasis on the calm and the moonlit land and sea. In seven short statements Arnold creates the visual picture and its emotional counterpart. He calls his companion to come and share the sweetness of air and scene. But at once the "grating roar" of the surf and the sound of the recurrent suck of the receding waves shatters the calm, and sends the poet's mind first to Sophocles, comparing the fortunes of Oedipus to the ebb and flow of the sea, and then to the retreating tide as an emblem of the loss of faith.

Like the moonlit radiance of the sea, Faith once "lay like the folds of a bright girdle furled" about the earth. Then, in lines echoing in sound his own despair, he creates the sense of emptiness and deprivation of the world without this hope.

In the last stanza he changes the metaphor. After the tormented cry to his love for truth and constancy as the only firm foundation for life, he interprets the calm and loveliness of the actual scene before them as an illusion, of which the reality is the "naked shingles" merging into the "darkling plain," while the "melancholy, long, withdrawing roar" turns to the "confused alarms of struggle and flight."

The sound pattern follows the sense, and the tranquil movement of the opening fades first into "the eternal note of sadness," and then into the harsh collision of consonants in the last two lines, to support the battle image.

It cannot be proved that Arthur Hugh Clough's "Say not the struggle naught availeth . . ." was written in reply to "Dover Beach," but it certainly sounds as if it were. The first two verses seem an answer to the battle metaphor at the end of Arnold's poem, while the third picks up the sea

[*Humanism*]   223

imagery and in the fourth Arnold's moonlight becomes daylight and the sun. Clough's vision, too, refuses to concentrate on "eastern windows only," the light of the classical past and the European tradition (east of Dover), and some critics interpret his look "westward" as a hope of the future cultural growth of America.

> Say not the struggle naught availeth
>   The labor and the wounds are vain,
> The enemy faints not, nor faileth,
>   And as things have been they remain.
>
> If hopes were dupes, fears may be liars;
>   It may be in yon smoke concealed,
> Your comrades chase e'en now the fliers,
>   And, but for you, possess the field.
>
> For while the tired waves, vainly breaking,
>   Seem here no painful inch to gain,
> Far back, through creeks and inlets making,
>   Comes silent, flooding in, the main.
>
> And not by eastern windows only,
>   When daylight comes, comes in the light,
> In front, the sun climbs slow, how slowly,
>   But westward, look, the land is bright.

Whether or no this is a conscious challenge to Arnold's passive despair, it voices the faith in positive action and the power of the human spirit to hold on that Arnold lacks, tender and heart-breaking though his poem is. This insistence on affirmation must always be the central faith of the humanist. It may appear in the ringing words of the Elizabethan George Chapman:

> Give me a spirit that on this life's rough sea,
> Love's t'have his sails filled with a lusty wind,
> Even till his sail-yards tremble; his masts crack,
> And his rapt ship run on her side so low
> That she drinks water, and her keel ploughs air;
> There is no danger to a man, that knows
> What life and death is: there's not any law,

Exceeds his knowledge; neither is it lawful
That he should stoop to any other law.

or at the end of Shelley's "Prometheus Unbound":

To suffer woes which Hope thinks infinite;
To forgive wrongs darker than death or night;
    To defy Power, which seems omnipotent;
To love and bear; to hope till Hope creates
From its own wreck the thing it contemplates;
    Neither to change, nor falter, nor repent;
This, like thy glory, Titan, is to be
Good, great and joyous, beautiful and free;
This is alone Life, Joy, Empire and Victory.

Tennyson creates it in the conclusion of "Ulysses," written
soon after the death of his great friend, Arthur Hallam.
He said of the poem: "It gives the feeling about the need
of going forward and bearing the struggle of life more
simply than anything in 'In Memoriam.' "

The lights begin to twinkle from the rocks:
The long day wanes: the slow moon climbs: the deep
Moans round with many voices. Come, my friends,
'Tis not too late to seek a newer world.
Push off, and sitting well in order smite
The sounding furrows; for my purpose holds
To sail beyond the sunset, and the baths
Of all the western stars, until I die.
It may be that the gulfs will wash us down:
It may be we shall touch the Happy Isles,
And see the great Achilles, whom we knew.
Tho' much is taken, much abides; and tho'
We are not now that strength which in old days
Moved earth and heaven; that which we are, we are;
One equal temper of heroic hearts,
Made weak by time and fate, but strong in will
To strive, to seek, to find, and not to yield.

Housman speaks in a different tone, that of wry, stoic
fortitude, in "The chestnut casts its flambeaux. . . ."

We for a certainty are not the first
    Have sat in taverns while the tempest hurled
Their hopeful plans to emptiness, and cursed
    Whatever brute or blackguard made the world.

*   *   *   *

Iniquity it is; but pass the can.
    My lad, no pair of kings our mothers bore;
Our only portion is the estate of man:
    We want the moon, but we shall get no more.

*   *   *   *

The troubles of our proud and angry dust
    Are from eternity, and shall not fail
Bear them we can, and if we can we must.
    Shoulder the sky, my lad, and drink your ale.

Yeats, in the last verse of "Two Songs from a Play," shows the creative and destructive oppositions at endless war, yet the strife is itself creative.

Everything that man esteems
Endures a moment or a day.
Love's pleasure drives his love away,
The painter's brush consumes his dreams;
The herald's cry, the soldier's tread
Exhaust his glory and his might:
Whatever flames upon the night
Man's own resinous heart has fed.

Like the act of love, every consummation is in a sense a death; something is consumed as well as consummated. The flames are the creative fires of the imagination and of the life-force, but also inevitably the fires that will finally burn out man's transient being.

Since to the humanist this life is all, he wants to live it as richly and fully as possible, to "animate / The trivial days and ram them with the sun," as Yeats says in another poem. The humanist welcomes every reminder of the wonders of the sense world and the mystery of his own response to them. Louis MacNeice's "Snow" is an original and engaging poem on that topic.

[*Poetry and the Human Condition*]   226

The room was suddenly rich and the great bay-
    window was
Spawning snow and pink roses against it
Soundlessly collateral and incompatible:
World is suddener than we fancy it.

World is crazier and more of it than we think,
Incorrigibly plural. I peel and portion
A tangerine and spit the pips and feel
The drunkenness of things being various.

And the fire flames with a bubbling sound for world
Is more spiteful and gay than one supposes—
On the tongue on the eyes on the ears in the palms of
    your hands—:
There is more than glass between the snow and the
    huge roses.

The poet has a sudden revelation of the wealth and va-
riety of the immediate world presented to his senses, and
of its "spawning" character, so that no one outer or inner
happening ever exists by itself, but immediately prolifer-
ates in various directions.

The visual impact of the bowl of pink roses in the win-
dow and the snowflakes outside brings a shock of delight;
but it becomes immediately an experience in the mind
too. "Soundlessly" applies to the picture, the window
"Spawning snow and pink roses against it / Soundlessly,"
but the sight also sets up "soundlessly" in the mind, the
abstract thought that the snow and the roses are "col-
lateral and incompatible." They are side by side and
therefore related in space, but yet incongruous and con-
tradictory in other ways. The comment, "World is sud-
dener than we fancy it," includes both the experience in
the eye and the mind.

Taste and touch bring the same reaction, in all the
various sensations that go to peeling, portioning and spit-
ting pips from a tangerine, and in the intoxication of ap-
prehending how "incorrigibly plural" everything is.

Then the ear joins with a further contradiction. The
flames sound both spiteful and gay, and he concludes:

[*Humanism*]   227

"There is more than glass between the snow and the huge roses." The glass divides the collateral and incompatible worlds of the snowflakes outside and the roses within the room; but there's something more than you can see through, something *not* transparent—in fact the whole wonder of outer and inner. The world exists in infinite external variety, and man responds to it sensuously, emotionally, mentally with equal richness and suddenness. MacNeice uses the pronouns *we, I, one* and *you*, for individuals too are "incorrigibly plural"; the whole spawning human race is alive in this way all the time.

The riches may be those of the inner life only, of serenity rather than of active excitement, of that peace which Arnold prayed for in his "Lines Written in Kensington Gardens":

> Calm soul of all things! make it mine
> To feel amid the city's jar,
> That there abides a peace of thine,
> Man did not make and cannot mar!

Siegfried Sassoon creates the joy of such a visitation and the sense of gratitude for it:

> A flower has opened in my heart—
> What flower is this, what flower of spring,
> What simple, secret thing?
> It is the peace that shines apart,
> The peace of daybreak skies that bring
> Clear song and wild swift wing.
>
> Heart's miracle of inward light,
> What powers unknown have sown your seed
> And your perfection freed—
> O flower within me wondrous white,
> I know you only as my need
> And my unsealèd sight.

Or the riches may be those of looking backward instead of forward as in "Ulysses," or of looking backward in order to go forward with more heart, as Edwin Muir suggests in his "Soliloquy."

[*Poetry and the Human Condition*]   228

When life's half done you must give quality
To the other half, else you lose both, lose all.
Select, select: make an anthology
Of what's been given you by bold casual time.
Revise, omit; keep what's significant.
Fill, fill deserted time. Oh, there's no comfort
In the wastes of empty time. Provide for age.

Robert Frost expresses something of the same thought in "I could give all to time," with its last line "And what I would not part with I have kept." But the finest poem in which he points the way to the serenity that can come to those who seek it is "Directive." Written at the end of the second World War, it is a parable aimed at "those who have ears to hear." Rather mischievously, Frost refers at the end to the confusing text in the fourth chapter of St. Mark's gospel, in which Christ declares that he speaks in parables so that only those worthy to be saved shall understand his real message.

Certainly Frost's message is a teasing one, and it has been variously interpreted: as an acceptance of the Christian doctrine of grace; as saying that salvation is make-believe; or that a child's toy comes to symbolize the acceptance of life; or that it's just about a walk in the hills with a drink from a mountain stream at the end of it. Yet in spite of the mixture of tones in it, from light banter to the quiet intensity of the conclusion, and the deliberate semi-playful mystification, so that one can't feel sure of interpreting details rightly, Frost is surely saying something about which he is deeply serious.

Back out of all this now too much for us,
Back in a time made simple by the loss
Of detail, burned, dissolved, and broken off
Like graveyard marble sculpture in the weather,
There is a house that is no more a house
Upon a farm that is no more a farm
And in a town that is no more a town.
The road there, if you'll let a guide direct you
Who only has at heart your getting lost,
May seem as if it should have been a quarry—

Great monolithic knees the former town
Long since gave up pretence of keeping covered.
And there's a story in a book about it:
Besides the wear of iron wagon wheels
The ledges show lines ruled southeast northwest,
The chisel work of an enormous Glacier
That braced his feet against the Arctic Pole.
You must not mind a certain coolness from him
Still said to haunt this side of Panther Mountain.
Nor need you mind the serial ordeal
Of being watched from forty cellar holes
As if by eye pairs out of forty firkins.
As for the woods' excitement over you
That sends light rustle rushes to their leaves,
Charge that to upstart inexperience.
Where were they all not twenty years ago?
They think too much of having shaded out
A few old pecker-fretted apple trees.
Make yourself up a cheering song of how
Someone's road home from work this once was,
Who may be just ahead of you on foot
Or creaking with a buggy load of grain.
The height of the adventure is the height
Of country where two village cultures faded
Into each other. Both of them are lost.
And if you're lost enough to find yourself
By now, pull in your ladder road behind you
And put a sign up CLOSED to all but me.
Then make yourself at home. The only field
Now left's no bigger than a harness gall.
First there's the children's house of make believe,
Some shattered dishes underneath a pine,
The playthings in the playhouse of the children.
Weep for what little things could make them glad.
Then for the house that is no more a house,
But only a belilaced cellar hole,
Now slowly closing like a dent in dough.
This was no playhouse but a house in earnest.
Your destination and your destiny's
A brook that was the water of the house,

Cold as a spring as yet so near its source,
Too lofty and original to rage.
(We know the valley streams that when aroused
Will leave their tatters hung on barb and thorn.)
I have kept hidden in the instep arch
Of an old cedar at the waterside
A broken drinking goblet like the Grail
Under a spell so the wrong ones can't find it,
So can't get saved, as Saint Mark says they mustn't.
(I stole the goblet from the children's playhouse.)
Here are your waters and your watering place.
Drink and be whole again beyond confusion.

The title is perhaps ironic. The simple meaning of "directive" is that which directs, therefore, a guide. But as a technical term in military or civil administration it has come to mean practical instructions for carrying out a plan or operation. It's a dry, abstract word. Perhaps the poet is hinting that what he has in mind can't be found by any such literal means, or in a context where such a technical term could be used. The poem is no cut-and-dried answer to a practical problem: it suggests a direction in which the poet has found his own destination and destiny and the reader may share it.

The sharp, clear first line, "Back out of all this now too much for us," with its whiff of Wordsworth's sonnet "The world is too much with us," suggests this direction. It has a double meaning; both "behind all this confusion" and *get* back, back out from this overwhelming "now." The last word of the poem is "confusion" and the second line points to a time (or an attitude of mind) "made simple by the loss / Of detail." The poet compares it in a vivid simile to weathered graveyard sculpture. Taken with other passages in the poem, maybe this is a hint that in a wide view of the past any particular religious symbolism dissolves into simple, more primitive outlines.

Anyhow this directive is taking us beyond the records of any recent civilizations or patterns of social relations, and the poet's aim is to get "you" sufficiently "lost" to conventional familiar standards so that, as he says later, "you're

[Humanism] 231

lost enough to find yourself"—the "self" that is part of the history of the human race, not just a fragment in the present chaos. The road along which we are guided is both a journey in time, back through history and pre-history, and also a quest for the spiritual values that have sustained man through the ages and which he has "quarried" along the way. It's been a long, hard, rocky road to hew. The personification of the "great monolithic knees" and the figure of the "enormous Glacier" bracing his feet against the Pole, give some idea of what the makers of the "iron wagon wheels" and their successors had to contend with. "A certain coolness" is natural in these primeval forces toward the modern over-civilized pilgrim.

The reference to the "serial ordeal," taken with the overt mention of the Grail at the end, gives us the clues to the "story in a book about it." Our journey too is a Quest, that age-old mythical pattern. The modern knight's "serial ordeal" is the remembrance of those who decided to go no further, the dwellers in the ruined cellar holes, and to imagine them watching him cynically. He must deal too with the comments of those who ignore the past and congratulate themselves on having superseded all that and knowing better.

The poet's advice in the face of such "ordeals" is to remember that we share the same humanity as all questers in all ages, and to rejoice in that: "make yourself up a cheering song" about the fellowship of man. By now we are reaching "the height of the adventure." We can forget the historical aspect of it all, "pull in" that "ladder road" behind us; forget the time-world and "all this now too much for us," and find ourselves "at home" with the poet in the world of his imagination. He will share his vision and faith with us, as he always has, though now his "farm" and "field" is "no bigger than a harness gall" compared with the ampler days of the past.

First we come to "the children's house of make believe." Is this mythology, legend, fairy and folk tales, and perhaps art in general, dismissed by so many as "little things"? The poet's remark, "Weep for what little things could make them glad," is again double-edged. At first reading, he seems to be scorning these playthings, but doesn't he really mean that we should weep if we have lost the imaginative spontaneity that delights in such things? The "house that is no more a house," but which was "a house in earnest," though its foundations are overgrown and steadily disappearing, sounds like the religious tradition which was at the heart of every civilization and art of the past. But *our* destination and destiny is the brook that was the original source of water for the house and around which the children played: the waters of life; perhaps the spirit of vitality and spontaneous living, that man shares with nature, serene above the turbulence of the valleys we have left. Is the broken drinking goblet like the Grail, that the poet has stolen from the children's playhouse and hidden by the brook, the human tradition handed down in its poetry, from which those who *can* respond will always drink the waters of healing and regeneration?

Frost is deliberately oblique in his presentation of moral insights. He doesn't say in direct Elizabethan fashion, "My mind to me a kingdom is," and proceed to catalogue its sovereign qualities. Rather he takes pleasure in the puzzle and indirection of his parable, slowing the reading so that we can enjoy listening to the vigorous colloquial flow of his voice and savor all the details of the journey; the "eye pairs out of forty firkins," the "few old pecker-fretted apple trees," the imaginary man ahead "creaking with a buggy load of grain," the belilaced cellar hole "now slowly closing like a dent in dough," the final scene at the brook. For the poem differs from any attempt at prose analysis in that Frost never loses touch with all the sensuous actualities that we can see and hear or touch. We are never away from the level of concrete narratives. Yet the "directive" is ultimately to the human spirit: that it should struggle on the upward path, and that it should ally itself with all that both man and nature have created in both past and present to bring peace and renewal out of contemporary chaos. It makes us feel that even if "our only portion is the estate of man" we have good reason to rejoice in that heritage.

[*Poetry and the Human Condition*]   233

14. Religion

"Turn but a stone and start a wing."

Francis Thompson

If there were no eternal consciousness in man, if at the foundation of all there lay only a wildly seething power which, writhing with obscure passions produced everything that is great and everything that is insignificant . . . what then would life be but despair?

So Sören Kierkegaard in *Fear and Trembling* commented on the necessity for religious faith. We have seen, however, that the humanist does not necessarily despair at facing this spectacle of an irrational fate: the situation summed up by Carl Becker in *The Heavenly City:*

What is man that the electron should be mindful of him! Man is but a foundling in the cosmos, abandoned by the forces that created him. Unparented, unassisted and undirected by omniscient or benevolent authority, he must fend for himself, and with the aid of his own limited intelligence find his way about in an indifferent universe.

Poets have created fine poetry from either attitude. Frost in "Design" (p. 186) faces the possibility that Becker's view may be the true one, where certainly the fall of a sparrow has no significance. Tennyson in "In Memoriam" (LIV), in the midst of ignorance and doubt, tries hard to believe the Christian message:

O, yet we trust that somehow good
   Will be the final goal of ill,
   To pangs of nature, sins of will,
Defects of doubt, and taints of blood;

[*Poetry and the Human Condition*]   234

That nothing walks with aimless feet;
   That not one life shall be destroyed,
   Or cast as rubbish to the void,
When God hath made the pile complete;

That not a worm is cloven in vain;
   That not a moth with vain desire
   Is shrivelled in a fruitless fire,
Or but subserves another's gain.

Behold, we know not anything;
   I can but trust that good shall fall
   At last—far off—at last, to all,
And every winter change to spring.

So runs my dream; but what am I?
   An infant crying in the night;
   An infant crying for the light,
And with no language but a cry.

Nor is the proportion of joy or suffering different within the two views. Arnold or Hardy may write out of the overwhelming sense of bleak human deprivation, but no poems could be more tortured than some of Hopkins or Eliot, written out of the sense of divine deprivation. At the other end of the emotional scale, Shelley exults in the glories of nature and of man's spirit in the triumph of his Prometheus, while Christopher Smart hymns the glories of nature and of his God at the conclusion of "A Song to David." Smart lived in the late eighteenth century and spent many years in Bedlam. Boswell reports Dr. Johnson's compassionate comment on his madness: "I did not think he ought to be shut up. His infirmities were not noxious to society. He insisted on people praying with him; and I'd as lief pray with Kit Smart as any one else." "A Song to David" radiates a wild rapture quite unlike anything else written at the time, and ends with these reverberating stanzas of praise:

Glorious the sun in mid career;
Glorious th' assembled fires appear;
   Glorious the comet's train:

Glorious the trumpet and alarm;
Glorious th' Almighty's stretched-out arm;
   Glorious th' enraptured main:

Glorious the northern lights astream;
Glorious the song, when God's the theme;
   Glorious the thunder's roar;
Glorious Hosannah from the den;
Glorious the catholic Amen;
   Glorious the martyr's gore:

Glorious—more glorious is the crown
Of Him that brought salvation down,
   By meekness called thy Son:
Thou that stupendous truth believed—
And now the matchless deed's achieved,
   DETERMINED, DARED, and DONE.

Dr. Johnson's opinion of Smart's poetry is not recorded, but he did not care for religious poetry in general, declaring that "religion clips the wings of the poet's imagination," and that "poetical devotion cannot often please." These seem strange judgments, but perhaps it is true that more bad poetry has been accepted on religious topics than on secular ones. Poets themselves give some reasons for this. Wordsworth points to one:

> Readers of moral and religious inclinations, attaching so much importance to the truths which interest them . . . are prone to overrate the authors by whom those truths are expressed and enforced. They come prepared to impart so much passion to the poet's language that they remain unconscious how little, in fact, they receive from it.

T. S. Eliot sees the same confusion between intention and accomplishment in the writers as well as the readers.

> Why, I would ask, is most religious verse so bad; and why does so little religious verse reach the highest levels of poetry? Largely, I think, because of a pious insincerity. . . . People who write devotional verse

are usually writing as they want to feel, rather than as they do feel.

The excellence of Eliot's own religious verse is in its unflinching truth to his moods of doubt as well as of faith. His acceptance of Christian faith was no easy leap from skepticism to assurance. The death of the old dispensation and the acceptance of the new was hard and uncertain, "wavering between the profit and the loss." It was "the time of tension between dying and birth," accompanied by a sense of ambiguity about which is which.

This flavor strongly pervades "Journey of the Magi," which, while it purports to be a dramatic monologue by one of the wise men, is full of subjective undertones. The old man recounts the experiences of the journey and its conclusion, in all the precision and clarity of its external sensuous detail, and with all the obscurity and perplexity of its ultimate spiritual significance.

'A cold coming we had of it,
Just the worst time of the year
For a journey, and such a long journey:
The ways deep and the weather sharp,
The very dead of winter.'
And the camels galled, sore-footed, refractory,
Lying down in the melting snow.
There were times we regretted
The summer palaces on slopes, the terraces,
And the silken girls bringing sherbet.
Then the camel men cursing and grumbling
And running away, and wanting their liquor and
    women,
And the night-fires going out, and the lack of shelters,
And the cities hostile and the towns unfriendly
And the villages dirty and charging high prices:
A hard time we had of it.
At the end we preferred to travel all night,
Sleeping in snatches,
With the voices singing in our ears, saying
That this was all folly.

Then at dawn we came down to a temperate valley,
Wet, below the snow line, smelling of vegetation;
With a running stream and a water-mill beating the
      darkness,
And three trees on the low sky,
And an old white horse galloped away in the meadow.
Then we came to a tavern with vine-leaves over the
      lintel,
Six hands at an open door dicing for pieces of silver,
And feet kicking the empty wine-skins.
But there was no information, and so we continued
And arrived at evening, not a moment too soon
Finding the place; it was (you may say) satisfactory.

All this was a long time ago, I remember,
And I would do it again, but set down
This set down
This: were we led all that way for
Birth or Death? There was a Birth, certainly,
We had evidence and no doubt. I had seen birth and
      death.
But had thought they were different; this Birth was
Hard and bitter agony for us, like Death, our death.
We returned to our places, these Kingdoms,
But no longer at ease here, in the old dispensation,
With an alien people clutching their gods.
I should be glad of another death.

The title reminds us of the many medieval and Renais-
sance paintings of the Adoration, and prepares us for
oriental warmth and color, and for the atmosphere of re-
joicing "with exceeding great joy" of the Gospels. The
insistent bleakness of the opening is therefore unexpected.
The first few lines are a direct-quotation from one of the
Nativity sermons of the seventeenth century Bishop Lance-
lot Andrewes, and the method of the poem follows a pat-
tern that Eliot discerns and admires in Andrewes's prose:
"Before extracting all the spiritual meaning of a text,
Andrewes forces a concrete presence upon us." We hear
nothing of the dream or the star of the Gospel story; the
cold, the distance, the hardships and the total lack of any

quickening presence blot out everything. The moments of regret for the ease and luxury they have left, the summer palaces and the silken girls, are the only personal emotions of the opening paragraph. Everything else is simple enumeration, without comment, of the things to be endured. One after another ("and" is repeated fifteen times in twelve lines), we hear of the obstacles provided by both nature and man to delay, embarrass or obstruct the journey. The adventure wins no support from others; they meet only dishonesty and suspicion, and they have little confidence in themselves as they push on in the darkness, haunted by doubts and with no sight of their goal.

The next paragraph opens with more hope. The rhythm softens and flows more easily. Dawn and dampness and a smell of growing things meets them in the valley, and a sudden intensification of energy, "with a running stream and a water-mill beating the darkness." Running water and the *beating* (suggesting the noise in the ear and the inner triumph of hope over doubt), bring the sense of a vital driving force at work, denying the voices that said it was all folly. These, and the trees and the galloping old horse and the vine-leaves over the tavern door speak of spring and freedom and fruitfulness. But behind the old man's straightforward enumeration of the facts, the reader senses the significance of the "three trees," of the sinister hands "dicing for pieces of silver." The Christian symbolism of the vine, ("I am the true Vine"), is contradicted by the "feet kicking the empty wine-skins." The promise of the "temperate valley" is shot through with ominous ironic signs. The transposing of hints of the crucifixion, of the dicing for Christ's garments and the thirty pieces of silver into the approach to Bethlehem foreshadow the basic ambiguity of the conclusion. Here, as among the mountains, is no clear guide, "no information." The final climax is baldly anticlimactic. The quest ends, not in failure, but in inadequacy. The fulfillment carries no *feeling* of fulfillment, or revelation. "Satisfactory" suggests a tone of flat disappointment, of recognition without illumination.

Instead, all the old man remembers is a bewildering

sense of paradox. His faith is firm. "I would do it again," but what was the *purpose* of it all? Was it only to nullify "the old dispensation," and destroy their former ease? What kind of Birth is it that brings only hard and bitter agony of mind, far worse than the earlier physical sufferings of the journey and the nostalgic regrets for the palaces and girls? Now they are alienated forever from their own people and their old beliefs. The old man doesn't doubt the profound importance of the new truth that has been vouchsafed to them. But if it has set them free from the bondage to old idolatries, it has left them adrift in a time-world now empty of significance. It has brought no *creative* change into life. The old man is now so weary and disillusioned that his only longing is to end this time-world altogether.

No "pious insincerity" here; nothing but painful and moving truth of a period of personal spiritual drought, skillfully dramatized and distanced into symbolic narrative. It illustrates well too Eliot's comment on the way to *read* religious poetry:

> If we learn to read poetry properly, the poet never persuades us to believe anything. . . . What we learn from Dante or the Bhagavadgita or any other religious poetry is what it *feels* like to believe that religion.

The whole question of poetry and belief has been much discussed. Many people find that they can't enjoy poetry if they disagree intellectually with the poet's position. Milton's theology, for example, destroys any pleasure in "Paradise Lost," or Pope's deism spoils "The Essay on Man." At the other extreme are those who declare that the poet's opinions play no part in poetic appreciation, and that as readers they can be completely objective about them. I doubt if that's really possible if the opinions are *argued* in the poem. But, as Eliot suggests, the only necessity is emotional sympathy and not intellectual assent. Religious feelings are like all other feelings created in poetry; we can share them to the extent that we can under-

stand them and put ourselves into the emotional shoes of
the writer. For instance, the last two verses of Robert
Burns's "To the Unco Guid" (the overly-good, the self-
righteous) is a plea for simple charity. Whether we accept
that "to step aside is human" as sufficient basis for that, or
hold that God alone can judge of human actions, makes
little difference.

> Then gently scan your brother man,
> Still gentler sister woman;
> That they may gang a kennin wrang,
> To step aside is human;
> One point must still be greatly dark—
> The moving *Why* they do it;
> And just as lamely can ye mark
> How far perhaps they rue it.

> Who made the heart 'tis He alone
> Decidedly can try us;
> He knows each cord, its various tone,
> Each spring, its various bias;
> Then at the balance let's be mute;
> We never can adjust it;
> What's done we partly can compute,
> But know not what's resisted.

It would be a hardened atheist who could not respond
to the simple protest of this anonymous sixteenth-century
poet.

> Yet, if his majesty our sovereign lord
> Should of his own accord
> Friendly himself invite,
> And say, "I'll be your guest tomorrow night,"
> How should we stir ourselves, call and command
> All hands to work! "Let no man idle stand.
> Set me fine Spanish tables in the hall,
> See they be fitted all;
> Let there be room to eat,
> And order taken that there want no meat.
> See every sconce and candlestick made bright,
> That without tapers they may give a light.

Look to the presence: are the carpets spread,
The dais o'er the head,
The cushions in the chairs,
And all the candles lighted on the stairs?
Perfume the chambers, and in any case
Let each man give attendance in his place."
Thus if the king were coming would we do,
And 'twere good reason too;
For 'tis a duteous thing
To show all honour to an earthly king,
And after all our travail and our cost,
So he be pleased, to think no labour lost.
But at the coming of the King of Heaven
All's set at six and seven:
We wallow in our sin,
Christ cannot find a chamber in the inn.
We entertain him always like a stranger,
And as at first still lodge him in the manger.

Or again, three hundred years later, who could not be
moved by Coventry Patmore's "The Toys"? For whether or
not the reader holds the religious faith of the writer, the
theme is universal.

My little Son, who look'd from thoughtful eyes
And moved and spoke in quiet grown-up wise,
Having my law the seventh time disobey'd,
I struck him, and dismiss'd
With hard words and unkiss'd,
His Mother, who was patient, being dead.
Then, fearing lest his grief should hinder sleep,
I visited his bed,
But found him slumbering deep,
With darken'd eyelids, and their lashes yet
From his late sobbing wet.
And I, with moan,
Kissing away his tears, left others of my own;
For, on a table drawn beside his head,
He had put within his reach,
A box of counters and a red-vein'd stone,

A piece of glass abraded by the beach
And six or seven shells,
A bottle with bluebells
And two French copper coins, ranged there with
    careful art,
To comfort his sad heart.
So when that night I prayed
To God, I wept, and said:
Ah, when at last we lie with trancèd breath,
Not vexing Thee in death,
And Thou rememberest of what toys
We made our joys,
How weakly understood,
Thy great commanded good,
Then fatherly not less
Than I whom Thou has moulded from the clay
Thou'lt leave Thy wrath, and say,
"I will be sorry for their childishness."

Similarly Christina Rossetti's "Uphill" has much the same theme and feeling as Frost's "Directive" (p. 229), though the tone and method is so very different. One poet finds strength in the idea of the fellowship of man and the human literary tradition; his journey is one that can be taken many times in life. Christina Rossetti is speaking of the journey of life itself and of future immortality, under the same metaphor of the mountain road with salvation at the end of the climb. But both bring the same sense of being in the presence of a courageous, understanding guide, whether the conclusion is a temporal or an eternal one.

Does the road wind uphill all the way?
    Yes, to the very end.
Will the day's journey take the whole long day?
    From morn to night, my friend.

But is there for the night a resting place?
    A roof for when the slow, dark hours begin.
May not the darkness hide it from my face?
    You cannot miss that inn.

[*Religion*] 243

Shall I meet other wayfarers at night?
   Those who have gone before.
Then must I knock, or call when just in sight?
   They will not keep you waiting at the door.

Shall I find comfort, travel-sore and weak?
   Of labour you shall find the sum.
Will there be beds for me and all who seek?
   Yea, beds for all who come.

A religious faith, like a humanistic one, is something that helps man in the living of life; helps him to face "the weariness, the fever and the fret" that any active living in the world of men will often bring. The humanist finds his help in the sense of creative powers latent in the natural world of which he is a part, and alive in human love. The religious believer in general finds it in the faith that a divine order exists in which all apparent human disorder has meaning, and the Christian believer finds it especially in the sense of the perpetual immanence of the divine in the temporal, in the figure of Christ.

The consciousness of an immortal order behind the "mere tempestuous debate" of this life is beautifully created by the seventeenth-century poet, Henry Vaughan, in "Quickness." He is the author of the poem "Man" (p. 135), where he laments that God has condemned man to restlessness and a sense of homelessness. But in "Quickness" he speaks of those moments when man's true home is revealed in the assurance of a mystical union between the temporal and the eternal.

False life! a foil and no more, when
    Wilt thou be gone?
Thou foul deception of all men
That would not have the true come on.

Thou art a moon-like toil; a blind
    Self-posing state;
A dark contest of waves and wind;
A mere tempestuous debate.

   [*Poetry and the Human Condition*] 244

Life is a fix't, discerning light,
> A knowing joy;
No chance, or fit: but ever bright,
And calm and full, yet doth not cloy.

'Tis such a blissful thing, that still
> Doth vivify,
And shine and smile, and hath the skill
To please without eternity.

Thou art a toilsome mole, or less
> A moving mist,
But life is, what none can express,
A quickness, which my God hath kist.

All the metaphors are simple and the poem shines with a clear brightness that matches the theme. Like most seventeenth-century lyrics, its structure is made up of oppositions and a final resolution. On the one side the falseness and deception of human appearances; and on the other, the true quality of spiritual reality. The "moon-like" toil means shadowy or obscure, which is enforced by the *blind* state and the *dark* contest, the moving *mist* and the toilsome *mole*. The other attributes of the false life are its self-conflict, its deception, its heavy labor. In opposition, the moments of eternity within life are lit by "a fix't, discerning light," the assurance of "a knowing joy," calm full peace that shines and smiles; and then in the wonderful last line all this quietness is transcended into the kiss of union, the "quickness." The word concentrates the feelings of swift ecstasy, and of piercing to the quick, the most living and sensitive part, and the original meaning of "quickness" as the principle of life itself.

George Herbert, the contemporary of Henry Vaughan, creates the same feeling of "a knowing joy" in his relations with the divine. This arises, though, not from the rapture of the mystic union but from the sense of a loving companionship. His Christ is the most gentle and human in all poetry, I think. "Love" is a little symbolic drama of personal experience, where the Christian ethic shines out in all its simple beauty.

Love bade me welcome; yet my soul drew back,
  Guilty of dust and sin.
But quick-eyed Love, observing me grow slack
  From my first entrance in,
Drew nearer to me, sweetly questioning
  If I lacked anything.

"A guest," I answered, "worthy to be here."
  Love said, "You shall be he."
"I, the unkind, ungrateful? Ah, my dear,
  I cannot look on Thee."
Love took my hand, and smiling, did reply,
  "Who made the eyes but I?"

"Truth, Lord, but I have marred them: let my shame
  Go where it doth deserve."
"And know you not," says Love, "who bore the
    blame?"
  "My dear, then I will serve."
"You must sit down," says Love, "and taste my meat."
  So I did sit and eat.

The figures are those of Christian sinner and savior,
but presented in the simple social metaphor of guest and
host. The host is warmly welcoming but the guest shy,
awkward, with downcast eyes, overwhelmed with his un-
worthiness, the memories of "dust and sin," of his unkind-
ness and ungratefulness. Love draws near "sweetly ques-
tioning" his trouble, but though the guest longs to re-
spond ("Ah, my dear") he can't meet Love's look. With
a touch of quiet humor the host smiles, "Who made the
eyes but I?" Again the guest stands shamefaced at his
sins, and again the loving host reminds him that they
have been redeemed. That reminder makes the guest ask
to stay as servant, but Love again gently welcomes him
as a sharer of all he has, as a partaker of "communion":
" 'You must sit down,' " says Love, " 'and taste my meat.' "
Finally, in full reversal of all the guest's former conflicting
feelings, comes the outgoing acceptance: "So I did sit
and eat."
  The whole miniature drama is presented entirely in the

tones of the speakers: the humble sense of unworthiness in the speech of the guest, the exquisite courtesy and encouragement of the generous host, and enclosing it all, the formal frame of the whole narrative movement, so simple and so sure.

The late-nineteenth-century poet Francis Thompson, in "The Kingdom of God," takes the same theme, the intimate presence of the divine in the lives of men. He creates it in a very different vocabulary and rhythm, but with the same conviction.

O world invisible, we view thee,
O world intangible, we touch thee,
O world unknowable, we know thee,
Inapprehensible, we clutch thee!

Does the fish soar to find the ocean,
The eagle plunge to find the air—
That we ask of the stars in motion
If they have rumour of thee there?

Not where the wheeling systems darken,
And our benumbed conceiving soars!—
The drift of pinions, would we hearken,
Beats at our own clay-shuttered doors.

The angels keep their ancient places;—
Turn but a stone, and start a wing!
'Tis ye, 'tis your estrangèd faces,
That miss the many-splendoured thing.

But (when so sad thou canst not sadder)
Cry;—and upon thy so sore loss
Shall shine the traffic of Jacob's ladder
Pitched betwixt Heaven and Charing Cross.

Yea, in the night, my Soul, my daughter,
Cry,—clinging Heaven by the hems;
And lo, Christ walking on the water
Not of Genesareth, but Thames!

The movement within the poem from the condition of religious doubt to that of assurance, which makes the drama in both "Love" and "The Kingdom of God," has

its most impassioned and intense expression—and its
most complex—in Gerard Manley Hopkins's "The Wind-
hover." This dramatic development is in part what gives
the poem its vitality, but the vitality lives too in the par-
ticular use of language and its rich power of extending
meanings. This was Hopkins's own favorite among his
poems and he considered it his masterpiece, yet ever since
its publication readers have been arguing about its inter-
pretation. Perhaps he was trying to compress more mate-
rial into a sonnet than the restricted form can contain,
which accounts for the various readings, but no lover of
poetry can fail to respond to both the humanity and the
magnificence.

THE WINDHOVER

To Christ our Lord

I caught this morning morning's minion, kingdom
    of daylight's dauphin, dapple-dawn-drawn Fal-
    con, in his riding
Of the rolling level underneath him steady air, and
    striding
High there, how he rung upon the rein of a wimpling
    wing
In his ecstasy! then off, off forth on swing,
As a skate's heel sweeps smooth on a bow-bend: the
    hurl and gliding
Rebuffed the big wind. My heart in hiding
Stirred for a bird,—the achieve of, the mastery of the
    thing!

Brute beauty and valour and act, oh, air, pride,
    plume, here
Buckle! AND the fire that breaks from thee then, a
    billion
Times told lovelier, more dangerous, O my chevalier!
No wonder of it: sheer plod makes plough down sil-
    lion
Shine, and blue-bleak embers, ah my dear,
Fall, gall themselves, and gash gold-vermilion.

Hopkins created patterns of metrical structure which were all his own. The number of syllables in the line is of no consequence; all that matters is the number of stresses or beats. For instance, the third line contains sixteen syllables but only five beats. Nor need the number of beats be regular: they vary from five to seven in a line. When Robert Bridges took him to task for these unorthodox practices, Hopkins declared that he used them because he was seeking "the nearest rhythm to the native and natural rhythm of speech." Certainly he succeeds in that, and the way the spoken flow counterpoints the traditional metric and rhyme scheme is very satisfying to the ear. But some of Hopkins's other practices are not those of natural speech. To get the utmost intensity of expression, he squeezes out what seem to him unnecessary articles and connectives, piles up adjectival modifiers, and uses elliptical concentrations whose obscurity provides the basis for variant readings. But all this is part of the fascination of the poetry and its strength. No one would trouble to argue about it if it were not so powerful and compelling.

The whole poem is constructed from interlaced images of *light* and *movement,* and the emotions they provoke. In the octet, the light of the morning and the movements of the bird are set against the darkness and stagnation implied in the poet's own condition, "my heart in hiding." This seems to be some state of withdrawal and sterility matching that in "Thou art indeed just, Lord . . ." (p. 141). In the sestet a new emotional response by the poet is suggested by quite different kinds of light and movement. Here the dappled sunrise of the opening is contrasted with the pale sheen of the plough and the "gash" of the fallen embers. In the same way the free splendor of the bird's flight contrasts with the "sheer plod" of the ploughman and the quiet falling in of the fire. Emotionally, the opposition is between the poet's first joy in the sheer beauty of the bird; his admiration and envy of its mastery in its own element; his apprehension of it as symbol of the triumph of the risen Christ (suggested by the capitalization of Falcon), and his final acceptance that

[*Religion*]   249

his own sphere cannot be mastery but must be humble service, though that can be lighted by the remembrance of Christ's life on earth, his crucifixion and resurrection.

The opening description is brilliant and intricate in its sensuous effects. *Minion* means lover, *dauphin* brings the idea of majesty, the *riding* suggests the figure of the "chevalier" mentioned later, and enforces the hint in *dauphin* of the Falcon's power and dominance in his realm. Then the movement changes from the steady hovering; the bird rises, "striding / High there," and "rung upon the rein of a wimpling wing." To "ring" is a term in falconry meaning to spiral in flight, but Hopkins keeps his *riding* metaphor alive too. The flight is guided (reined) by the quick beating of the rippling wings. Then again another physical image, the wide arc of a skating "edge," and the open vowels in "sweeps smooth on a bow-bend" match the motion. All the mingled force and grace of the bird is summed up in "the hurl and gliding / Rebuffed the big wind."

The poet sees and feels all this and his heart comes out of hiding and speaks. The question is, what does he say? First, he is stirred by "the achieve of, the mastery of the thing!" but what do the first three lines of the sestet mean? The interpretation depends on the sense in which we read the word "buckle," and on the reference intended in the "thee."

Some critics take "buckle" as a continuation of the dauphin-chevalier motif, with its association of "buckler," and then read "thee" as the bird, with its overtone of the son of God (Kingdom of daylight's dauphin). The first line of the sestet then becomes a prayer that all the active, vigorous, masterful qualities in the Falcon's flight shall be buckled to the poet's "hidden" heart, and become a spiritual power (fire) as the image of the physical bird becomes merged with that of Christ. The spiritual qualities are "a billion times lovelier" than the physical bird, because the fire is that of divine grace, and "more dangerous" since the perils of the spiritual quest are greater than those of any "chevalier" who buckles on his armor for a physical combat.

I can't accept this reading myself, as it seems to destroy the pattern of the complete dramatic contrast between the two parts of the poem, in emotional feeling and in the metaphors of light and movement. It is very tempting to link "buckle" with the chivalric "rider" of the octet and to give it the sense of "buckle on or together," but the quite contrary meaning "to crumple, to collapse" seems to me to make an equally valid reading and to work in much better with the last three lines. If we take it that way, the poet is making a choice between a temptation to self-assertion, to achievement and mastery, and the dedication to lowly service and sacrifice. Since the poem is addressed to Christ, the "thee" can be no other, but surely it is in *opposition* to all the "brute beauty and valour and act" of the soaring bird. The poet gives a cry of regret (oh) for the "air, pride, plume" that he must forgo, but nevertheless bids them imperatively to be gone. The capitalized AND represents the kind of miraculous change that then occurs. We must strongly accent *thee* and "*my* chevalier," to distinguish them from the bird, the chevalier who rides in glory in the sunrise. The revelation (fire) that breaks from the spiritual example of Christ's life *on earth* is far lovelier to the poet than the splendor of the bird in the heavens, and more dangerous because it needs so much more courage than mere hurling and gliding to rebuff the big wind. It's quite possible, indeed necessary, to keep the implication that the Falcon is an emblem of the risen Christ; the point, however, is that it is the example of Christ as man on earth that the poet knows he must follow, and whom he addresses in the words of George Herbert, "ah my dear."

A quotation from a sermon of Hopkins on the manhood of Christ is apt in helping with the last three lines: "Poor was his station, laborious his life, bitter his ending: through poverty, through labour, through crucifixion his majesty of nature more shines." Here in statement is exactly what the poet says in metaphor. Christ in his heavenly majesty is reflected in the Falcon. The presence of the divine "flaming out" in the beauties of nature is a favorite theme in Hopkins's poetry. But it is Christ as example of humble labor and human suffering that he has chosen as "chevalier," and it is through toil and pain that "his majesty of nature more shines." There's none of the "wonder" of the flashing "kingdom of daylight's dauphin" in this shining, but neither is his heart still "in hiding" or cooled to "blue-bleak embers." Humbly he accepts "sheer plod," but notes that even this slow labor keeps the plough bright as it pushes through the soil (sillion). And though his embers fall and gall themselves into wounds, yet the sequence of "fall, gall, gash," with its suggestion of the crucifixion, is followed by the triumphant shining "gold-vermilion." From blue-bleak embers can spring the fire of rebirth and resurrection—another dawn—so that the final resolution sweeps back to the sunrise of the opening and to the celestial Falcon who will be the poet's final "chevalier."

None of these poems attempt to "persuade us to believe anything"; they embody in language "what it feels like" to believe a religion. The poets all trust in a transcendent value beyond any temporal human one. In the individual poem they may, or may not, reach communion with it, but their ladders start, as Yeats says all the ladders start, "in the foul rag and bone shop of the heart." The humanists cannot accept the doctrines implicit in the poems, but can give full emotional sympathy, since they experience the same feelings of despair and of resolution in their own struggles and acceptances. They may even wish sometimes, as Hardy does in "The Oxen," that their own faith could include the supernatural.

> Christmas Eve, and twelve of the clock.
> "Now they are all on their knees,"
> An elder said as we sat in a flock
> By the embers in hearthside ease.
>
> We pictured the meek mild creatures where
> They dwelt in their strawy pen,
> Nor did it occur to one of us there
> To doubt they were kneeling then.

[*Poetry and the Human Condition*]   252

So fair a fancy few would weave
   In these years! Yet, I feel,
If someone said on Christmas Eve,
   "Come; see the oxen kneel,

"In the lonely barton by yonder coomb
   Our childhood used to know,"
I should go with him in the gloom,
   Hoping it might be so.

15. The Poets on Poetry

"The complete consort dancing together."

T. S. Eliot

"Poetry is what is lost in translation," says Robert Frost. That is the *poetry* is not in the story or the theme or the moral message or in the emotions aroused or in any abstraction that can be made in prose. Poetry can't be talked about without speaking of these things; they permeate and pervade it inextricably, and no one would read poetry unless it enclosed them. Its *function* is a vindication of the worth of the world, of living human experience. But poetry lives in its own language and can't be separated from the original words in which it is created. That is its *nature*. As we saw in an earlier chapter (p. 20), the "familiar compound ghost" who appears in the last of Eliot's *Four Quartets* speaks for all poets:

> Our concern was speech and speech impelled us
> To purify the dialect of the tribe
> And urge the mind to aftersight and foresight.

The ghost puts the responsibility to language as the poet's first "concern," since his work preserves what Yeats calls "gradual Time's last gift, a written speech," the whole literary tradition of a people.

We think nowadays of the Elizabethans as contributing more to the wealth of the English vocabulary than any other age, and indeed they did. They were the first writers to be conscious of the potentialities of the English language and of the responsibilities of the poets to expand and refine it. In the fifteenth century, English was still far behind French and Italian as a literary medium. Some writers still thought of Latin as the really civilized and lasting means of communication. The new poetic forms from the continent stumbled along at first most stiffly and clumsily in the English language. But it grew apace. Samuel Daniel, writing in 1599, makes a plea to that "power above powers, O heavenly Eloquence," to come and inspire the English people, for, he says, it is thus only that the English genius will be able to fulfill itself, and give life to yet unborn literature in "the yet unformèd Occident."

Thou that canst do much more with one poor pen,
    Than all the powers of princes can effect;
And draw, divert, dispose and fashion men,
    Better than force or rigour can direct!
Should we this ornament of glory then,
    As th' unmaterial fruits of shades, neglect?

Or should we careless come behind the rest
    In power of words, that go before in worth;
When as our accents equal to the best
    Is able greater wonders to bring forth?
When all that ever hotter spirits express'd
    Comes bettered by the patience of the north.

And who, in time, knows whither we may vent
    The treasure of our tongue, to what strange shores
This gain of our best glory shall be sent,
    T' enrich unknowing nations with our stores?
What worlds in the yet unformèd Occident
    May come refined with th' accents that are ours?

Or who can tell for what great work in hand
    The greatness of our style is now ordained?
What powers it shall bring in, what spirits command?
    What thoughts let out, what humours keep re-
        strained?
What mischief it may powerfully withstand;
    And what fair ends may thereby be attained?

It is fitting that the modern poet who cares most openly and passionately about the poet's responsibility to his medium should come from America. T. S. Eliot has declared:

> To pass on to posterity one's own language more highly developed, more refined and more precise than it was before one wrote it, that is the highest possible achievement of the poet *as poet*.

His medium is the poet's inseparable partner, and only through a constantly refreshed collaboration between living and writing can poetry function fully. This developing comradeship, the need for truth in it, and its difficulty, because of the complexities of both the man and the language, is eloquently stated by Eliot in "East Coker," the second of the *Four Quartets*. The poet writes here in a mood of near despair, for he feels that his personal struggle to keep alive the strength, richness and variety of his medium goes on in the midst of a culture that cares nothing for "the treasures of our tongue," but is quite willing to leave it to deteriorate into poverty, imprecision and "general mess."

> So here I am, in the middle way having had twenty
>   years . . .
> Trying to learn to use words, and every attempt
> Is a wholly new start, and a different kind of failure
> Because one has only learnt to get the better of words
> For the thing one no longer has to say, or the way in
>   which
> One is no longer disposed to say it. And so each ven-
>   ture
> Is a new beginning, a raid on the inarticulate
> With shabby equipment always deteriorating
> In the general mess of imprecision of feeling,
> Undisciplined squads of emotion.

In the face of this sad glimpse of what Eliot has called elsewhere "the pains of turning blood into ink," it is no wonder that serious poets should decry the popular idea that their work is a pastime that need not be taken too seriously. Yeats spoke of "the chief temptation of the artist, creation without toil," but no one could accuse *him* of that. He agonized over composition:

> The fascination of what's difficult
> Has dried the sap out of my veins, and rent
> Spontaneous joy and natural content
> Out of my heart.

His aim, he said, was "a speech so natural and dramatic that the hearer would feel the presence of a man thinking and feeling." But this apparent spontaneity was bought with incessant labor.

> A line will take us hours maybe;
> Yet if it does not seem a moment's thought,
> Our stitching and unstitching has been nought.
> Better go down upon your marrow bones
> And scrub a kitchen pavement, or break stones
> Like an old pauper, in all kinds of weather;
> For to articulate sweet sounds together
> Is to work harder than all these, and yet
> Be thought an idler. . . .

No wonder too that poets should be jealous of their trust to preserve the "dialect of the tribe" from decay, and should speak out in protest against those who debase it. William Meredith has done this today in "To a Western Bard Still a Whoop and a Holler Away From English Poetry."

> I read an impatient man
> Who howls against his time,
> Not angry enough to scan
> Not fond enough to rhyme.

> And I think of the terrible cry
> The brave priest Hopkins raised
> The night he raided the sky
> And English verse was praised.

> And the infinite, careful woe
> That informs the song of Blake,

[*The Poets on Poetry*]   257

The stricter because he knew
The jog the madmen take.

Or our own great poet's rage
Yeats', in his decorous care
To make singing of old age
And numbers of despair.

It is common enough to grieve
And praise is all around;
If any cry means to live
It must be an uncommon sound.

Cupped with the hands of skill
How loud their voices ring,
Containing passion still
Who cared enough to sing.

The care for the tradition knits the past with the present. It also knits the present with the future, for good poets are proud enough to know that their voices *will* ring when they and the subjects of their verse are long dead.

Not marble, nor the gilded monuments
Of Princes, shall outlive this powerful rhyme,
But you shall shine more bright in these contents
Than unswept stone, besmear'd with sluttish time.
When wasteful war shall statues overturn,
And broils root out the work of masonry,
Nor Mars his sword, nor war's quick fire, shall burn
The living record of your memory.
'Gainst death, and all-oblivious enmity
Shall you pace forth, your praise shall still find room,
Even in the eyes of all posterity
That wear this world out to the ending doom.
   So till the judgement that yourself arise,
   You live in this, and dwell in lovers' eyes.

Shakespeare is not really so much intent on his love as on the power and glory of his verse, on the fact that his lines will "pace forth" in all their majesty when all else is swept away. Or Pope knows that however trivial Belinda herself and the story of the rape of her lock may be, they have become immortal in his poem.

> For, after all the murders of your eye,
> When, after millions slain, yourself shall die:
> When those fair suns shall set, as set they must,
> And all those tresses shall be laid in dust,
> This Lock the Muse shall consecrate to fame,
> And 'midst the stars inscribe Belinda's name.

This is the historical value of poetry; that at all times it has cherished language and has been engaged in the task of enlarging and enlivening man's consciousness through it. But art exists and functions both in and out of time. A poem is a document written by a particular person in a particular period on a particular theme—an item in a long historical sequence. It is also an individual work of art, a thing that has a separate timeless existence from that of the poet himself, begotten and made in the union between him and his medium. "It adorns nature with a new thing," says Emerson. The poet is Maker. "God hath bestowed his perfectest image on poets. None come so near to God in wit," says Thomas Nashe. Francis Thompson echoes him.

> Poet! still, still, thou dost rehearse,
> In the great *fiat* of thy verse
>   Creation's primal plot.

A poem is made of words, "the complete consort dancing together," but the words are the end result of what has produced them, "blood, imagination, intellect running together"; an organic harmonious energy that has transformed the incoherence, the fragmentariness, the wastefulness of living, into the clarity, the shapeliness, the precision of art. To the poet, the poem may be an occasion to rise beyond the prison of raw personal emotion. As Donne says:

> Then as th' earth's inward narrow crooked lanes
> Do purge sea water's fretful salt away,
>   I thought, if I could draw my pains,

Through Rime's vexation, I should them allay,
Grief brought to numbers cannot be so fierce.
For he tames it, that fetters it in verse.

The poet, through "Rime's vexation" tames the tyranny
of his own fierce feelings into the fetters of his poetic
form. But whatever the occasion, the process is the same.
Henry James declares that "it is art that *makes* life, makes
interest, makes importance . . . and I know of no substi-
tute whatever for the force and beauty of its process."

This process and its result are so satisfying because
they answer a basic impulse in human consciousness; the
search for organic order. Yeats said of the revelations that
came to him in symbolic visions and dreams, "the setting
of it all in order has given me a new framework and new
patterns. One goes on year after year, getting the disorder
of one's mind in order, and this is the real impulse to
create." This is the same faculty that Coleridge describes
when he says that the creative process combines "a more
than usual state of emotion with more than usual order."

Man craves for a sense of harmony. Psychologists tell
us that we spend our lives, consciously and unconsciously,
in one long effort to find an equilibrium within our en-
vironment. Certainly all the larger satisfactions that visit
mortality are rooted in the sense of reconciliation and co-
ordination. This impulse has made humanity seek at all
times to find some principle of harmony in the universe
we inhabit; to conceive of, and believe in, some scheme
in which man plays an essential part in a universal de-
sign. Theologians have devised elaborate systems of dogma
to uphold it and philosophers elaborate systems of abstract
thought, while science has been built from the conviction
that unity must underlie the diversity of nature. Civiliza-
tion in general has been the process of imposing order
on chaos; the effort to control force into form, to achieve
a patterned society of diverse units working harmoniously
together.

But man never achieves this more than partially in po-
litical, economic or social relationships and rarely in his
personal life. His religions and philosophies too decay

and change. In art alone he sees the symbol of harmony in its perfection; in that he can *contemplate* it, though he may not be able to explain it. Abstract esthetics is an unsatisfactory subject and we have to admit reluctantly that though criticism may help toward apprehension, any words that we use to talk about a poem, a picture or a piece of music may build a road toward the revelation, but cannot bring it about. The ultimate experience has to be an individual and direct communication from the work of art to the beholder, the listener, the reader.

Yet if anyone can communicate the experience of poetry it must be the poets themselves, and in conclusion let us listen to three of our modern poets as they make poetry out of what poetry is and does. Wallace Stevens in "The Idea of Order at Key West" opens by setting the scene: a girl singing beside the sea. It is immediately clear that the girl and the song and the sea are symbols; they are the poet, the poetry and the life out of which it springs. The poet subdues life to his song:

> It may be that in all her phrases stirred
> The grinding water and the gasping wind;
> But it was she and not the sea we heard.

> For she was the maker of the song she sang.
> The ever-hooded, tragic-gestured sea
> Was merely a place by which she walked to sing.
> Whose spirit is this? we said, because we knew
> It was the spirit that we sought and knew
> That we should ask this often as she sang.

The voice of the spirit differs from "the dark voice of the sea" and from "the outer voice of sky / And cloud" and from "the heaving speech of air." But it isn't in sound alone that the voice differs:

> It was her voice that made
> The sky acutest at its vanishing.
> She measured to the hour its solitude.
> She was the single artificer of the world
> In which she sang. And when she sang, the sea,

Whatever self it had, became the self
That was her song, for she was maker. Then we,
As we beheld her striding there alone,
Knew that there never was a world for her
Except the one she sang and, singing, made.

Ramon Fernandez, tell me, if you know,
Why, when the singing ended and we turned
Toward the town, tell why the glassy lights,
The lights in the fishing boats at anchor there,
As the night descended, tilting in the air,
Mastered the night and portioned out the sea,
Fixing emblazoned zones and fiery poles,
Arranging, deepening, enchanting night.

Oh! Blessed rage for order, pale Ramon,
The maker's rage to order words of the sea,
Words of the fragrant portals, dimly-starred,
And of ourselves and of our origins,
In ghostlier demarcations, keener sounds.

Not only is the singer making a new thing, a new world
apart from the natural world about her and from the hu-
man listeners, but the song has a particular quality. It
intensifies a natural experience, making "the sky acutest
at its vanishing," and it *orders* it, "arranging, deepening,
enchanting night."

Of the final address, Stevens said: "I used two every-
day names. As I might have expected, they turned out to
be an actual name." But the name is just a rhetorical
flourish to pose to an imaginary listener the question of
how the imaginative vision brings mastery of material,
finer human insights (ghostlier demarcations), and a
keener ear.

We would not find any poem that is a more beautiful
piece of poetic architecture than Yeats's "Sailing to By-
zantium." The poem is sometimes read as an account
of Yeats's theories of reincarnation after death, but I
doubt if that is the theme. Yeats, like anyone else, could
only have opinions about, or a faith in, the life after
death, but he *knew* all about the process of reincarnation

that takes place in this world, the reincarnation of life into art; the reincarnation of the mind and spirit of the creative artist into a new sense medium, a new, living physical form in language.

He tells us himself that this is the analogy *in life* to what he believes to be the progress of the soul after death. After death, he says:

> Finally . . . the soul attains the condition of fire, time comes to an end and the soul puts on a rhythmic or luminous body and contemplates all the events of its memories in an eternal possession of itself in one single moment.

And again he speaks of this spiritual state "where all fuel has become flame, where there is nothing but the state itself, nothing to constrain it or end it." And immediately he adds: "We attain it always in the creation or enjoyment of a work of art . . . but it passes from us." It passes because humanity is doomed to time and change, but the work of art itself remains, in which the soul has been caught forever in its rhythmical and luminous body, and where all fuel has become flame and there is nothing but the state itself—the poem.

To Yeats, Byzantine culture represented the apex that man has ever achieved, and he regarded Byzantine art as the flower of that culture. But Byzantium in this poem is only very faintly a geographical entity. It represents much more a state of mind or being. Yeats wrote the poem when he was in his sixties. He felt himself growing old. He hated to grow old, and Byzantium represents a condition where physical age is of no consequence. It is the state of mind in which the artist creates and the atmosphere in which a work of art lives. The "holy city of Byzantium" is very close to Blake's "holy city of the Imagination." Its most important aspect is that it is a timeless condition. The work of art is apart from the world of physical change and decay and corruptibility: it is immortal, it doesn't grow old and die. And the artist in the act of creation is existing in a world of mind and spirit, alone with the sense medium in which he is creating. He is in "the condition of fire," fashioning a new body in the symbolic fire of inspiration, illumination and purification. The central symbol in the poem is this fire, which is in opposition to the earth, the air and the water, the symbols of physical life.

> That is no country for old men. The young
> In one another's arms, birds in the trees,
> —Those dying generations—at their song,
> The salmon-falls, the mackerel-crowded seas,
> Fish, flesh, or fowl, commend all summer long
> Whatever is begotten, born, and dies.
> Caught in that sensual music all neglect
> Monuments of unageing intellect.
>
> An aged man is but a paltry thing,
> A tattered coat upon a stick, unless
> Soul clap its hands and sing, and louder sing
> For every tatter in its mortal dress,
> Nor is there singing school but studying
> Monuments of its own magnificence;
> And therefore I have sailed the seas and come
> To the holy city of Byzantium.
>
> O sages standing in God's holy fire
> As in the gold mosaic of a wall,
> Come from the holy fire, perne in a gyre,
> And be the singing-masters of my soul.
> Consume my heart away; sick with desire
> And fastened to a dying animal
> It knows not what it is; and gather me
> Into the artifice of eternity.
>
> Once out of nature I shall never take
> My bodily form from any natural thing,
> But such a form as Grecian goldsmiths make
> Of hammered gold and gold enamelling
> To keep a drowsy Emperor awake;
> Or set upon a golden bough to sing
> To lords and ladies of Byzantium
> Of what is past, or passing, or to come.

[*Poetry and the Human Condition*] 264

The mental climate the poet has reached is Byzantium and "that" is the country he has sailed *from*. But it's no place on the map. It's the country of youth and mortal joys and spontaneous animal fertility; the country of the creatures of water, earth, air, "fish, flesh, or fowl," which is going to be contrasted with the condition of fire.

In this first verse the poet creates a series of physical images which are going to be paralleled in the rest of the poem with a similar series of spiritual images. On the one side the birds in the trees, the dying generations, the song "commending" mortal life, the images of teeming natural reproduction, the spontaneous joy of all those "caught in that sensual music." On the other side we are to have the golden bird on the golden bough, the immortal generation of art, the soul clapping its hands, "commending" its new life, the singing *school* in which it must learn its hammered and enameled craftsmanship and be gathered into "the artifice of eternity." Song appears in every verse, for this is a poem about poetry.

In the first six lines we are in a lovely summer world of youth and sex and natural abundance. But in the midst of all this movement we are brought up short in the last two lines where the sound pattern hardens into the final heavily accented "monuments of unageing intellect." In contrast to the "dying generations," monuments are objects made by man to commemorate the dead and their values; solid permanent objects that outlast the individual life. The basis of these monuments is the immortal element in man, his mind and spirit, which is not re-created into natural physical offspring, but is re-created into inanimate objects not subject to natural laws. But at the same time these things too belong to the sense world: the soul can live only by finding a new *body*. The artist must use a sense medium and create sensuous images in order to *communicate* the values of the spirit. He makes a changeless and incorruptible body instead of one that decays and ages.

So the poet points the difference. In contrast to the dignity and grandeur of the "monuments" is the spectacle of how paltry a "thing" an old man's body is. In the place of the flowing grace of "the young in one another's arms" is this solitary, rigid scarecrow, its garment of flesh in rags. It is quickly followed by the picture of the soul as an animate body, clapping its hands and singing as loudly as the birds. But it has to *learn* its new song; it has to study its different order of being, the monuments of its own magnificence; the arts man's spirit has begotten and which don't die. So he comes to the "holy city," which does not carry a religious significance. It is hallowed, existing in the illuminating and purifying fire, away from the creatures of earth, air, water.

The sages to whom the poet prays have been old men too but now they are sources of inspiration. They stand "as in the gold mosaic of a wall," in fact he has to visualize them in a work of art, to give them *body* before he can imagine them communicating with him. He prays them to "perne in a gyre." In another poem Yeats tells us that "perne" is a dialect word meaning a bobbin on which thread is wound. Here he seems to use it as a verb, and the phrase means "come spiraling down." This symbol of a gyre is deeply embedded in Yeats's imagination as the pattern of all dynamic activity. So the sages and their fire are to take possession of him, and consume his *heart* away, the carnal element in him. His heart is "sick with desire / And fastened to a dying animal," so that "it knows not what it is." It is still regretting the world of the first stanza, longing to be young again and fulfill itself sexually; yet it is also sick with desire to be rid of the dying animal and gathered into "the artifice of eternity" instead of "caught in that sensual music."

"The artifice of eternity" allows of several meanings. We can turn it round and call it "the eternity of art." But Yeats may be suggesting further subtleties. Art itself is artifice. Not in the bad sense of "artificial" but it is a man made thing, an artifact—not a product of nature. He may further imply that even in creative art, man cannot escape from time. The idea of eternity itself is an artifice, for man can know only time. In creating or experiencing art we feel we have abstracted ourselves, but the minutes tick away. Nevertheless that state is an analogy of the timeless, and in the final verse the poet passes "out of nature" into the figure of the golden bird singing on the golden bough. Yeats had read a description of this in a book on Byzantine art. The bird and its song are indivisible, the soul and the poem it makes, both fashioned in the fire.

But though the song will be eternal, living out of time, yet it will still remain in time, because poetry doesn't exist without an audience of mortal men and women. Perhaps the "drowsy Emperor" is the dull human world that needs awakening to the fiery song; or perhaps the song is for all those who can escape to Byzantium, the world of art. But the final paradox is that the immortal song can only be about time, "of what is past, or passing, or to come." Though itself beyond time and change, it sings in its imperishable form *to* human beings, and can sing only about the condition of being human.

Auden's poem "In Memory of W. B. Yeats (d. Jan. 1939)," again takes up the subject of poetry and its nature and function. The opening verse of the first part evokes the natural and the cultural weather of the time of Yeats's death, the winter before the outbreak of the second World War. The metaphor of landscape as symbolic of inner qualities is sustained throughout:

> He disappeared in the dead of winter:
> The brooks were frozen, the airports almost deserted,
> And snow disfigured the public statues;
> The mercury sank in the mouth of the dying day.
> O all the instruments agree
> The day of his death was a dark cold day.

In the world of time and space it's "a dark cold day," and in symbolic terms Auden suggests that the cultural climate matches the time of year. He sees civilization as cold and dead; the free-flowing waters of life are frozen, the aspirations of men earthbound, the great tradition muffled and disfigured. The day is dying, as the sinking thermometer notes, and the old poet is dying, but the "instruments" are not only those of scientific measurement. As the poem develops they include also the "mourning tongues" that grieve over the death of the individual poet as the creative instrument, and finally the poem turns to praise of poetry itself as the instrument of man's spirit.

The second part distinguishes between the man and the poet. The death of the man is unimportant, for as Auden saw him the man himself had very human weaknesses. He was open to flattery and enjoyed being lionized; he was the victim of his own temperament and of the social and political "weather" of Ireland. But what survives (survival comes in three times in these ten lines) is the poetry.

> You were silly like us: your gift survived it all;
> The parish of rich women, physical decay,
> Yourself; mad Ireland hurt you into poetry.
> Now Ireland has her madness and her weather still,
> For poetry makes nothing happen: it survives
> In the valley of its saying where executives
> Would never want to tamper; it flows south
> From ranches of isolation and the busy griefs,
> Raw towns that we believe and die in; it survives,
> A way of happening, a mouth.

In the realm of action, of "executives," poetry makes nothing happen, and "Ireland has her madness and her weather still," in spite of Yeats's passionate attacks on her decay. Poetry survives "in the valley of its saying," that is, its rich soil is language. It arises in ugly and arid places of the heart, "ranches of isolation and the busy griefs"; it arises from actualities, "raw towns" that seem reality as we live and die in them. But poetry doesn't die. It survives and flows *south* from its source in the pains of living, bringing everything that we associate with "south" in the wintertime: warmth, comfort, release. Poetry is an instrument, a "mouth" that interprets by its "saying"; that is its own "way of happening."

For the concluding part Auden chose a simple form of rhyming quatrain that some readers find trivial. But he is fond of taking a simple traditional pattern and loading it with an unexpected concentration of force. Here what appears to be the metric of a nursery rhyme becomes weighted with the rhythm of a funeral march or a ritual incantation.

> Earth, receive an honored guest;
> William Yeats is laid to rest:
> Let the Irish vessel lie
> Emptied of its poetry.
>
>   *   *   *   *
>
> In the nightmare of the dark
> All the dogs of Europe bark,
> And the living nations wait,
> Each sequestered in its hate;
>
> Intellectual disgrace
> Stares from every human face,
> And the seas of pity lie
> Locked and frozen in each eye.
>
> Follow, poet, follow right
> To the bottom of the night,
> With your unconstraining voice
> Still persuade us to rejoice;
>
> With the farming of a verse
> Make a vineyard of the curse,
> Sing of human unsuccess
> In a rapture of distress;
>
> In the deserts of the heart
> Let the healing fountain start,
> In the prison of his days
> Teach the free man how to praise.

Yeats's body lies dead, "emptied of its poetry," returned to earth; he exists no longer as a man, but lives forever in his poems. In the last five verses Auden again contrasts the contemporary situation and the eternal mission of poetry. On the one hand the darkness, the frozen imprisoned emotions, the disfigured human race, the sense of isolation, the atmosphere of war. On the other the creative, affirmative, liberating voice of the poet. Free, not locked in the prison of his times; unconstrained, not sequestered.

Then farm, vineyard, healing fountain replace the deserts of the heart and the "ranches of isolation and the busy griefs" of the second part. Poetry makes beauty out of tragedy, singing of "human unsuccess / In a rapture of distress." The atmosphere of the poem's opening is exactly reversed in its close. The dark cold day of the poet's death in the time-world is transfigured into the joy, the praise, the fertility of art's timeless achievement.

Like everyone else the poet must put up with the society in which he finds himself, and like everyone else he would like to feel of some use to it. But his use must be through his particular form of action, "getting the better of words." So there is a sense in which the only creed to which he must be true is art for art's sake. The poet can give us that "wonderfully full, new and intimate sense of things" because he removes us from the world of doing to the world of being, where things do not change and where we can contemplate them instead of taking part in them. The writer himself inhabits our world, full of "the general mess of imprecision of feeling / Undisciplined squads of emotion." But the world he *creates* is a kind of Utopia where every part is individually alive and at the same time functioning in a vital, organic pattern: "the complete consort dancing together." It is not subject to time or change or chance because, though it seems so warm and living, it is an image-world, existing only in its own imperishable medium. But that is its triumph. E. M. Forster puts it well. He declares that the work of art is the only material object in the universe that possesses forever internal stability and vital harmony:

> The work of art stands up by itself, and nothing else does. It achieves something which has often been promised by society, but always delusively. Ancient Athens made a mess—but the *Antigone* stands up Renaissance Rome made a mess—but the ceiling of the Sistine got painted. James I made a mess—but there was *Macbeth*. Louis XIV—but there was *Phèdre* Art for art's sake? I should just think so, and more

[*Poetry and the Human Condition*]   270

so than ever at the present time. It is the one orderly product which our muddling race has produced.

Robert Frost also emphasizes "the figure a poem makes," its vital order:

> It assumes direction with the first line laid down, it runs a course of lucky events, and ends in a clarification of life—not necessarily a great clarification, such as sects and cults are founded on, but in a momentary stay against confusion.

That seems a very modest claim for literary art, but it is a profound one. Literature is, as James Joyce said, "the eternal affirmation of man's spirit." It supplies no more final answers than life itself does. We have to leave the moral certainties to the theologians and the politicians. But whatever its content—whether its song is of triumph or despair, serenity, stoicism or frustration—the very fact of its existence testifies to man's power to create something from his experience, something that possesses its own vitality and order. It declares that whether or not there is some supernatural creative order behind the confusion of living, in which man can have faith, he can have faith that he himself is the soil and source of fertile creative forces and forms. His poetry stands, in matter and manner, in form and content, as an indestructible proof, not only that man suffers and endures and re-creates himself, but also that he can create cosmos from chaos, and bring into being at least "a momentary stay against confusion." Momentary perhaps, for the maker himself, and for his individual readers, but nevertheless immortal, as generation after generation shares it and it becomes part of the collective consciousness of the race—the written speech of men and women of all countries, all ages, all temperaments, all creeds, all classes, all callings—the human tradition.

Appendix

Meters and Verse Patterns

Meter means measure, and the unit of measurement in English verse is the *foot*. We have borrowed the classical names for describing the number and order and character of the syllables that form "feet." Feet may be either disyllabic (formed of two syllables), or trisyllabic (formed of three syllables). They are named as follows:

Iamb: an unaccented syllable followed by an accented one:

> The plówman hómeward plóds his wéary wáy. (Gray)

Trochee: an accented syllable followed by an unaccented one:

> Lífe is réal! Lífe is éarnest! (Longfellow)

Spondee: two accented syllables together, as in the last two feet of this line:

> The cumbrous elements—eárth, flóod, aír, fíre (Milton)

Dactyl: an accented syllable followed by two unaccented ones:

> Toúch her not scórnfully (Hood)

Anapest: two unaccented syllables followed by an accented one:

> And the soúnd of a voíce that is stíll. (Tennyson)

Although it is not difficult to find illustrations of all these types of feet, by far the most popular and all-pervasive movement in English verse is the iambic. It suits the nature of the language better than any other, and probably nine-tenths of English poetry uses this foot as its basic metrical unit.

The *line* of verse contains one or more feet. Again, the classical names are officially used: *monometer*: one foot; *dimeter*: two feet; *trimeter*: three feet; *tetrameter*: four feet (often called octosyllabics); *pentameter*: five feet; *hexameter*: six feet (also called alexandrines); *heptameter*: seven feet.

Two measurements are therefore involved in meter: the *kind* of foot and the *number* of feet in the line. These can be combined in any possible ways. "The plowman homeward plods his weary way" is iambic pentameter; "Life is real! Life is earnest!" is trochaic tetrameter; "Touch her not scornfully" is dactylic dimeter; "And the sound of a voice that is still" is anapestic trimeter.

RHYME AND OTHER METRICAL DEVICES

Verse patterns may be either rhymed or unrhymed. Rhyme is an identity of sounds at the end of lines. This may be in the last syllable of the line (*single or masculine rhyme*),

> And hears the Muses in a *ring*
> Aye round about Jove's altar *sing*.

or in the last two syllables (*double or feminine rhyme*)

> And add to these retirèd *leisure*,
> That in trim gardens takes his *pleasure*. (Milton)

Dactylic verse requires a triple rhyme

> Touch her not *scornfully*,
> Think of her *mournfully*

but in serious verse the rhyme is seldom more than double. Triple rhymes come more often in comic or satiric verse, as in Byron's "Don Juan":

> Her plan she deem'd both innocent and *feasible* . . .
> Not scandal's fangs could fix on much that's *seizable*.

or as in so many of the verses of Ogden Nash today.

The rhymes may be *internal*, within the line as well as at the end:

> And a good south *wind* spring up *behind*;
> The Albatross did follow,
> And every *day*, for food or *play*
> Came to the mariner's hollo!
>
> (Coleridge)

Or the rhymes may be *half-rhymes* or *slant-rhymes*, where the sounds are similar, but not identical:

> Little Tommy *Tucker*
> Sang for his *supper*.
> What did he have?
> Brown bread and *butter*.

Modern poets are particularly fond of using *assonance,* a chiming of the vowel sounds only, while the consonants play little part in the sound pattern. In these lines by Louis MacNeice, the sound pattern is in the uses of "i," "o" and "a."

> Not the twilight of the gods but a precise dawn
> Of sallow and grey bricks, and the newsboys crying
>   War.

The alternative to this is *consonance,* where the position is reversed. The consonants dominate the pattern of identical sounds while the vowels differ. This is from "Strange Meeting" by Wilfred Owen.

> It seemed that out of battle I *escaped*
> Down some profound dull tunnel, long since *scooped*
> Through *granite* which titanic wars had *groined.*
> Yet also there encumbered sleepers *groaned.*

Other verbal devices are used to give variety to the meter. In some lines the sense is enclosed within the single line, which is then called *end-stopped*. If the sense flows over into two, or several lines, they are then called *run-on*. A couplet where the sense is complete is a *closed couplet* (as in the lines from Pope below). If a sentence, or clause, ends in the middle of a line, the break which then occurs is called a *caesura*, and makes a pause in the reading of the line. Other common sound effects are those of *alliteration,* the repetion of consonants; and *onomatopoeia,* the imitation of natural sounds in words. A succession of harsh, slow-moving syllables is called *cacophony;* and of light, harmonious ones, *euphony.* The following famous passage from Pope's "Essay on Criticism" gives illustrations of all these devices.

> True ease in writing comes from art, not chance,
> As those move easiest who have learned to dance.
> 'Tis not enough no harshness gives offense,
> The sound must seem an echo to the sense:
> Soft is the strain when Zephyr gently blows,
> And the smooth stream in smoother numbers flows;
> But when loud surges lash the sounding shore,
> The hoarse, rough verse should like the torrent roar:
> When Ajax strives some rock's vast weight to throw,
> The line too labors, and the words move slow;
> Not so, when swift Camilla scours the plain,
> Flies o'er th' unbending corn, and skims along the
>   main.

There is alliteration throughout the passage (which should be read aloud), and in the fifth and sixth lines, where the repetition of the "s" sound creates the softness and smoothness of wind and stream, it is combined with onomatopoeia. The lines on the torrent and on Ajax illustrate cacophony, and those on Camilla, euphony. In all, carefully and skillfully, Pope makes the sound of the words echo the actions described.

These can vary from the single couplet to an elaborate arrangement such as Edmund Spenser's "Epithalamion," which has a varying stanza of sixteen lines.

The *couplet* is any rhymed pattern of two lines, but its most popular forms are the iambic tetrameter or octosyllabic (see the quotations from Milton's "L'Allegro" p. 276), and the iambic pentameter. This form is usually called the *heroic* couplet, though that name was not used for it until late in the seventeenth century, when it was associated with the popular "heroic" plays of the time. (See Chapter 3 for a full discussion of its varieties.)

A three-rhymed pattern is called a *triplet* or *tercet*. The three lines may use one set of rhyming words, as in Tennyson's "The Eagle":

> The wrinkled sea beneath him crawls;
> He watches from his mountain walls,
> And like a thunderbolt he falls.

Or the rhymes may be linked from verse to verse. This form is called *terza rima*, and is famous as the pattern of Dante's *Divine Comedy*. The rhymes run aba-bcb-cdc-ded —and so on. Few English poets have used it, but an illustration is Shelley's "Ode to the West Wind."

> If I were a dead leaf thou mightest bear;
> If I were a swift cloud to fly with thee;
> A wave to pant beneath thy power, and share
>
> The impulse of thy strength, only less free
> Than thou, O, uncontrollable! If even
> I were as in my boyhood, and could be
>
> The comrade of thy wanderings over heaven,
> As then, when to outstrip thy skiey speed
> Scarce seemed a vision; I would ne'er have striven
>
> As thus with thee in prayer in my sore need.
> Oh! lift me as a wave, a leaf, a cloud!
> I fall upon the thorns of life! I bleed!

With the *quatrain* (any arrangement of four lines), we pass into patterns usually called *stanzas*, and the variations of four, five, six, seven, and eight line stanzas are too numerous to list. But there are certain "named varieties": *rhyme royal,* a French form, first used in English by Chaucer, is a seven line stanza in iambic pentameter, with the rhymes running ababbcc. It is the meter of Shakespeare's "The Rape of Lucrece."

> From the besieged Ardea all in post,
> Borne by the trustless wings of false desire,
> Lust-breathèd Tarquin leaves the Roman host,
> And to Collatium bears the lightless fire,
> Which, in pale embers hid, lurks to aspire,
>   And girdle with embracing flames the waist
>   Of Collatine's fair love, Lucrece the chaste.

Ottava rima was introduced from Italy in the sixteenth century and used first by Sir Thomas Wyatt. It is an eight lined stanza, also in iambic pentameter, rhyming abababcc. For two very different uses of it, see Byron's "The Vision of Judgment" (p. 160) and Yeats's "Sailing to Byzantium" (p. 264).

The *Spenserian Stanza* has nine lines, eight in iambic pentameter, and the last an alexandrine, with the scheme ababbcbcc. Keats uses it in "The Eve of St. Agnes":

> A casement high and triple-arched there was,
> All garlanded with carven imag'ries
> Of fruit, and flowers, and bunches of knot-grass,
> And diamonded with panes of quaint device,
> Innumerable of stains and splendid dyes,
> As are the tiger-moth's deep-damasked wings;
> And in the midst, 'mong thousand heraldries,
> And twilight saints, and dim emblazonings,
> A shielded scutcheon blushed with blood of queen
>   and kings.

The *sonnet* is a complete poem of fourteen lines in iambic pentameter. Though poets have evolved many variations of it, the two general types are the Petrarchan and the Shakespearean. The *Petrarchan*, introduced from Italy in the sixteenth century, is divided into an *octave,* the first eight lines, usually playing on two rhymes, and a *sestet,* the last six lines, using either two or three rhymes. Illustrations of this form are "Thou Art Indeed Just, Lord . . ." (p. 141) and "The Windhover" (p. 248) by Hopkins, and Wordsworth's "Surprised by Joy . . ." (p. 123). The *Shakespearean* form divides into three quatrains, each with its own two rhymes, and a final couplet with another rhyme. As well as the examples from Shakespeare, Donne's "Batter My Heart . . ." (p. 58), Drayton's "Since There's No Help . . ." (p. 205), and Frost's "A Silken Tent" (p. 54) are all in this pattern.

The *ode* is the most loosely used term in metrical description, and covers a wide variety of poetic forms. Odes may be *regular* or *irregular.* Regular or *Horatian* odes have a stanzaic pattern. The first to be written in English were Spenser's "Prothalamion" and "Epithalamion." Milton's "On the Morning of Christ's Nativity" uses another stanza form, and Keats created a form of his own, a quatrain, followed by a sestet, which is the pattern in "To a Nightingale," "On a Grecian Urn," and "To Melancholy." In the "Ode to Autumn," he introduced an extra line.

Another regular form of ode is the *Pindaric,* which Gray copied faithfully in his *Progress of Poesy.* But what Abraham Cowley introduced into England under the name of Pindaric Odes are not true Pindarics. He was too ignorant of classical meters to recognize that though intricate and elaborate, the structure was quite regular. "His idea of an ode," says Sir Edmund Gosse, "was of a lofty and tempestuous piece of indefinite poetry conducted without sail or oar in whatever direction the enthusiasm of the poet chose to take it." As a result, many odes in English poetry are lofty but indefinite forms, offering great freedom in metrical arrangment and rhyme schemes. Wordsworth's "Intimations of Immortality" is generally considered the finest of these irregular odes.

Many other specialized poetic schemes have been invented. During the fourteenth and fifteenth centuries, the courtly poets of Provence elaborated a number of highly stylized and difficult rhyming patterns, such as the *bal-*

lade (not to be confused with the ballad), the *sestina*, the *villanelle*, the *triolet*, the *rondeau* and the *rondel*. These never took root in England, but at the end of the nineteenth century a passing fashion for these forms was promoted by a group of minor poets, of whom the chief were Swinburne, Austin Dobson, Andrew Lang, W. E. Henley and Edmund Gosse. The poems themselves are not interesting, but students interested in the subject should consult Andrew Lang's *Ballads and Lyrics of Old France,* and Gleeson White's anthology *Ballades and Rondeaux.*

Bibliography

This short book list describes the most important criticisms by poets themselves on other poets and on poetry in general. The starred items are available in paper-back editions.

ARNOLD, MATTHEW: *Essays in Criticism.* 1865–1888. Arnold was the most influential critic of the late nineteenth century, as T. S. Eliot has been of our own day. His subject matter ranges very widely from classical literature to his own contemporaries. A selection of the essays is in the Everyman edition.

AUDEN, W. H.: *The Enchafèd Flood.* Random House, 1950. Three lectures dealing with the symbolism of the city and the sea, the contrasted universes of rational order and imaginative chaos, particularly in relation to the Romantic poets. *Poets at Work.* Harcourt Brace, 1948. Auden wrote one section in this called "Squares and Oblongs." It is a collection of notes about poetry, often searching and always original.

COLERIDGE, S. T.: *Biographia Literaria.* Chapters xiv, xv, xvii, xviii. These chapters discuss the poetic material in the *Lyrical Ballads,* with Coleridge's disagreement about Wordsworth's theory of poetic diction. He writes fully, too, on the qualities of poetry in general.

ELIOT, T. S.: *Selected Essays 1917–1932. The Use of Poetry and the Use of Criticism.* 1933. *Essays Ancient and Modern.* Harcourt Brace, 1936. *On Poets and Poetry.* Farrar, Straus and Cudahy, 1957. These essays, particularly the earlier ones, have probably affected contemporary criticism more deeply than any other writings.

*EMPSON, WILLIAM: *Seven Types of Ambiguity.* 1930. Points out the extreme subtlety and complexity of poetic language.

FROST, ROBERT: "The Constant Symbol": an introductory essay to *The Poems of Robert Frost* in the Modern Library edition, 1946. "The Figure a Poem Makes": the introduction to *Collected Poems.* Holt, 1949. Both full of insights into the poetic process.

HOPKINS, G. M.: *Letters to Robert Bridges. Letters to Canon R. W. Dixon.* 1935. *Notebooks and Papers.* Oxford University Press, 1937. Hopkins wrote no formal criticism, but his scattered remarks are full of interest and insight.

HOUSMAN, A. E.: *The Name and Nature of Poetry.* Cambridge University Press, 1933. A controversial and provocative declaration that the real nature of poetry is inexplicable.

*JARRELL, RANDALL: *Poetry and the Age.* Vintage Books, 1953. Some brilliant essays on modern poets.

*JOHNSON, SAMUEL: *Lives of the Poets.* 1779–1781. Gateway Books. Full of sound wisdom and good sayings.

KEATS, JOHN: *Letters.* A selection with an excellent introduction by Lionel Trilling, is in the *Great Letters Series.* Farrar, Straus and Co. His informal discussions often say more than whole volumes.

SHELLEY, P. B.: *A Defence of Poetry.* 1821. The most transcendental of the critics, but full of fiery idealism about the poet's calling.

SIDNEY, SIR PHILIP: *Apology for Poetry,* 1595. A defense of poetry because it "beautifies our mother tongue," and brings delight and wisdom to man. Both this and the Shelley essay above, together with a fine collection of other essays on poets and poetry, are in *Criticism,* edited by Schorer, Miles and Mackenzie. Harcourt Brace, 1948.

STEVENS, WALLACE: *The Necessary Angel.* Knopf, 1951. Stevens's prose is as subtle and elaborate as his poetry, and these essays are not easy reading. They appeal particularly to those interested in abstract questions of esthetic appreciation.

WORDSWORTH, WILLIAM: "Advertisement" to the Lyrical Ballads, 1798. "Preface" to the Lyrical Ballads, 1800. "Preface" to Poems and "Essay Supplementary to the Preface," 1815. Defenses of his own revolutionary theories and experiments in poetic forms, with an analysis of his distinction between the Fancy and the Imagination, and much on the nature of poetry.

*YEATS, W. B.: *The Autobiography of W. B. Yeats,* Anchor Books. *Discoveries.* 1907. *The Cutting of an Agate.* 1919. The scattered critical essays have the same mystical quality as the poems, but with flashes of practical advice, and highly individual opinions.

List of Poets

Page numbers refer to references and quotations.

[*List of Poets*] 287